MY PRIVATE WAR

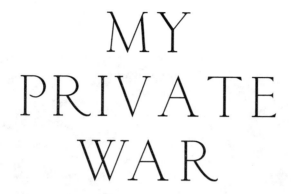

Liberated Body, Captive Mind:
A World War II POW's Journey

NORMAN BUSSEL

PEGASUS BOOKS
NEW YORK

For Melanie, known to me only as Sucre, who saved my life, endured difficult years watching the agony of a guilt-tortured soul, yet refused to be driven away.

As it was in the beginning, so shall it be at the end. All I can offer you that will be everlasting . . .
    is my undying love.

I can think of few experiences worse than being captured by your enemy but, oh Lord, how I wish my crew members who died that day had become POWs, too. In loving memory of:

Sgt. Joseph Guida, Sgt. Vasilios C. Mpourles, Lt. Sherwood W. Landis, Lt. Wynne M. Longeteig

MY PRIVATE WAR

Pegasus Books LLC
45 Wall Street, Suite 1021
New York, NY 10005

First Pegasus Books edition 2008

Interior design by Maria Fernandez

Library of Congress Cataloging-in-Publication Data is available.

ISBN: 978-1-60598-015-7

10 9 8 7 8 6 5 4 3 2 1

Printed in the United States of America
Distributed by W. W. Norton & Company, Inc.
www.pegasusbooks.us

Contents

As a Clinical Psychologist with the Department of Veterans Affairs, my primary practice over the past thirty years has involved treating combat veterans for anxiety, depression, and Post Traumatic Stress Disorder (PTSD). I have had the privilege of sitting with about a hundred men each week, either individually or in group therapy, helping them explore, work through, and reframe traumatic combat experiences, and deal with the residual effects that still impact their lives.

Norman Bussel's book, *My Private War—Liberated Body, Captive Mind: A World War II POW's Journey*, is the chronicle of a typical 1940s American teenager who went off to war. You will read about him learning to fly a B-17 bomber, become wounded when his plane explodes over Berlin, and lose four crewmates who were as close to him as brothers. Captured and beaten by German civilians, he became a prisoner of war for a year, living under abominable conditions. Finally liberated by American troops, he returned home expecting to resume a normal life, only to discover that, while his body had been set free, his mind was still held captive by survivor guilt and the memories of his horrific experiences.

Reading this compelling story of one man's long battle with PTSD, and his ultimate victory, can be a first step toward improvement for all combat veterans who suffer from this disorder. At the same time, this book is not just for combat veterans, because everyone needs to know the horrors of war, the terrible ordeal that our young people experience in battle, and the crippling emotional baggage they bring back with them.

This story is, in many ways, as fresh as today's media coverage of the War in Iraq. Every day, we read of young men and women serving extended tours in a conflict where there is no clear battle line, no down time, and no safe place. They must always be on alert for a suicidal insurgent intent on taking their lives, a well-hidden sniper waiting to make them a target, or a deadly IED that may be hidden anywhere, ready to blow apart life and limb.

I started work with PTSD sufferers as a young psychology intern reaching out to Vietnam veterans in the 1970s in a VA system that was just beginning to explore their needs and their PTSD symptoms. It was an engrossing experience to begin to understand the pain, the fear, the feelings of isolation, shame, anger, resentment, intrusive thoughts, night terrors, relationship failures, and emotional liability that characterized most of these young American men.

Many were able to keep traumatic memories hidden except for times when they were awakened by a nightmare, or with cold sweats, or when they reacted harshly to a loved one. Often, when their tempers flared, they weren't really sure why. In the next decade, especially after the intense media coverage of the fiftieth anniversary of significant World War II combat invasions dredged up hidden memories, many more of these older veterans sought help and were sent to the VA by their internists to be treated for delayed PTSD.

Retirement brought WW II veterans a well-deserved leisure, which turned out to be a mixed blessing because it provided time not only to reflect upon their tumultuous wartime past, but also to contemplate the growing demise of friends and family. Troubled by thoughts they had previously been able to ignore, they came to the VA in large numbers, puzzled because they thought PTSD symptoms were related only to Vietnam veterans.

Another group of combat veterans who began to be identified as needing treatment for PTSD were former prisoners of war from WW II, Korea, and Vietnam. Their symptoms included delayed PTSD causal to trauma of their capture and the horrors they experienced while in captivity. For many years, these men did not share their experiences with anyone except other POWs, and even then there was often a reticence to talk about feelings of vulnerability, anger, resentment, and shame.

POWs suffered the physical and mental trauma of knowing that they could be abused and killed at any moment at the whim of their captors. The tension was unrelenting. They were in a constant state of vigilance, because survival depended upon instant reaction to enemy commands. They witnessed the abuse, starvation, and murder of fellow POWs. Those who survived, freed by their fellow American soldiers, looked like—and were perceived in the same manner as—the holocaust concentration camp survivors.

Even after they returned home and regained their weight and physical health, they felt different—and sometimes were treated differently—than those veterans who never suffered the inhumanity and indignity of captivity. Rather than feel the pain of their memories and feelings, and face the ignorance of some who labeled them cowards, they remained mostly silent about their experiences and even their POW identity, as if it was a cause for shame.

They were home from the war, but the battle inside them continued for years and significantly affected their everyday lives.

Most thought that life would finally be better after a year or more in hell, but a hidden internal struggle was just about to begin. It wasn't long before they noticed that they were always ON. A learned hypervigilance continued to track everything and everyone even in normal, safe environments.

Even the most intimate relationships can become more distant and less affectionate, while ties to family and friends suffer from the strain of a veteran's withdrawal. Unable to explain his mental turmoil, the combat veteran becomes more introverted; many turn to alcohol and drugs for relief from the anxiety and depression that surround their emotional pain and physical isolation. We need to look closely at our returning combat veterans, examining both the obvious and the subtle changes that have occurred.

Veterans returning from the highly stressful environment of Iraq or Afghanistan have the same challenges as all those combat veterans before them, especially those who returned from Vietnam and the POW camps of other wars. They exhibit a variety of behaviors, including hypervigilance, exaggerated startle response, denial, emotional detachment, and insomnia. Many of these conditions will not improve without professional help. What this book offers is great insight into their PTSD and an impetus to get treatment today, so they will no longer be men with liberated bodies but still-captive minds.

—Kenneth E. Reinhard, PhD, A.B.P.P.
Diplomate in Clinical Psychology
Director, Anxiety Disorders Clinic
VA Hudson Valley Healthcare System

Chapter One

"BIG B," 1944

I was the last one to bail out of our B-17 bomber alive that day. It was around noon on April 29, 1944, and our target was Berlin. "Big B," we called it. It was probably the most heavily fortified city in Germany, with thousands of accurate and deadly 88mm anti-aircraft guns pointed at the sky. Pointed at the Allied planes that came to drop their bombs on Hitler's glorious city. Pointed at my Bomb Group, the 447th. Pointed at my squadron, the 708th. Pointed at my plane, the *Mississippi Lady*. Pointed at . . . me.

This was a mission that I was not supposed to fly. If I had used the pass I'd been issued the day before, I would have been in London. But I had opted to stay the night at RAF Rattlesden, our base field. Around four A.M. that Saturday, I was awakened by the sound of gravel crunching under the soles of GI shoes outside our

Nissen hut. Our door was opened and a sergeant came in, shining a very bright flashlight on a roster pad. As he began calling out names for that day's mission, I pulled my blanket over my head and waited for him to leave, because I wasn't scheduled to fly. I had the weekend off.

The first time he called my name, I didn't answer. I felt that I had misheard him. Then, when he yelled "Bussel" again, I jerked my blanket down and shouted, "I'm not flying today! I got a pass last night to go to London."

"Then you shoulda gone to London last night," he said. "All passes cancelled. Everybody's flying today."

As I stood barefoot and shivering on the cold concrete floor and began to dress, I reflected that the sergeant's announcement was very ominous. "All passes cancelled. Everybody's flying today." This had to be a damned important target if no one was excused from flying. He was right. I shoulda gone to London last night.

After the previous day's long mission, I felt I'd better eat a substantial breakfast, because there was no telling when we'd get back. Even though I wasn't very hungry at that early hour, I packed in the food purposefully, preparing for a long day by downing cereal, juice, fried eggs (fresh, not powdered), toast, bacon, potatoes, and black coffee. Actually, the food in our small mess hall was better than that served on most bases in the States.

I met our pilot, "Daddy," at the briefing center. We dubbed him with this venerable nickname because, at twenty-eight, he was the oldest member of our crew. "This will be our first mission as a crew," he said. "It'll be good flying on the same plane with you guys again."

There were two briefings before every mission. The first was a general briefing for the entire crew. Afterward, the pilots and co-pilots remained for additional instruction, and navigators and bombardiers each met in separate rooms for specialized briefing on their positions. The noncoms suited up and checked out their equipment.

The general briefing room was very large, with wooden folding chairs lined up in rows of ten so each crew could sit together. There were no loud voices. All you could hear was a low murmur. There was a palpable air of tension as we waited for the target to be announced.

Finally a lieutenant colonel climbed the four steps to the podium, holding a long wooden pointer in his hand. He walked over to a large wall map that had been covered with thick black cloth and pulled the cloth aside. We were seated too far away to see the markings on the map, but when he touched the end of his pointer to its face, we knew that it was resting on our air base. Slowly, the pointer followed a black line across the map, and when it stopped he turned to face us and said, "Gentlemen, your target today is . . . Berlin."

A groan filled the room, then a muttering as crew members swore softly and talked with each other about the dreaded prospect of bombing "Big B." We already knew that Berlin was teeming with anti-aircraft batteries, and in April 1944 the Luftwaffe could loft many fighter planes to attack our slower, heavy, bomb-laden B-17's. Our fighter escort was still quite thin compared with what it would reach in the coming months, when large numbers of reinforcements were scheduled to arrive from the United States.

Our instructions from the podium continued. We were ordered to maintain tight formations so we would be less vulnerable to German fighters; we were advised that flak would be heavy over the target; we were told that there would be cumulus clouds at 14,000 feet over the city; and we were wished good luck. Dawn was breaking just as our crew boarded a truck to the flight line.

The mission started out very badly for my crew and continued to get worse as the day progressed. First, there was the problem with our navigator, Sherry. The day before, Lt. Sokol, who was also in our bomb squad and a close friend of Sherry's in navigation school, had been hit in the neck by shrapnel while on a mission. His crew had been unable to stop the blood flow, and Sokol died on the flight back to Rattlesden. Sherry's face was still ashen as we rode out to our plane.

I went to the radio shack to pick up our crew's equipment. Hurriedly, I looped the ten headsets over my left arm and grabbed the ten throat mikes with my right. When I reached the hardstand, our crew was standing outside the plane, and I began passing the headsets out to them.

When I handed Sherry his, I heard him gasp, "Oh my God! Oh my God!"

"What's wrong?" I asked.

Speechless, he could only point to one earpiece as he shoved the headset back into my hand. I saw that one of the wires had been cut and there was dried blood on it. Also, a name had been written on a piece of adhesive tape applied to the earpiece: Lt. Sokol.

I was horrified and Sherry was in shock. I grabbed the ground crew chief by the arm, leading him over to his jeep as I explained why I needed to get back to the radio shack in a hurry. The chief drove like a maniac and I picked up another headset. When we got back to the plane, I handed it to Sherry.

"How do you feel?" I asked.

He was trembling. "Got to pray, boy," he said. "Got to pray."

When Daddy started the B-17's four powerful Pratt & Whitney engines, the tremendous force of the backdraft made it impossible to climb on board without holding on to the side door and pulling yourself inside. I was just behind Sherry, and I helped boost him into the waist of the plane. All strength seemed to have drained from his body. As the throttle gunned higher, the plane began to buck on the hardstand like a restrained animal, and the roaring engines made me think of Pegasus: four huge winged horses raring to break free.

Just before takeoff, the control tower told us by intercom that our group was early and we were ordered to take off and do a 360-degree turn. By the time we completed the turn, the tower said, we would in position to join up with the main formation.

As we taxied out to the runway, Daddy called Sherry on the intercom and asked him to direct us when we were airborne, so we could quickly form with the rest of our squadron. Sherry's voice was hoarse and scarcely more than a whisper. Daddy couldn't understand a word he said. I listened in anxiously for a while. I was familiar enough with Sherry's voice that I could make out what he was saying. Finally, I spoke up and offered to relay Sherry's instructions to Daddy. He agreed, and this was the way we managed to form with our squadron.

The plan to do a 360 turned out to be a catastrophe. By the time we had completed our turn, the rest of the wing that we were supposed to join was minutes ahead of us, and we never caught up. As a result, the fighter planes that were slated to escort us ended up flying with the larger group and we were left to defend ourselves.

The B-17 wasn't named the Flying Fortress for nothing. We had seven formidable .50-caliber machine guns for defense, but the loss of our "Little Friends," as we affectionately called our fighter escort, would make the German fighters even more daring in attacking us that day.

Anyone who has fought in a war can think of many times when death was cheated because of the slightest change in plans, in routines, in circumstances. Such an incident took place as we began our mission to Berlin. As we flew over the English Channel, Little Joe, our ball-turret gunner, came into the radio room and sat on my chest chute, which was just in back of my chair. I could understand why he did it: it was a helluva lot softer than the hard, cold floor of the plane. I turned and said, "Little Joe, don't sit on my chute. What if I have to use it today?"

Annoyed, Joe tossed the chute across the radio room and it landed next to the door leading to the bomb bay.

"It won't hurt the damned chute to sit on it!" he said.

As it turned out, if Little Joe hadn't tossed my chute across the room, it would have been consumed by flames, because fire later started in the exact spot where my chute had been lying and I would have had nothing to bail out with. I never got to thank Little Joe for saving my life. A few minutes later, this sweet little kid from Brooklyn was dead. He was just nineteen years old.

Flying over the English Channel, my radio suddenly came alive with the voices of pilots reporting that they were about to abort and return to base. Some claimed engine problems; some alluded to other mechanical malfunctions. I didn't count the number of reports I heard, but it struck me as being quite disproportionate. I wondered how many of the aborts were legitimate, how many crews just didn't want to go to Berlin. As much as I dreaded this mission, I was superstitious enough to believe that the crews who avoided Big B that day were likely to get shot down on a milk run later on.

We didn't begin to encounter flak until we crossed the German border, and even then it was sporadic. When the flak increased, I opened a carton of "chaff" and began stuffing the silvery strips through the chaff slot in the radio room. Chaff came in small packages, open at both ends; it looked like the tinsel used to decorate Christmas trees. As thousands of strands dispersed in our wake, it interfered with the radar that the Germans used to track us and direct their anti-aircraft fire. It was too late to benefit our formation, but it could help the planes following us. I hoped that the planes in front of us were pushing out chaff just as diligently.

As we flew deeper into Germany, the sky began to fill with black puffs of smoke as flak shells exploded all around us. Any notion that these bursts were innocuous was quickly dispelled with the occasional "ping" of shrapnel fragments bursting through the aluminum skin of the plane. It sounded like gravel being thrown against a tin roof.

Then Bill reported incoming fighters, and Daddy began to call each gunner on the intercom to check if he was firing at the attacking Me 109's. I was shooting my overhead gun in the radio room when Daddy called for me to report. I got out two words, "Yes, I—" when a burst of flak, which must have been right on top of us, blew a huge hole just above the desk where I had been sitting. Fragments splattered over my body, knocking me down and ripping off my throat mike.

When I abruptly stopped talking, Daddy knew that I was hit, and I heard him yell, "Norm's hit! Somebody from the waist get in there and help him."

I could feel blood running down my face, my leg, and my ribcage, but I didn't believe I was gravely wounded, so I snapped my throat mike back on as quickly as I could and said, "I'm okay, guys. Repeat: I'm okay. Stay with your guns, I'm getting back on mine."

I had just started firing at another fighter when our plane was rocked again and I was thrown against the side of the ship. As I stood up, I realized that I was no longer getting any oxygen, and then I saw the flames behind my chair, and the plane's skin began dripping molten aluminum. It was surreal to watch the aluminum skin, the metal that appeared to surround us so protectively, suddenly drip, drip, drip like soldering lead. My plane was melting before my eyes. Obviously, our oxygen lines were burning because the fire was so intense. I tried to use the intercom, but it was dead. I never heard an order to bail out.

Flying at 28,000 feet without oxygen can do weird things to your mind. I seemed to be moving in slow motion. With the plane burning around me, I didn't feel rushed or afraid. Nor did I sense any danger. In fact, my impaired brain even flirted with the idea that the flames would go out and we would fly back to England.

After all, our engines were still intact . . . still emitting their low, powerful, steady tone. I opened the door to the waist to see if I could help anyone back there and I was confronted by a solid wall of flame. I tried to peer beyond it but I could see nothing. As I slammed the door shut, I heard explosions inside the radio room and felt powder burns on my face as the raging fire caused my ammo to cook off. The blasting of the .50-caliber shells jerked my ammo belt violently, and it danced like a large metallic snake writhing in the flames . . . contorted with anguish.

I still didn't think about bailing out. The plane was flying along on a smooth, level course. I realized that the intercom was out, but I never even heard the alarm bell. I thought Daddy was still controlling the plane. What I didn't know was that the plane was set on automatic pilot and I was flying with four dead buddies as my sole companions.

I decided to head for the cockpit to see if anyone there needed help. First, I hooked on my chest chute, not realizing the left clip was not completely locked. As I opened the forward door, I saw that the bombs had been salvoed. The empty racks gave silent testimony that our deadly cargo had been dumped on Berlin and the bomb bay doors were wide open. I looked down, and far below I could see thick layers of clouds. I don't know why I noticed the large chocolate D-bar lying on my desk, the one I planned to eat as we crossed the English Channel on the way back to Rattlesden. I stared at it for a moment, my muddled mind trying to figure out why I was so enchanted at the sight of a chocolate bar lying next to my radio, in the middle of our burning plane flying high over Berlin. I made no move to pick it up, but I sensed that something was missing. It was. I had forgotten to bring LaVerne's lucky bra, a going-away present from the beautiful stripper who stole my heart in West Palm Beach. It was back in Rattlesden in my footlocker.

As I stood in the doorway, I turned and looked through the huge hole in the left side of the ship and saw that flames had engulfed the entire wing. The wings, of course, are where the plane's fuel is stored. By now my clothing was on fire, and I knew I'd never make it to the cockpit. I stepped out onto the catwalk in the bomb bay and for a brief instant remembered my famous last words, "I'll never bail out. I'll go down with the plane first." Then I jumped.

I began a count to ten, delaying pulling my ripcord so the force of the air would make my flying suit stop burning. I was falling on my back and I could see the plane moving away. I had reached the count of seven when the ship veered wildly out of control, then exploded into a million burning pieces. I had been seven seconds away from eternity.

The 447th lofted twenty-nine B-17's that day; seven of the crews were on their first mission, and three were on their second. Eleven planes were lost, with one crew making it back to the English Channel where they ditched and were picked up by a British air-sea rescue unit. The rest returned to our base, to mourn their buddies who were lost, while guiltily glad that they were another mission closer to the end of their tour.

Chapter Two

In Uniform, 1942

I was on a train with about two hundred other, mostly teenaged, draftees from the Memphis area, headed for the induction center at Fort Oglethorpe, Georgia. I don't know what train graveyard this relic had been reclaimed from, but I had never before been on a passenger car that was heated by a potbellied stove. It was in the center of the car, its four contoured, cast iron legs embedded in several inches of sand, which kept the wooden floor from catching fire. The sand was kept in place by four two-by-fours forming a square around the stove. If you were seated too close, you would roast. If you were at either end of the car, you were very cold.

It was just after midnight when we arrived at Fort Oglethorpe in a cold, wind-driven rain. We were ordered off the train and told to form a four-deep column. There was no shelter. It was considered a sign of weakness for us young men to wear raincoats or carry umbrellas. In just a few minutes, we were all soaked to the skin.

A sergeant (wearing a rainhat, long raincoat, and rubber boots) faced the formation, holding a clipboard on which another soldier aimed a flashlight while balancing a large umbrella over both of them. The sergeant then proceeded to growl out each name on the roster. Names, other than Smith, Jones, or Brown, were so badly mispronounced they had to be repeated several times before recognition finally prompted a response of "Here!"

The roll call took the better part of an hour, and then the sergeant pointed out the barracks where we were to sleep and said that since we hadn't had any dinner, he would take us to the mess hall.

As we trooped in, there was not a soul in sight and a single light bulb made the rows of long wooden tables look even more stark. The sergeant disappeared into the kitchen and in a few minutes reappeared, arguing with a very large mess sergeant who glared at us as we dripped water all over his floor.

The mess sergeant made it clear that we were not expected and that he would have to serve us "what's available." What was available turned out to be stale bread, cold gravy, and lukewarm black coffee left over from dinner. If this was an example of how we could expect to be treated in the service, I didn't think I was going to make it.

The next day we had our physical exams and aptitude tests. The physicals didn't take long. New recruits were sorely needed, so unless you had a serious disability, you were quickly passed through. The aptitude test involved many vocabulary questions that were quite easy for me, as I had always been an avid reader and English was my best subject back in school. However, I didn't like the part of the exam that asked you to determine how many little cubes were hidden behind other little cubes. I also frowned on math problems that seemed as nonsensical as: "If Bill is 14 and Fred is 11 . . . how old is Janet?"

On the trip back home two days later, the tenor of our conversations had changed and we were not the same quiet group who had embarked on this adventure. We were loud and vocal about what we had experienced. Although we didn't even know the term at the time, we had fallen victim to a service-connected disease called "red ass," whereby one gripes about everything and anything that displeases him, real or imagined.

Chapter Three

KEESLER FIELD

A few weeks later, I received orders to report to Keesler Field, Mississippi, for basic training. Keesler Field was not far from Biloxi, Mississippi, which was a resort of sorts on the Gulf of Mexico.

Although there were many barracks on the base, they were for permanent troops, not for inductees. We were assigned to "tent city," which was located near the beach. There were four men to a tent and we slept on canvas cots. We had our meals trucked down from a mess hall and ate out of aluminum mess kits. No matter how well we cleaned our mess kits after each meal, we all ended up with the runs. Our latrines were slit trenches, which we filled in with dirt every weekend. Then we dug new slit trenches for the coming week. Therein lies one of the most embarrassing moments I experienced while in the service.

Our tents were set up in rows, separated by aisles about fifteen feet wide, with the tent openings facing the aisle. Every thirty feet, in the middle of every aisle, was a Lister bag holding about twenty gallons of water, with a spigot at the bottom. Invented by a man named Lister, this canvas bag was suspended from a tripod and kept full of fresh water, so we could fill our canteens.

The slit trenches were located about a hundred yards beyond each row of tents. You squatted down and straddled the sucker. Since most of us were suffering from bouts of diarrhea, we didn't pay much attention when we heard someone galloping toward the slit trenches in the middle of the night, other than to think, "Poor bastard."

One overcast night, when you couldn't see your hands in front of your face, I awoke with the instant realization that I needed to get to the slit trenches without the slightest delay. We all kept our flashlights and toilet paper beneath our cots and, although I found the tissue right away, I couldn't locate the flashlight. Aware that I couldn't wait a second longer, I dashed out of the tent and went flying down the aisle through the pitch black darkness.

I thought that I was running to the right of the Lister bags, until I smashed into something at full tilt. At first, I thought I had hit a tree, because it barely budged. Then it sloshed water all over me . . . and suddenly I knew. I had run smack into a Lister bag. Lying on the ground, with the wind knocked out of me, soaking wet, I was soon engulfed in the glaring illumination of many flashlights as guys poured out of their tents to see what had happened.

As the laughter and hooting died down, I was helped to my feet, still dazed and too late to visit the slit trenches. I went back to my tent, got soap, a towel, and clean shorts, then started on the quarter-mile hike to the showers.

The routine of basic training consisted of learning the manual of arms with the .30-caliber rifle, marching (close-order drill), calisthenics, obstacle course, and finally an overnight hike of about twenty-five miles round-trip with a forty-pound pack.

The time frame for basic was usually about a month, depending on the urgency of requests for new recruits from various branches of service. Unfortunately someone had gone through my records and discovered that I taken high school ROTC for three years, and all at once I was a celebrity. The lieutenant was painting a rosy picture of my future as a drill sergeant and I was assigned to introduce draftees, with two left feet, to the intricacies of close-order drill.

Most of my trainees were Mexican immigrants who spoke no English, so my two years of high school Spanish served me well. One kid in my platoon, Gilberto Villareal, was being chewed out by the sergeant one day for failing to make his bed properly. Of course, the sergeant was shouting in English and poor, cringing Gilberto didn't understand a word he was saying. I politely interrupted the sergeant's tirade to say that Gilberto spoke no English and that I would explain the problem to him later.

I showed Gilberto how to make his bed so that when a quarter was dropped on it, it would bounce. He thanked me profusely, but I didn't know how grateful he was until the next morning.

When I returned from my trek to the shower, I found my bed had been made so tightly that a penny would have rebounded a foot and my shoes were shined to a finish that would have caused a fly to break a leg trying to land on one.

I thanked Gilberto for his expression of appreciation and figured that was the end of it. The next morning, I returned from the shower to find that he had done the same thing again. This time I explained to him quite firmly that I really didn't want him to do this any more. It took a week for me to convince him that I didn't want a personal valet. Upon completion of basic, all the Mexican immigrants were sent to school at Gulfport, Mississippi to learn English. I'm sure Gilberto turned out to be an excellent soldier.

Because German submarines had been sighted offshore in the Gulf of Mexico with some frequency, security on the base was not taken lightly. Each of us was required to serve on guard duty and, since they usually began at the head of the alphabet in their selection, my name came up often.

By coincidence, most of my guard duty took place at night. It was a lonely assignment, but I rather enjoyed the quiet of patrolling the beach at night with only the sound of the waves lapping at the shore and an occasional creature scurrying along the sand.

Each guard was issued an armband, a flashlight, a billy club, and a Colt .45 automatic pistol. This equipment made a young recruit feel very important. Each guard position could be checked on several times in one night, and we were under strict orders to let no one pass unless they knew the password for the night. One evening, as I received my instructions, the sergeant told me it was rumored that some "high brass" might be making the rounds and that I was to let no one get past me without being given the password. "That means no one, even if he's a general."

A short while later, as I was walking my post, I saw the headlights of a jeep approaching. I stopped and waited until they were about twenty-five feet away, then called out, "Halt! Who's there?" As I shined my flashlight at the jeep, I stopped breathing. It was occupied by a lieutenant and a one-star general.

"It's Lieutenant Brown and General Dawkins. Let us pass."

"May I have the password, sir?"

"General Dawkins doesn't require a password, Private. Step aside."

"I'm sorry, sir. I can't let you continue without the password." I hoped they couldn't hear my knees knocking.

The lieutenant was suddenly threatening. "You know you could be court-martialed for refusing the general passage. Step aside now!"

I was trying very hard to keep my voice from trembling. "I'm sorry, sir. I cannot let you proceed without the password." I reached down and unfastened the flap on my pistol scabbard. I had no idea what I was going to do next.

The general heaved himself out of the jeep and came forward. "What's your name, Private?"

"Bussel, sir," I stammered.

"Congratulations, Private Bussel. You've done exactly the proper thing." Then he climbed back into the jeep and they headed back in the direction from which they had come. It took me quite a while to calm down enough to feel pleased with myself.

Almost three months passed, and I continued instructing close-order drill and taking different groups on overnight hikes once a week. I was still a private.

When I complained about my situation to the lieutenant, he told me to be patient, that I was doing a good job and that I would be promoted shortly. I finally made it clear that I didn't want to be a drill sergeant, and he responded, "You're going to end up going overseas."

"That was my intention when I came into the service," I said. Ten days later, I got my orders and was surprised, and very pleased, to find out that I was going into the Air Force.

I had graduated from high school in 1941, and that fall I enrolled at Memphis State College. Three months later, after the Japanese attack at Pearl Harbor, many of my friends were volunteering for the armed forces, and two of them were going to take tests for the Naval Air Force.

I had long been fascinated with flying, and I wanted to join them, but I was only eighteen years old and needed my parents to sign my application papers. My father was a World War I United States Army veteran and, though he was reluctant, I could see that he could be persuaded. My mother was a different problem: she simply refused to sign.

For weeks, I kept the pressure up. I told her that if I was drafted,

I would have no choice of where I went and how miserable I would be if I were sent to a branch of the service I didn't like. That did the trick, and, with great reluctance, she agreed to sign the papers.

I did well on my examinations for the Naval Air Force and rushed home with the application for my parents' signatures. I was not prepared for what happened next. My mother said that she had changed her mind and categorically refused to sign. Plead as I might, she would not give in. I was devastated.

My interest in college was gone and I wanted to do something to help the war effort, so I went to aircraft riveter's school and, upon completing the course, got a job in Memphis at Fisher Body, formerly an automobile plant, building B-25 bombers.

The B-25 was a two-engine bomber and early in the war was much in demand. The plant was open twenty-four hours a day, seven days a week. Although shifts were eight hours, everyone was urged to work longer, and I averaged twelve hours and often more.

My special area was the bombardier nose and, in our haste to speed up production, it was not uncommon to drill an off-center hole in the frame. Most of the time, we could substitute an oversized rivet, but a written approval from an engineering inspector was required. Even though it was legitimate, I was often uncomfortable with these decisions and concerned about those who would ultimately fly these planes.

Just after I turned nineteen, I was notified through the mail that my draft number had been called and I was to report to the induction center in six weeks. I brought the notice to my supervisor at the aircraft plant. He told me that he would get me a deferment, because my job at the plant was important. I quickly explained that I had always planned to go into the armed forces and did not want a deferment.

Chapter Four

SCOTT FIELD

All through basic training, I worried that my three years of infantry ROTC would surely land me in some branch of the ground forces. Of course, I didn't yet understand that military decisions rarely followed what most people would consider logical patterns. There was an immediate need for personnel to man the planes that would soon be bombing Germany in increasing numbers, and it would take time to train these crews. Anyone whose test scores qualified them for one of these positions was slated for the Army Air Force. I was very pleased that I would realize my dream to become a flyer. Since my tests showed an aptitude for learning Morse code, I was selected for radio school.

There were a number of students who washed out early on because they found it maddening to listen to the constant sound of dit, dits and dah, dahs that constitutes Morse code. I found that the quicker I could identify each series of dits and dahs for the letter of the alphabet they represented, the better I was able to concentrate on the message; that way, the sounds were not nearly so distracting. We also had to learn "Q" signals, which expedited the transmission of commonly used words. For example, the "Q" signal for "static" was "QRM."

Classes were conducted in four six-hour shifts, on a rotating basis, with the midnight-to-six A.M. stint being the most difficult. Our instructors on the midnight shift were constantly berating us for dozing off in class, but it was almost impossible to stay awake. Our barracks housed about seventy men, representing every shift, and with the constant comings and goings, no one got enough sleep.

As chance would have it, almost everyone in my barracks was from New England, with most coming from Massachusetts. As the only Southerner, I took a constant ribbing, such as: "Norm, I'll bet that's the first pair of shoes you've ever worn."

"It sure is," I would reply, "but I've worn knee pads to pick cotton since I was four years old." I think a few of the teasers were convinced that this statement was true, although I'd never picked cotton in my life.

Some of the guys in my barracks had odd, yet impressive, talents. One was a weight-lifter who could chin himself several times with one hand, holding on to a wooden girder. Another was a guy named Denino, who could climb up and scamper around on the rafters like a monkey. This capability was very important to his health, because he got a great kick out of throwing a bucket of cold water into the communal shower stall, then racing for the rafters before several wet, naked, and enraged bathers, trailing suds and water, could catch him and retaliate.

The routine at Scott Field was structured on a cadet type of discipline. The day started with physical training: a twenty-minute run, followed by calisthenics. Since we weren't issued running shorts, everyone was required to wear their GI issue, khaki-colored boxer shorts over their jock strap.

On our morning runs, we would often pass young women, civilian employees of the PX, on their way to work. One day, one of the women cast a sidelong glance at our attire, and one of our guys called out, "Yes, lady, we're wearing our underwear!" The hapless woman shrieked, blushed, and hurried away.

Another day, we passed a pretty teen-aged PX employee who was very well endowed and wore a tight T-shirt with a high school logo superimposed over a football. Beneath the football, emblazoned in bright red letters, were the words "state champions." Some joker in the rear ranks yelled, "Honey, those ain't *state* champions: those are *world* champions!" We passed her again a few days later, wearing a different shirt, and her cheeks turned rosy red.

Following the cadet system, it was required that ten men be seated at the same time at tables in the mess hall. Bread, water, and milk were already on the table, and if you ran out of one of the three, you held up the empty package, or pitcher, and more was brought to your table. You were not permitted to replenish the supply on your own.

On leaving the chow line, you seated yourself at your table, and going back for seconds was permitted. The problem was that if you were a slow eater, or returned for seconds, you could finish your meal after the others and would be the recipient of dirty looks, because all ten men at a table had to leave at the same time.

I could understand the need to emphasize the importance of discipline to a group of youngsters brimming with testosterone, but I felt that some aspects of our existence were deliberately devised to humble us. A good example was our toilet. The thrones were lined up in a row of ten across . . . no stalls, no partitions. They were simply placed on one side of the room, right out in the open, separated by about three feet of space. I can't think of a more effective way of inducing constipation. If the occupants of the moment were inclined to join hands and strain in unison, it could have been accomplished with barely a stretch. I felt a good deal more privacy using the slit trenches in Tent City. There, at least, with everyone observing the protocol of facing in the same direction, you didn't have to concentrate on avoiding your neighbor's eyes.

Another needlessly degrading ritual was the inevitable, monthly "short arm" inspection. Lined up single-file with fellow sufferers, in a long room, completely naked except for your shoes and socks, you waited for your turn to be told by a doctor, "Okay, skin it back and milk it down." This referred to your grasping your penis with one hand and squeezing it as you brought your hand forward. If there was any discharge, you were taken aside for a venereal disease test. The next order was, "Bend over and spread your cheeks." The proper procedure here was to bend over at the waist, then reach back with both hands to pull your buttocks apart, so the doctor could see if you had crabs.

As mortifying as this process was, it did not approach the humiliation of the method used at Keesler Field. There, we were required to assemble on a grassy hill, attired in only shoes and our thick and heavy rubber raincoats. Nothing was to be worn underneath. The temperature was usually around 100 degrees, and we often waited for more than half an hour to be called into a large tent for the "short arm." A sergeant would yell, "At ease," allowing us to sit on the grass. "Smoke if you got 'em." We would slide cigarettes out of our raincoat pockets and sit there smoking, while rivulets of sweat ran down our rib cages, trickled down our backs, and flowed between the "cheeks" we would ultimately be called upon to "bend over and spread."

Once in a while, the military will do something sensible. Since these occasions are rare, it is only fair to acknowledge one when it occurs. Because we were being trained as radio operators, to serve on Air Force combat crews, it made sense to determine how each of us would react to flying.

To check out our air aplomb, there were several Piper Cubs at Scott Field, which were used to take future radio operators on short flights. The pilots were lieutenants who were probably considered too old for combat duty, as they were in their late thirties or early forties. They would take up one student at a time and at the end of the flight would note on a pad your reaction to flying.

My first flight in the small plane was a real thrill. We weren't allowed to use the runways for takeoff or landing; they were reserved for the heavy traffic of larger planes. We took off and landed on the grass. After getting clearance for takeoff, we would bump along on the uneven ground and, as we lifted into the air, the light plane would bounce this way and that, depending on the vagaries of the wind. As we gained altitude, we were still subject to being blown around by air currents. At times, it seemed we had completely relinquished control of the plane and were being thrown about at the whim of the wind. Flying over the farmland of southern Illinois gave me an entirely different perspective of the topography of the area. From the air, each farm seemed to be laid out in precise squares, and the shades of color of the various crops made it resemble a huge patchwork quilt. To be airborne for the first time is an exciting moment that is forever remembered.

At Scott Field, because we were students, we didn't have to do KP or other base-related assignments. We were, however, responsible for keeping our barracks in condition to pass inspection, and there were daily details such as latrine duty or policing the area around our barracks.

One enjoyable aspect of Scott Field was its proximity to St. Louis. We had weekends off and the Air Force supplied bus service to the city. Once there, city buses and public jitneys provided fast and affordable transportation. St. Louis had much to offer servicemen, with its museums, parks, excellent zoo, and the Cardinal baseball team, which was having a great year. Most GI's, however, were seeking female companionship, and since the industrial war effort had attracted many young women to local war plants, it wasn't difficult to meet members of the opposite sex, financially independent and out on the town.

When I went into the city, depending on how flush I was, I could stay at the Statler for $3.50, or the Lenox, across the street and slightly more posh, for $4.75 per night. After I checked in, I would head up the street a couple of blocks for Carl's Bar, a favorite watering spot for the Rosie-the-Riveter crowd. Carl's served excellent steaks and reasonably priced drinks. Usually, I would leave Carl's Bar with a date; or, if my date had to change for the evening, I would set a time to meet her later.

I recall leaving Carl's Bar late one afternoon without a date, which meant that I had been drinking alone for a couple of hours and was feeling no pain. As I tipsily made my way down the sidewalk, I was boxed in by two guys who suddenly grabbed me by my arms and elbows and lifted me high into the air.

Turning my head, I could see that each set of hands belonged a sailor wearing a black armband with the large white letters "SP" emblazoned on it. "Put me down," I sputtered, "the Shore Patrol doesn't have any jurisdiction over me. I'm in the Air Force." The Shore Patrol was the Military Police arm of the Navy.

I was gently set back on the ground and I turned to face two giants well over six feet tall who were doubled over with laughter. The two jokers who had scared the piss out of me were John Glass and Bill Price, a couple of years ahead of me in high school and Memphis policemen before going into the Navy. I had never expected to have a mini-high school reunion on the sidewalk in front of Carl's Bar in St. Louis. We filled each other in on information we had heard from Memphis about other Humes High

School friends. I was very sad to hear that several guys we knew had already been killed overseas.

One thing that I did find shocking in St. Louis was a blatant example of bigotry, which I'm sure was only the tip of the iceberg in that city. I was exploring a neighborhood with friends one day when we passed a swimming club that had posted a large sign announcing "Jews and Niggers not allowed!" Was this the Spirit of St. Louis?

I had encountered occasional anti-Semitism in Memphis, but it was never this overt. Memphis racism, of course, was an entirely different matter, with signs on street cars directing "Colored Passengers Will Move to the Rear of the Car," and the Overton Park Zoo's posting: "Reserved for Colored on Thursdays." Public water fountains, of course, were reserved for "White Only" every day of the week.

I was not aware, at the time, of the truly psychopathic anti-Semitism that existed in Germany. So far, we were only receiving rumors of Hitler's "Final Solution" for Jews, and it was so abstract, no one really understood its true nature. I had no idea that I was destined to experience this madness firsthand.

Our barracks was a two-story structure, housing about thirty-five men on each level, with bunks arranged in two rows on either side of a large open room. There was a footlocker at the foot of each bunk, and at the head was an open closet with a rack for hanging clothing.

There was a wide aisle running down the center of the barracks, and there was a door at either end. Because the doors were never locked, anyone had access to any barracks at any hour of the day or night. In order to protect our belongings, it was necessary to have one person on duty as a Barracks Guard at all times. Each day, a new guard was assigned by the Barracks Chief. The guard could study or read while on duty, and could be relieved to go to the mess hall.

The job of Barracks Chief was a highly desirable one, mainly because of several perks, some of which were legitimate and some that were not. One attractive feature was that the Barracks Chief had his own private room on the first floor, complete with a door that could be locked. Also, the Barracks Chief could appoint himself Barracks Guard whenever he wished and get a day off.

Actually, no one was supposed to be Barracks Guard more than once a month, but no one kept track. It was unwise to do this too frequently, however, because you would miss too many classes.

The illegitimate perk involved the Barracks Chief taking the Barracks Guard job himself, then assigning several guys from various shifts to fill in for him when they were not in class. The Barracks Chief could then sneak into town for the day.

Since St. Louis was less than three hundred miles from Memphis, I could not resist the temptation to go home from time to time. It was a risky thing to do, because we weren't allowed to travel more than a hundred miles from camp. Whenever I made the trip, my mom was a nervous wreck until I got back to Scott Field. I would usually take Barracks Guard duty on Friday and spend the weekend at home.

When I became Barracks Chief, I began to think about who I would choose as my replacement when I graduated, and I finally settled on a fellow named Picard. Picard was not only a friend, but he was also at the top of his class and set a good example for others by keeping his area of our barracks spotless. Our record for inspection demerits was always at a minimum.

One Saturday, I went to St. Louis with Picard and two other guys from our barracks. As usual, we headed for Carl's Bar for lunch and a few drinks. Then we went to a "While You Wait" laundry to have our summer khakis cleaned and pressed and our shoes shined. We sat in little, curtained booths, in our underwear, reading newspapers while we waited. It usually took about thirty-five minutes. We all lucked out that evening: everybody hooked up with a date and we went our separate ways.

On Sunday, we all slept late, and that afternoon we went bar-hopping, looking for girls who were interested in having dinner with us, but no one seemed able to connect. The four of us ended up having dinner together, then stopped by the Lenox Hotel for a drink before going back to the base. The tables were all taken, but there were three stools available at the bar. I knew that I had already had enough, so I said, "Look, I don't want anything else, why don't you guys take these seats and I'll sit right outside in the lobby and have a cigarette. Just stop by and pick me up when you're ready to leave."

I sat down on a soft chair, lit up a Camel, and probably dozed off immediately, because the next thing I remember was waking up to someone picking up my hand and removing the cigarette just as it was about to burn my fingers. I stared into the deep blue eyes of the prettiest girl I had ever seen, and knew that I must be dreaming. She had shoulder-length blond hair and wore a simple black dress with a single strand of pearls.

"I'm sorry I disturbed you," she said softly, "but you were about to get a bad burn." Then she turned to go.

Now, I was wide awake and I wasn't going to let this dream get away. "Oh, no, I thank you for not letting me set myself on fire. How about having a drink with me?"

She hesitated. "No, it's getting late and I really ought to turn in."

"It won't take long to have a drink. What can I get you?"

She smiled. "A Coke would be fine."

"You sit right here and I'll pop over to the bar and get you one."

I ran over to the bar and got a couple of Cokes. "Put this on your tab, Picard. This is for an angel I just met." I nodded at the two-seater couch in the lobby and all three looked over and gulped. "How in the hell did you find her?" said Picard. Over my shoulder I said, "She came to me in a dream."

Her name was Debbie, and she had come to St. Louis to visit her father, who was a major at Scott Field. We sat there chatting, and my heart was pounding and I was awash in those enormous blue eyes.

My friends came over from the bar, and Picard brought me back to reality. "Norm, we're gonna have to get back to the base. You know our shift changes today and we have a six A.M. class in just a few hours."

I had a sinking feeling in my stomach. I asked Debbie how long she was going to be around, and she said, "A couple of days." My mind was racing ahead, and I told her that I would sneak into town the next day and meet her.

"Look, guys, I'm gonna walk Debbie to her room and I'll be right down."

Picard wanted to know her room number. "If you're not down in five minutes, we're coming up for you. We've gotta catch the next bus. If you miss class, you're going to be in deep trouble. Especially being Barracks Chief."

"I promise you, I'll be back in five minutes."

When we got to her room, she handed me the key and I opened the door. As we stepped inside, she closed the door and walked into my arms. Her soft lips met mine in the most passionate kiss this nineteen-year-old had ever experienced, and she drew me gently down to the bed.

I was startled by three loud knocks at the door. "Norm, we're going to miss our bus. We have to leave *now*," said Picard through the door.

"You guys go on back. I'll see you later."

This time Picard was banging on the door with a closed fist. "If you don't get back to the base, you're gonna flunk out of school. Come on out!"

At that moment, no threat short of the firing squad—and I

would have to think about that—was going to induce me to come out. "I'm not coming."

"Then I'm going to knock the door down," Picard yelled, and he was big enough to do it.

I got up, kissed Debbie good-bye, and opened the door. "I'll see you tomorrow," I said. I never thought to ask her surname.

On the elevator, Picard said, "You'll thank me for this tomorrow."

"Go to hell," I growled.

When we got to the bus station, we waited for an incoming bus to unload so we could board it for the trip back to the base. I noticed a friend from our shift waiting on line. "Hi, Tony, six A.M. is gonna come around real quick, huh?"

Tony gave me a puzzled look. "We don't pull a six o'clock tomorrow. That shift ended Friday. We don't have be in class till noon."

I whirled around toward Picard, and he ducked. "I'm sorry, Norm, I forgot the shift was changing today," he said apologetically.

"I'll deal with you later," I said, and went racing back to the Lenox Hotel. As I entered the lobby, it occurred to me that I didn't remember the number of Debbie's room. I knew that it was on the fifth floor. I stopped at the front desk and asked if anyone named Debbie was registered on the fifth floor. "We're not permitted to give out that information," said the clerk.

I went up to the fifth floor and began knocking on doors. Gently. "Debbie?" I whispered. Some rooms were apparently vacant and the silence was prophetic. At the rooms that were occupied, the responses I received through closed doors were by no means cordial.

As I continued down the hallway, my desperation grew and my door rapping became louder, as did my voice. I guess I was hoping that even if I was at the wrong door, Debbie would hear me calling and come to my rescue.

At the other end of the hallway, an elevator door opened and a very large person, wearing the badge of hotel security, got off and headed in my direction. "Who are you looking for, soldier?"

"I was trying to find Debbie's room."

"Debbie who?"

"I don't remember her last name."

"If you don't know her last name, we have no way of knowing what room she's in. You can't go around waking up everybody in the hotel at one o'clock in the morning. I'm going to have to ask you to leave."

It was a long ride back to the base. When I got there, I took the duty roster into my room and entered Picard's name for latrine duty for the next two weeks. Later in the day, Picard was abjectly apologetic. "Norm, it was an honest mistake. You know I wouldn't blow you out of the water like that on purpose!"

I was unrelenting, and Picard cleaned the latrine every day without complaint. A couple of months later, when I graduated, I appointed Picard to be the next Barracks Chief. I often wondered whatever became of Debbie. And I often dreamed about how that evening would have played out . . . if I had stayed.

One day, when I was on the six A.M. to noon shift, I returned to my barracks to find a large sign on the bulletin board ordering everyone to fall out in front of our barracks at 1600 hours, attired in fatigues, for flood duty. We were all milling around, speculating on where we were going, when an officer arrived in a jeep. He told us that a small town nearby was being threatened by the rampaging Mississippi River, and we were going to reinforce the levee with sandbags in hope of saving the town from being flooded out.

Trucks arrived shortly, and we were transported to the flood site. The rushing water was lapping at the tops of the sandbags already in place, and it seemed impossible that we would be able to add enough new bags to fend off the rapidly rising stream. Our contingent was dropped off at various points along the levee and instructed to work as quickly as possible.

I was assigned to one of several railroad handcars that were propelled by two men pumping handles in an alternating fashion, similar to a seesaw. My partner and I were to take our cars to an area where hundreds of sandbags had been dumped, load up our car, and return to the spot where our group was placing them on top of the old bags.

Although we were handling the sandbags at a frenzied pace, none of us had much hope that we would be successful. We worked throughout the long night, breaking only to use the men's room at a nearby gasoline station. We hadn't had any supper, and exhaustion was starting to take its toll when we noticed that we were finally beginning to make some progress. The water was leveling off. Invigorated by the first signs of success, we worked even harder; after another hour, we had won the battle.

As we wearily climbed the hill to the town, we were a bedraggled group, GI shoes caked with mud, clothes soaked with sweat, our hair plastered to our heads, but it was a great feeling to know that we had turned the floodwaters away from this small town. The sun was just rising as we reached the top of the hill. Then we all stopped dead and stared in amazement at the folding chairs; the card tables, each neatly topped with a tablecloth; the napkins and utensils for four place settings. The whole town had turned out to greet us. The men came over and shook hands, patted us on the back, and earnestly thanked us for saving their town. The women brought us over to a breakfast buffet that, far from our accustomed Air Force grub, caused us to salivate with memories of home cooking.

There were huge piles of hot-from-the-oven biscuits; real butter, honey, and homemade preserves; fresh-from-the-farm slices of cured ham, bacon, and sausage; real, not powdered, eggs; fresh milk; and gallons of glorious hot, strong coffee and heavy cream. For dessert, there were home-baked pies, cakes, and cookies. We sat and gorged on this wonderful meal, and our hostesses kept coming over with refills until we were unable to find room for another bite. It was such a perfect way to say thank you. One year later, in an entirely different environment, I would be wistfully remembering that feast and wondering if I would ever experience such gustatory delight again.

When I graduated from radio school, I was promoted to private first class.

I guess they wanted to show us that the single stripe didn't mean much, because each of us was assigned to some kind of duty while we were waiting to ship out to gunnery school. It was the luck of the draw whether you were sent to do KP, clean furnaces, "police the area," which meant picking up cigarette butts and trash, or some other equally demeaning task. I, and another unfortunate, ended up working at the coal piles. This was just a case of bad luck. We weren't even being punished.

The time was late August, and Scott Field was swelteringly hot and humid. The person we reported to at the coal-storage area was a civilian, which didn't please me any more than the assignment, but I was determined to be agreeable. The civilian showed us where coal had been dumped from rail cars and told us to transport it in wheelbarrows to a large shed about fifty feet away.

In less than fifteen minutes, our fatigues were soaked with sweat and our faces and hair were coated with coal dust. Although we worked steadily until noon, we had barely made a dent in the huge pile of coal. On the way to the mess hall, we stopped at the latrine to wash up and were startled on seeing ourselves in the mirror. Rivulets of sweat had run down our blackened faces, and we looked grotesque. We removed as much of the grime as we could, then went to lunch.

It was probably just over an hour when we returned to the coal pile. We picked up our shovels and began loading the wheelbarrows, when the civilian showed up and began berating us.

"What took you guys so long? Did you have fish for lunch? I could have moved more coal in an hour than you two have in half a day. Let's step it up now. And before you go, be sure you sweep the floor of the shed."

Suddenly, I was past my flash point, and I confronted him, shovel in hand. "Look, you creep, we've worked our butts off today in this filthy coal pile and we don't need you telling us what to do. If you don't get the fuck outta my face right now, I'm gonna split your head open with this shovel."

The civilian wheeled around and headed for the gate and we returned to the coal pile. In a few minutes he was back with a lieutenant, who walked over to us and said, "Are you guys having some kind of problem over here?"

We put our shovels down and saluted. "No, sir. We're not having any problem. I'm just not going to put up with any civilian yelling at me and giving me orders."

"Well, he's in charge of this area, Private, and he has to tell you what needs to be done. I understand that you threatened him."

"Yes, sir, I did. We've been moving coal from here to that shed all day, just like he asked, and then he comes over and gripes that we're not working fast enough. Look, Lieutenant, in a few months we're going to be flying combat missions and this civilian will still be here running the coal yard. Does the Air Force require us to take orders from civilians?"

The lieutenant stared at me for a moment. Then he turned to the civilian. "Leave these guys alone and let them do their job." They both went back through the gate, the civilian a few paces behind the lieutenant. We finished up for the day and left, but I had no intention of returning to the coal yard again.

The next day, all the recent graduates assembled at the duty pool for assignment. I was talking with several classmates about my disastrous experience the previous day, when the duty sergeant asked for six volunteers to clean a vacant barracks in preparation for occupancy by incoming students. I immediately raised my hand and encouraged five of my friends to come along. At least we knew what this assignment involved.

When we reported to the vacant barracks, we were met by a staff sergeant who instructed us on what needed to be done, then left. We swept the floors, cleaned the latrine, and washed windows. After lunch, we came back and made a few finishing touches and the place would have passed any inspection. Late in the afternoon, the sergeant returned, commended us on doing a good job, and dismissed us.

On the following day, before handing out new assignments, the sergeant at the duty pool asked if any of us had been instructed to report back to complete our job of the previous day. I quickly raised my hand. "We need to finish up a barracks cleaning detail."

The sergeant asked, "Do you know who else was on that job with you?"

"I sure do," I replied.

"Good. You guys can take off."

On the way back to the vacant barracks, my friends weren't too sure. "Norm, we could get in trouble over this."

"Yeah, but KP or the coal pile would be worse," I said. When we arrived, the staff sergeant was on his knees, fixing a loose spring on one of the beds. As we trooped in, he gave us a puzzled look. "What are you guys doing back here?"

"We got to thinking after we left, Sarge, that the cigarette butt cans have dirty sand in them and need to be refilled," I said. "We'll also be glad to check out all the beds and see if any of them need repairing. And the furnace room is a mess and needs cleaning badly."

The sergeant straightened up and grinned knowingly. "All right, if you want to work here today, go ahead. When you're finished, I don't mind your hanging around the barracks, just be sure you don't leave any candy wrappers or other trash lying around. And don't sit on the beds."

We spent all of the remaining days, before we shipped out to gunnery school, at the vacant barracks and the sergeant never showed up again. We read magazines, ate candy bars, shoved the wrappers in our pockets and left the place clean. We also learned a valuable lesson on how to manipulate the system.

Although I was very anxious to leave for gunnery school, when it came time to ship out, I would have given anything to spend just one more week at Scott Field. The World Series was about to start between the St. Louis Cardinals and the New York Yankees, and the Cards had donated a number of tickets for distribution on our base. A drawing was held, and I was lucky enough to win a free ticket. I was elated. I had never been to a World Series. Alas, it was not to be. I left for gunnery school at Laredo, Texas, the day before the game, and gave my ticket to a friend. I have still never been to a World Series game.

Chapter Five

LAREDO

Our accommodations for the trip from Scott Field to gunnery school at Laredo, Texas were far from first class: they were a string of boxcars that had been converted into a troop train by installing rows of bunk beds in them. There were no other amenities, not even lights; so, not long after sundown, we were in the pitch dark except for our cigarettes, which glowed like lightning bugs. Some of us had flashlights, but the batteries went too quickly to allow playing cards, so we went to sleep early every night. We usually kept the sliding doors open for ventilation, which allowed soot from the coal-burning engine to fly into the cars, much of it ending up under our fingernails and in our hair. It was fun to sit in the doorway, with our feet dangling, but it was best to avoid looking forward toward the engine, because you were sure to get soot in your eyes and each tiny cinder felt like glass. We had our own mess car, and the food was no better and no worse than the chow in most mess halls.

When we arrived in Laredo, the Armed Services "logic" once again took charge and I was told that I, a radio operator/gunner, would be trained as a ball-turret specialist. Some paper-shuffler had apparently placed my name in the wrong file and, although a radio operator on a bomb crew had absolutely no need to learn to operate the ball turret, I knew it was futile to question the end decision. Consequently, I learned much more than I ever needed to know about the ball turret.

Our training consisted of learning to use the shotgun and to fire the .50-caliber machine gun from turrets mounted on the backs of trucks. After we had mastered these weapons, we were scheduled to be taken up on air training missions, where we would fire at targets towed by other planes.

Some of the trainees who had grown up on farms or in the country felt right at home firing the shotgun, as they had been hunting for years. For the rest of us, each day was increasingly painful, as our shoulders and chests absorbed the mule-like kick of the shotgun. No matter how I held the gun, tight against my shoulder or an inch or two away, I would receive a powerful punch each time I fired. I even tried firing from my left side, but the impact was the same and soon both shoulders were black and blue.

One phase of our training involved skeet-shooting, in which we used our shotguns to down clay targets, projected from three different angles, in a manner resembling the flight of birds. In order to strike and explode the target, we had to lead these clay "pigeons" in the same manner we would use to hit enemy fighter planes in combat. If you fired directly at the moving target, the shotgun pellets would arrive just behind the pigeon and you wouldn't have a hit. The correct way is to lead the target by just enough distance that the gradually widening pattern of pellets will converge with the target and blow the pigeon to bits.

I quickly mastered the technique of leading the target. In fact, I had an opportunity to prove the concept one night. Several of us were sitting on my bunk playing poker, when someone yelled, "Rat! Rat!" I turned and saw a large rodent running along the wall across the room. I reached down, picked up my heavy size-12 GI shoe, calculated the lead distance, and threw as hard as I could. Perfectly timed, the shoe and the rat met just at the right moment. Result: one dead rat.

A roar of appreciation echoed throughout the barracks and I was invited to the PX to be toasted for my prowess, with quart mayonnaise jars filled with 3.2% beer.

Despite my success with the rat, my shoulders were in such pain from the pounding they had already taken from the shotgun that I was doing very poorly with my trapshooting. The routine required the shooter to yell "Pull" each time he wanted target to fly out of the projector, and an attendant would trigger the device. Once, with my shotgun at my waist, I called for the clay disk too soon. Suddenly it went flying past and, automatically reacting, I fired from the hip. Boom! The target exploded into many tiny fragments and I felt like a gunslinger at high noon in an old-time Western movie. After that incident, my propensity for trapshooting increased dramatically.

Soon, I was calling for targets more rapidly than anyone else and blasting them out of the air consistently. I became the hero of the skeet-shooting range and acquired the nickname "Trigger."

The day finally arrived when we were to begin the part of our program we were most apprehensive about: air-to-air firing tests. If you were going to wash out of gunnery school, this would be the point where it was most likely to happen.

Despite our worries about failing to get a passing score on target shooting, we felt that the flying portion of our training should have been the most exciting part of our course. As it turned out, our anxiety was heightened from an unexpected source: the pilots who flew us on our firing missions.

These "hot-shot" pilots were second lieutenants, fresh out of pilot training, who were bitter because they were assigned to fly gunnery students on training flights rather than fly P-47 fighter planes into combat. They were flying AT-6 single-engine, two-seater fighter/trainer planes with open cockpits, and AT-11 twin-engine trainers, which held about twelve passengers.

The AT-11's were equipped to pull a tow target, which was fired at by gunners on the AT-6's from .50-caliber machine guns mounted on the back of the rear cockpit. Each AT-11 would also take up about ten gunners who took turns firing at tow targets pulled by other AT-11's. Each gunner was given .50-caliber bullets that had been marked with the color he had been assigned for the day, and he was responsible for loading them in his gun.

When the planes returned from their missions, instructors were on hand to count the number of hits on the tow targets by color; then the students were graded accordingly.

The shavetail pilots, bored to death with ferrying a bunch of privates first class around, were always trying to show off their skills. I had no fear of flying, but I had a healthy respect for flight safety and I resented it when these "aces" were reckless. There were usually about fifteen to twenty AT-6's on a training mission, and we flew to the target area, then back to the airfield, in formations of three or four planes. En route, the pilots got a kick out of tapping their wings on the wings of other planes in the formation. They also thought it was great fun to get close to the AT-11's and spin the tow targets around with their wings, ostensibly to show the gunner they were flying how many hits they had gotten.

I came close to getting a huge blemish on my record one day, because I got stuck with a very impatient pilot who probably had a date that evening and was annoyed that my gun was malfunctioning. The AT-6 is an open-cockpit, two-seater plane, and pilots and gunners must wear goggles or else feel like the air slipstream is ripping their eyeballs out.

I was in the rear seat, belted in, but still dealing with the wind tearing at my body and, try as I might, unable to close the cover on my gun sight. If I held my thumb on the inner leaf of the gun sight, I could bring the top portion down, but when I removed my thumb, the inner leaf flew back up and I couldn't fire the weapon.

The pilot kept yelling at me to fire and I kept telling him that I couldn't get the sight down. Then he would dive the plane about two thousand feet and I felt that I'd left my stomach back at four thousand feet. Of course, I couldn't work on my gun while he was careening all over the sky, and he was becoming more and more impatient with me.

Then he began threatening to take me back to the base, and I knew that would be disastrous, so I kept asking for a few more minutes. I had one leg hanging out of the cockpit as I leaned over the gun, but I could not get the sight closed. Finally, I knew what I had to do. I left my thumb on the inner sight and, with my other hand, smashed the cover down on my thumb. The cover locked and I was finally able to fire my gun. I actually made quite a good score that day, but that night the fingernail on my thumb turned black, and it eventually came off.

One day, a very tragic event stopped the pilots' horseplay forever. We were returning from a firing mission, at an altitude of about five thousand feet, and were close enough for every plane to be within sight of the others. There was one three-plane formation where the two pilots who were wingmen happened to be cousins and the plane in the middle was flown by a pal. By some strange coincidence, the two wingmen decided to clown around at the same instant and both of them performed an inside peel-off. The two planes locked wings and spun toward the ground. One of the gunners was able to bail out before the planes crashed. The two cousins and the other gunner were killed.

Immediately, all the planes were called down. As the planes approached the airfield and began to circle for landing, a dramatic change came over the daring pilots who, only minutes before, had been so unflappable. I had never seen an aborted landing of an AT-6 at our airfield. Suddenly, no one seemed able to land on the first try. Plane after plane would hit the runway, bounce into the air and then take off again. It was clear how much the crash had affected everyone's nerves. It took three times as long to get all of the planes back on the ground that day.

Later, we heard that the commanding officer of the base, a general, had all the pilots assemble in his office that afternoon. He addressed them as anything but officers and gentlemen. He warned that the slightest hint of aerial horseplay in the future would result in a quick and decisive court-martial. That ended the escapades of the feckless would-be fighter pilots. I expect that the general's threat had less effect on their metamorphosis than the sudden realization that they were not immortal.

A few days later, it was my turn to fire from an AT-11. There were ten of us on board and, before we took off, the pilot said that the last shooter to finish would come forward and sit in the co-pilot's chair. Then he would know we had all fired and he could head back to the base. He seemed to be a reserved guy, unlike the hyper AT-6 pilots. I wondered if his quietness was at all related to the alcohol on his breath.

I happened to be the last one to shoot, and when I slid into the co-pilot's seat, he turned and asked: "All done?" I nodded, and he slowly turned the plane in the direction of the airfield.

After about ten minutes, the right engine began to sputter; soon its twin propellers were no longer a blur as they froze to a stop. The pilot managed to steady the plane on one engine, but suddenly became very agitated and told me, "Yell back and tell them to cut the tow target." I relayed his order at once, and the guys began to scramble around looking for the wire-cutter. He obviously felt that the extra pull of the long cloth sleeve would drag us down even faster. Then he called the tower, told them we were at 3,500 feet and were coming in for an emergency landing.

Someone from the rear came running up. "We can't find the wire-cutter."

The pilot's face was turning red. "Pull the lid up on the compartment near the door!"

Just as the yell came from the rear, "We found the wire-cutter," the right engine sputtered to life again. Obviously wanting to save the tow target if possible, and with both engines now working, the pilot said, "Tell them to hold up on cutting the wire."

I relayed the latest order just as the right engine began to falter again. We must have been at about 2,500 feet by then and the pilot began to look around for his parachute. He spotted mine just in back of my seat and I was quick to say, "No. That's mine."

Again the engine caught and we soon touched down on the runway. After we had taxied over to a hardstand, the pilot looked over at me rather sheepishly and said, "I had a dental appointment this morning and I'm still a little out of it." I didn't mention that I found it odd that the dentist would have given him alcohol as an anesthetic. The way he was reeking, I was sure that he was still suffering from a bender the night before. Had he been sober, he might have acted more decisively, cutting the tow target the first time the engine failed rather than putting all on board in danger.

When we graduated from gunnery school, each of us was awarded a pair of "silver" wings, separated by a single replica of a machine gun bullet. We were also promoted to buck sergeant, which meant three stripes, at that time the lowest rank held by anyone scheduled for combat flying status. We immediately had our stripes sewn on every shirt and jacket. With our wings pinned to our shirts and the rims removed from our hats, which were then crushed to give them the rakish look of a pilot, we were transformed into flyers. For a long time, it was difficult for us to resist lingering at any mirror or window, which gave back our new reflection.

Chapter Six

MEMPHIS

My two-week furlough in Memphis was not what I had
expected. For months, I had eagerly looked forward to
going home; but when I got there, everything seemed
changed. There were men and women in uniform all over the
place. The Naval Air Station at Millington was right outside the
city, so sailors were much in evidence, along with khaki-clad troops
from nearby Army camps.

By now, all my male friends were also in the armed services and
it was rare that I ran into a guy I knew who was also on furlough.
Of course, the girls were still around and many were working in
manufacturing plants producing supplies for the military. They
were lonely with all the men away and the servicemen who wanted
to date them after USO dances made them feel as if they were
being "picked up." They were delighted to go out to dinner, or to a
dance with someone they knew from before the war; someone they

wouldn't have to fight off later in the evening. Most girls I asked out were old friends from high school, so there was no romance involved. Almost every girl had a boyfriend in the military, and he was usually someone I knew. Besides, I wasn't hunting tail; I just wanted a friend and good company.

There was something strange about my hometown. Even with industry booming and downtown flooded with people every night, Memphis still seemed like a ghost town to me. All my friends had vanished into the military. In the past, I could never have walked the length of Main Street without stopping to speak with, or wave to, a dozen or more friends. Now, though the landmarks were familiar, the occupants could have been transported here from somewhere else.

No matter whom I dated, we inevitably ended up talking about the "War." One date said, "It's hard to really have a good time any more. You fellas come home on leave just before you go overseas, and you ask us out. We both know that in a matter of weeks, you're going to be in combat. Neither of us can forget that long enough to be ourselves." Truer words were never spoken.

The fabric of our lives had changed so much, we often found it comforting to just sit and reminisce about our high school days. That, at least, had been a time of stability; of sanity; of continuity; of knowing what you would be doing tomorrow, or next week, or next month. We talked about friends who were overseas, and we struggled to accept the fact some of our classmates had already been killed in action. Sometimes we would look at their pictures in our yearbook; not that we didn't recall how they looked, but the book was something tangible, something that we could hold in our hands. It was hard to imagine that these teenagers we remembered as being so vibrant and so carefree had been thrust into the most challenging and grave situation of their short lives and, in a single instant of bewilderment, suddenly realized that their lives were over. How did they face those final seconds? How did they react? How would I react?

Before I went into the Air Force, I had worked at Fisher Body, a former automobile plant that had been converted to a factory manufacturing B-25 bombers. One afternoon, at the beginning of my old shift, I drove by to say hello to any former colleagues who might still be around. Other than two supervisors, who had been declared essential by the draft board, there was just one riveter I had worked with, and he had enlisted in the Marines and was reporting for duty in a month.

I soon began to feel out of place . . . restless. Everyone had a job to do during the day, while I was at loose ends. I was bored with movies. I didn't enjoy drinking alone. I kept running into the parents of my friends who were in the service, but those conversations were trite at best. Relatives invited me over to dinner, but that soon became an ordeal and I began to beg off.

I knew that my future was dangerous and uncertain, but I was anxious to confront it. The waiting was beginning to bug me. I couldn't stay home with my family every night. My sister was eleven and my brother three, so there wasn't much I could discuss with them. Whenever I did stay home, my parents sat around and awkwardly tried to pretend that everything was normal . . . but nothing was normal. I had a hard time keeping myself from clock-watching.

A couple of times I went to the zoo at Overton Park and felt sorry for the animals pacing back and forth in their cages. I passed the pony ride and watched the kids sitting uneasily atop their steeds, as bored attendants led the ponies around the track by their bridles. I remembered once, when I was old enough to ride solo, the pony I was on suddenly decided to kneel and I slid forward onto his neck. Fortunately, a stable employee ran over and pulled him up just before he started to roll over on his back. I strolled through the quiet park grounds calmly thinking about my future—which was so obscure that I wasn't afraid to face it, because I didn't have a concrete idea of what to expect. I felt like I was watching a movie in which I was the lead actor and the film was moving inexorably toward its unpredictable conclusion.

The day before I left for Avon Park, Florida was a Sunday, and my grandmother had the whole family over for lunch. She made my favorite dishes, and the noisy conversation at the table helped to break the tension of my imminent departure. After lunch, I went for a walk with my uncle David and he wished me good luck and a safe return home. I told him that if the family was notified I was KIA (Killed in Action), they could believe it, because the Air Force investigated very carefully before issuing such a statement. But if they received word that I was MIA (Missing in Action) . . . I would be back. I don't know what brought this intuition into my nineteen-year-old head, but I had a very strong belief in what I said.

Chapter Seven

THE CREW

I had never been to Florida until I was shipped to Avon Park in December 1943 to join a B-17 crew as radio operator/gunner and go through transition training. Friends who had gone there on vacation had almost always picked Miami over Tampa or Fort Lauderdale because, back in the late thirties, it seemed the more prestigious resort. Their descriptions of beautiful beaches, penetrating sunshine, warm ocean water, coconut and palm trees, and lush gardens left me with a skewed mental image that every town in Florida was located right on the beach. Of course, this wasn't true, and the only bodies of water near the air base were the numerous freshwater lakes and the backyard swimming pools. Avon Park was situated smack-dab in the middle of the state, about seventy-five miles from either the Gulf of Mexico or the Atlantic Ocean.

When I graduated from gunnery school at Laredo and received orders telling me where to report after my furlough, I found out that Avon Park was a B-25 bomber base. I felt that the chickens were coming home to roost. Before going into the Air Force, I had built B-25's at the Fisher Body plant in Memphis, and had been a "troubleshooter," responsible for putting oversized rivets in holes that had been drilled badly and had to be redrilled to accommodate a larger rivet. Before I installed a larger rivet, it was necessary to get approval from an engineer. Sometimes it was decided that a larger rivet could not withstand the stress and the part was scrapped but, more often than not, the process was approved. I often had grave misgivings about the justification for some of the decisions and was concerned about the airworthiness of the planes. Now I was going to have to fly in these babies, and I was not looking forward to the experience.

On the day I arrived at Avon Park, I was at the bus station waiting for transportation to the base, and two lieutenants were standing next to me waiting for a bus to the train station. Suddenly the air was filled with the sound of a plane taking off, and we watched a B-25 slowly climbing into the sky. The two officers looked up, and one said, "Well, there goes the last one of 'em."

My curiosity got the better of me, and I couldn't help but ask, "Excuse me for butting into your conversation, Lieutenant: the last of what?"

"The last of the B-25's. Tomorrow morning, this becomes a B-17 base."

I broke into a big grin, and he said, "You seem pleased, Sergeant."

"I used to build B-25's," I said.

"That bad, huh? We've found them to be very reliable."

"Oh, I'm sure they are, sir. I guess I'll just feel more comfortable with B-17's, because I didn't see how they were put together."

I spent my first night at Avon Park in one of several barracks reserved for newcomers just reporting for duty. The next day, crews would be formed and, thereafter, the crew's six noncommissioned officers would be assigned to one barracks and the four commissioned officers to another.

The hardstands where the planes were parked all had numbers, and I received a notice to report to a certain hardstand at eight the next morning. When I arrived at the site, eight men were already there, four officers and four noncoms. I saluted the officers and introduced myself. Then the last man arrived, and the pilot, Lt. Edgar Farrell, began a roll call of the crew from a clipboard he held. "Lt. John Benedict, copilot, Lt. Wynne Longteig, bombardier, Flight Officer Sherwood Landis, navigator, Staff Sgt. William Peters, engineer, Staff Sgt. Norman Bussel, ball-turret specialist—"

When I hesitated, Lt. Farrell turned to me and asked, "You are the ball-turret specialist, right?"

"Well, yes, sir, I am—but I don't think we can fit the radio equipment into the ball turret."

"My God! You're the radio operator as well? How in the world did that happen?"

"I don't have the faintest idea, sir. That's what they assigned me to in gunnery school."

"Well, let's go on and we'll deal with that in a minute," Farrell said. "Robert Palumbo, tail gunner?"

"Right, sir."

"Merle Rumbaugh, waist gunner?"

"Yes, sir."

"Waide Fulton, waist gunner?"

"Yes, sir."

"Joseph Guida, gunner. What position are you, Joe?"

"I was told I would be a waist gunner, sir."

"Well, we already have our waist gunners. You're small, so you could fit easily into the ball turret. Do you think you could do that?"

"I can try, Lt. Farrell."

Farrell grinned. "I'm sure Sgt. Bussel will give you some pointers, right?"

"I'd be happy to," I said.

"Good. Then we have our crew. We'll fly our first training mission tomorrow morning at eight. For now, let's all climb on the plane and just get familiar with our positions."

The Boeing B-17 Flying Fortress with a hundred-foot wingspan and four huge engines looked immense compared with the little Piper Cubs and AT-6 fighter/trainers I had flown on. The radio compartment was the most private place on the plane. It was shut off by a forward door to the bomb bay and another door at the rear leading to the waist. I had my own small desk and chair, and loads of radio equipment.

The bomb bay was crossed by an eighteen-inch-wide catwalk with a single thick rope, strung about waist-high to hold on to as you walked across. Just past the front end of the bomb bay was the engineer's position and his top turret gun. Farther forward was the pilots' cabin, and to the left and below was an opening to the bombardier and navigator's station and the forward escape hatch.

The waist section housed the two waist gunners, the ball-turret gunner, and, farther back, the tail gunner. The plane was boarded from a door in the waist, also intended as an escape hatch for everyone aft of the bomb bay.

Like most air crews, ours was an interesting mixture of places of origin and personalities:

The pilot, 2nd Lt. Edgar Farrell, was from Atlanta. A former insurance agent, he had powerful wrists and forearms, which were a real asset in wrestling with the controls of a B-17. His Southern drawl and quick soft laugh soon put everyone at ease. It was amazing how fast each of us ended up with a nickname or contraction. Our six noncoms openly called each other by their newly coined names, but the officers' nicknames were only spoken when they were out of earshot. At 28, Farrell was the eldest on our crew and we secretly referred to him as "Daddy."

The copilot, 2nd Lt. John Benedict, 27, was from California. A former sergeant in Chemical Warfare, he had applied for pilot's school, transferred to the Army Air Forces, and, after training, received his commission. His primary topic of conversation was, "We have enough chemicals to gas to death every Kraut and Jap bastard that breathes and this war would be over in six weeks. I don't know what the hell we're waiting for." He looked a bit like Fred Astaire. A sardonic character with a scatological vocabulary, his favorite expressions were "bat-shit, cat-shit, gnat-shit, and rat-shit." We referred to him as "Benshit." He was also a racist and used the "N" word freely and frequently.

The bombardier, 2nd Lt. Wynne Longteig, 25, hailed from Idaho. Tall, quiet, and unassuming, recently married, he did his job with as little conversation as possible and vanished as soon as we were dismissed every day. We called him "Long John."

Our navigator, Flight Officer Sherwood Landis, 22, from Pittsburgh, had just graduated from college with a degree in engineering when he was drafted into the Air Force. Tall, with a brush of auburn hair, he was friendly and outgoing with a good sense of humor. Only in the service for six months, he felt that the rest of us were much more experienced and didn't hesitate to ask questions, even of the noncoms. He suggested that we call him "Sherry."

The engineer, Staff Sgt. William Peters, 22, was from Bristol, Virginia. Short, muscular, and tough, with flaming red hair, it was inevitable that he became "Red." A teller of tales, most of them tall, we never knew when to believe his stories. He said that he was a bootlegger, running moonshine between Virginia and Tennessee. A true skeptic, he believed nothing we heard in training lectures; he had to prove it himself. Red was also a master of appropriation.

Mention that we needed a broom to sweep our barracks, and he would soon show up with one.

Our left waist gunner, Sgt. Merle Rumbaugh, 20, was a farm boy from Pennsylvania. "Rum" always had this big, engaging smile on his face, and nothing seemed to get him down. Conscientious, popular with everyone on our crew, he was the first to volunteer to help if you had a problem.

The right waist gunner, Sgt. Waide Fulton, 27, was a former postal worker from Oxford, Pennsylvania. A serious fellow who had his girlfriend visit him in Avon Park, he frowned at the boisterous behavior of the younger members of our crew. Because he didn't like to be teased, we other noncoms made it a point to needle him, and he always obliged by barking back at us. We just called him Waide.

The ball-turret gunner, Sgt. Joseph Guida, 19, was from Brooklyn, and we all delighted in his accent. Quiet and shy, he never went pub-crawling with the rest of us, preferring to stay in the barracks and write letters. His parents were dead and he lived with his older sister. A friend he had gone to gunnery school with, also a quiet young man, often came by, and they would sit around and chat or go to the PX together. Because he was so introspective, "Little Joe" often seemed lonely and we always made sure to include him in our conversations.

I guess I had no strong distinguishing characteristics, at least none that the guys latched on to, because my name was merely shortened to Norm. Actually, this was a nickname to me, because in Memphis I had always been called Norman.

Our tail gunner, Sgt. Robert Palumbo, 21, was from Detroit and a very pleasant and agreeable guy, but we really didn't get to know him well: less than two weeks after we started flying, he began to have severe earaches and went on sick call. The doctors found that he had burst his eardrum and removed him from flying status.

In a couple of days, a tail-gunner replacement joined our crew. It's hard to explain why the new man didn't fit in. He wasn't unpleasant; he just didn't seem to want to be part of our crew. He was detached, never accepted our invitations to join us for lunch or for a beer at the PX. After work each day, he never went back to the barracks and would usually show up after we had all gone to sleep.

We didn't know then that if a crew member was incompatible, the rest of the crew could ask the pilot to remove him and request a replacement. So we set about trying to motivate this gunner to ask for a change on his own.

Although it was never far from our minds that every passing day brought us closer to the time when we would be facing the unknown challenge of engaging an enemy in mortal combat, most of us were in, or barely out of, our teens and could still be easily diverted to boyish pranks.

We were pretty inventive, but not very nice in our actions. When the tail gunner returned to the barracks each night, he didn't know what he might expect to find in his bed. Once it was a garbage can. Another time it was an old suitcase we had found and filled with soda bottles.

One night after dinner, I asked Red, "How would you feel if you came back to the barracks one night and found your bunk sitting up on the roof, completely made up, with your duffel bag hanging from the end of the bed?"

Red said, "You don't mean—?"

"Yes, I do mean."

"That's a great idea. Maybe then he would take the hint."

"Yeah, but how would we get it up on the roof and perch it on the gable?"

"With a ladder," said Red.

"But we don't have a ladder."

"We will," said Red as he headed for the door.

In less than ten minutes, Red was back with a very long ladder, and we began to move the bed to the roof. It fit nicely, with the legs on either side of the gable. Since it wasn't dark yet, we were able to make up the bed perfectly. A quarter would have bounced up from the blanket. Then we tied his duffel bag to the head of the bed, climbed down, and hid the ladder.

About an hour later, our unfortunate tail gunner showed up. We had started a poker game at the opposite end of the barracks and didn't look up when he came in.

He came over to where we were playing and said plaintively, "I can't find my bed."

Red and I looked up and said in unison, "Can't find your bed?"

"No. It just disappeared."

Red and I became very helpful and walked around the barracks with him looking for his bed. "Maybe somebody was playing a prank and took it outside," said Red.

I got a flashlight out of my footlocker and we all went outside.

We looked all over the area and expressed our commiseration with the tail gunner over his loss.

Then, I suggested that we return to our barracks and look up on the roof.

"Why in hell would anybody put his bed up on the roof?" asked Red.

"I don't know," I said, "but some nuts around here will do anything."

I shined the light up on the roof and—lo and behold—there it was.

"Well, don't this beat all," said Red.

"How can we get it down?" asked the tail gunner.

"Don't worry," said Red. "I know where there's a ladder."

In a few minutes, we had the bed back in the barracks and the tail gunner couldn't thank us enough for our help. So much for that plan.

The next day, Red and I spoke with Lt. Farrell and told him the new guy just wasn't working out and was it possible to ask for someone else. Daddy said that he was authorized to request a replacement and that he could get us another tail gunner—and he did.

The new guy in the tail was about the size of Little Joe, but that's where any resemblance ended. Sgt. Vasilios Constantine Mpourles, 24, was an irrepressible, bubbling bundle of energy who was never quiet. The son of a lawyer in Lowell, Massachusetts, he was an expert on Army regulations and planned on going to law school after the war. He had been in the Army for about a year when he signed up for pilot training. Like so many others who weren't quite coordinated enough to be pilots, Bill flunked out and was sent to gunnery school and then on to Avon Park to join a crew. He told us that Vasilios, in Greek, is William, so he became Bill.

On bomber crews, the protocol of saluting and adhering to the codes of procedure, such as those followed by infantry units, soon became cumbersome. With ten men crammed into small quarters, it was difficult not to become chummy and abandon the ceremony of hierarchy. The noncoms on my crew noticed that other crews had ceased to salute their officers every morning at the flight line, so we gradually stopped as well.

One day, after we returned from a training flight, Daddy asked the noncoms to remain behind for a few minutes.

"Lt. Benedict has complained to me that you've stopped saluting the officers on our crew. I think you know me well enough by now to believe me when I say I really don't give a shit. But he was Regular Army before he became a pilot, and he's a stickler for the rules. If I don't ask your cooperation on this, he could go to the colonel and force me to comply. So, rather than stir up a whole beehive, I'm gonna have to knuckle under to his demands and ask for your help. I apologize for having to do this, but I hope you'll understand. Can I count on you?" Everybody said, "Sure, Lieutenant," and he thanked us and left.

We all headed for the PX to drink beer. "That's pretty chickenshit," said Bill. "I don't see the other crews throwing highballs every time their officers fart."

Red said, "I knew Benshit had a bug up his ass. Next thing, he'll have us spit-shining our shoes. And maybe his, too."

"Look," I said, "we're gonna make him sorry he ever started this crap. From this minute on, we'll salute Benshit till his arm falls off, but we'll stop all casual conversation with the officers. While we're on duty, we'll answer any questions they ask about our work; but after that, we'll make ourselves scarce. They'll get the idea soon enough."

Everybody agreed, and we all went to chow. Later that evening, Sherry stopped by our barracks. "I just want to say that I had nothing to do with what Farrell was pushed into telling you guys today. Frankly, it embarrasses me. You have a lot more time in the service than I do."

I walked him to the door and said, "Look, Sherry, just remember that whatever happens after today is not directed against you personally."

Most of the noncoms on our crew walked to the flight line together every morning. I suggested to the guys that from now on, we arrive singly, so that the officers would have to salute six times.

The first day after Daddy's protocol announcement, we were standing on the hardstand waiting for the last guy to arrive and the officers were making small talk, but other than an occasional nod, there was no response from the noncoms. It was awkward.

Before a flight, it is the radio operator's job to pick up headsets and throat mikes at the radio shack. The rule is that an officer must sign out the equipment. I was glad that Sherry or Long John had been accompanying me to sign out, but on the fourth day of our silent rebellion, Benshit volunteered to go with me. On the way over to the radio shack, he tried chatting and I simply nodded at appropriate times.

While he signed out, I hooked the equipment over my left arm and started back. He ran to catch up with me. About a hundred feet from the radio shack and about twenty feet apart were two small snack stands.

As we approached, Benshit asked, "Like a soda?"

"No, thanks," I said.

"How about a candy bar?"

"No, thank you."

There were about ten people waiting at each stand, and Benshit got in line at the stand on the right. I got in line at the stand on the left. I saw him look over at me, but I was talking with the guy behind me. When I got to the front of the line, I ordered a Coke and a Baby Ruth. As I shifted the equipment on my arm to reach my wallet in the top pocket of my flight suit, one of the headsets fell to the ground.

As I put my wallet back, Benshit walked toward the fallen headset and said, "I'll get that."

I reached down quickly, scooped it up, and said, "I've got it."

We walked back to the plane in silence.

Later that night, Daddy came to our barracks. All of us jumped to attention. He smiled. "At ease, guys. It's over, and I'm glad. Whatever your plan was, it worked. Benedict asked me to lighten up on the regulations. In the very near future, we're going to be depending on each other for our lives. I want to depend on a buddy, not a robot. We've got a good crew. I'm proud of every one of you. Have a good night." We were all glad that things were back to "normal," but Benshit had acquiesced to the relaxation of protocol only because it created an awkwardness that our other officers complained about and he seemed to crave their acceptance. His superiority was barely concealed, but we could deal with that, as long as the robot-like saluting process had been waived.

With everyone more relaxed, we were now free to enjoy flying the B-17, and what a thrill it was. The purr of the four powerful engines drummed a unique sound into your brain that you would never forget. Our training missions were quite a bit of fun. Sometimes we flew bombing missions over the Atlantic, where Long John would drop dud bombs on targets already set up for us. Sherry would plot the course to our target, and when we reached it, Long John would take over and drop a "bomb."

Other times we would fly gunnery missions over the water. This required two B-17's working together. Each plane had a white cloth tow target hooked to its tail by a long cable, and the planes would take turns shooting at each other's targets from a predetermined distance. Each gun position on the plane was loaded with a different color .50-caliber bullet. When the target was hit, the bullet hole was smudged with the paint color assigned to each gunner. When the plane landed, the bullet holes were counted by color and each gunner was given his score.

The day before we flew our first gunnery mission, an instructor met us at the plane to explain the fine points of operating each gun position. Positions such as the waist guns and the radio operator's gun were moved manually by the gunner. The other positions—tail turret, ball turret, engineer's top turret, and the "chin" turret—were moved by automatic controls.

The top turret, with twin .50-caliber machine guns, faced aft toward the vertical stabilizer. As the instructor explained the top turret, which was Red's position, he said, "Now, don't worry about shooting holes in the vertical stabilizer. This turret has an automatic cutoff. Just before your guns reach the vertical stabilizer, they will stop, momentarily, until they get past it, then firing will automatically continue. So you couldn't hit the tail assembly even if you tried."

I looked over at Red, and he had a quizzical expression that bothered me. Walking over to the mess hall, I asked him, "Do you have some doubts that the cutoff on your gun won't work like the instructor said?"

"As a matter of fact, I do. How do I know the damn cutoff won't malfunction?"

"Red, you don't. But do you know what I would do if I were firing your gun?"

"What?" he said belligerently.

"I would take my finger off the trigger just before I came in line with the vertical stabilizer. Then, as soon as I got past it, I would start shooting again."

"Yeah, but I still don't believe the cutoff will work every time. Nothing's perfect. We know that. That instructor's full of shit."

A couple of days later, we were on a gunnery mission and Daddy was on the intercom calling out to each gunner when it was time for him to fire. He started at the tail and worked forward.

After my turn was over, he called out, "Okay, Red, go for it."

I listened to the brrrp, brrrp sound of Red's gun. Then, I heard a loud sproing and the plane shuddered and momentarily rocked from one side to the other. Daddy got it back under control, but I jumped up and looked out the Plexiglas gun blister in the radio room. Why was I not surprised to see a very large hole in the vertical stabilizer?

I opened the door to the bomb bay and raced across the catwalk to Red's position.

"Red, goddamit, you shot a hole in the vertical stabilizer!"

"I told you it wouldn't work! I told you!"

"Well, I didn't ask you to prove it to me, asshole. You coulda gotten us all killed."

Daddy was on the intercom. "Red just shot a hole in the tail and obviously clipped a cable. We're returning to base."

We landed at Avon Park without any problem and taxied to the hardstand. Everybody got out, and Daddy said, "Let's just don't say anything about this accident. The ground crew will see the hole and fix it."

We went to dinner and then were playing cards in the barracks when the door opened and two stern-looking officers came in. "Where's Crew Six?" one of them barked. We were all already standing at attention. Bill raised his hand. "Right here, sir."

"Air Force Intelligence. Come with us," the other officer said.

We tromped behind them to the office of the colonel who commanded our group. As we entered the office, we saw Daddy, Benshit, Long John, and Sherry standing at stiff attention. I couldn't decide which one was more pale. We moved next to them, turned to face the colonel, and came to attention.

What followed was a dressing-down that none of us would ever forget. The colonel ranted about the possibility that the plane could have taken the lives of another crew if the damage had not been discovered by the ground crew. He raved that every single one of us was complicit in failing to report the hole in the tail and could be held responsible if this led to an accident. Then he lowered his voice and, in measured words, said, "If I ever hear the faintest hint that you guys have returned a damaged plane, with even the slightest scratch on the skin, without reporting it, I'll court-martial you so goddamned fast you won't know what hit you. Dismissed! Now get your sorry fuckin' asses out of my sight before I change my mind." We all certainly learned our lesson and scooted back to the barracks with our tails between our legs.

One very hot morning, we were assigned to fly cross-country on a training mission that would take at least eight hours. Although it was only 7:30 A.M., our flight fatigues were already soaked with sweat. Daddy suggested that we pick up a bottle of 3.2% beer for everyone on the crew. "By the time we get to 7,000 feet, the beer will be cold."

We all thought that was an excellent idea and hurried over to the

PX. We stashed the beer in the radio room and I was to let the crew know when it was cold. At about half-hour intervals, I would reach over and touch the bottles, testing for drinking temperature. After a while, I began getting calls asking "How's the beer coming?" Since the intercom didn't work station-to-station, the whole crew would hear my progress reports.

Finally, I decided that the brew was just right, and I announced, "Beer call!"

It wasn't long before the radio room was crowded with suds-sippers. Then I noticed Daddy and Benshit raising bottles to their lips, and I panicked. "Who the hell's flying the plane?"

Daddy grinned, "It's okay. We're on automatic pilot."

"Automatic pilot, shit," I said, "somebody's gotta be in the cockpit."

"C'mon. I'll show you," Daddy said, and opened the door leading to the pilot's compartment.

I followed him forward and couldn't believe what I saw. The pilot and copilot's steering wheels were moving very slowly, in unison, as the plane adjusted to the set course. It was an eerie, ghostlike sight and my feelings about the trustworthiness of this system were about the same as Red's when he was asked to accept that the cutoff on his guns would work flawlessly. We headed back to the radio room and our cold beers, but I was not even a little at ease with the phantom pilot at the wheel.

"Look, guys," I said, "the cutoff on Red's gun didn't work and I don't trust this automatic pilot to always work, either. Until a warm body's up there flying this plane—no more beer." Daddy laughed, picked up his beer, and made his way back to the cockpit.

All B-17's were equipped with a "relief tube," which is a fancy term for a makeshift toilet. It was located in the bomb bay and was simply a long rubber tube with one end extending outside through an opening in the side of the plane and the other end fashioned with a small metal funnel for you to pee into. It was an acrobatic feat to hold the tube with one hand, your penis with the other, and try to urinate while balancing yourself on the narrow catwalk with the plane bouncing around in the sky. As if that wasn't enough of a problem, you were fair game for anyone else coming across the catwalk who decided it would be fun to push you in the back and make you pee all over your hands. Not that anyone *ever* did that. . . .

On the day of our cross-country flight, we were surprised to find a portable toilet in the waist compartment for an emergency. When Daddy saw the potty, he told the crew, "Look, if anybody needs to use the toilet, feel free. Just remember, whoever uses it will be responsible for cleaning it when we land. I'm not gonna be on latrine duty for you guys."

A couple of hours into the flight, the door to the bomb bay opened and Daddy came into the radio room, headed for the waist.

"Are you going where I think you're going?" I asked.

"Oh, shut up," he growled.

Since Daddy was disconnected from the intercom, I took the opportunity to announce to the crew that he was using the potty. After we landed, we all gathered around and razzed the hell out of him as he washed down the toilet with a hose.

It was Daddy's idea that Sherry, Long John, Red, and I should be able to fly the plane in an emergency on a combat mission. Choosing us made sense, because we were closest to the cockpit. His plan was that, in the event both he and Benshit were incapacitated, one of us could take over and fly the plane back to friendly airspace. "You won't be able to land, of course, but the crew could bail out and whoever is flying the plane could set the automatic pilot for the plane to return to enemy territory and then bail out himself. It's simply a case of can't hurt, could help."

So, the four of us took turns getting flying lessons from Daddy. When it was my turn to take over the pilot's seat and I was confronted by all the gauges and levers, I felt that the task was impossible.

Daddy said, "Now, just relax. This is a lot less complicated than it looks. First, to get the feel of it, I want to set you on a straight course. Tell you what. See that train over to your left? Turn over that way; then just follow the track. It's straight as an arrow for miles."

Since I had been driving a car for over four years, I didn't hesitate a second to turn the wheel to the left, in order to align the plane with the train. That's when my heart suddenly stopped beating, because the right wing immediately dipped to the right and the plane was making a right turn.

Benshit was standing behind my seat and said, "Batshit."

Daddy was laughing so hard, he could barely speak. "Sorry, I forgot to tell you. This doesn't work like a car. You turn the wheel in the opposite direction from where you want to go."

"Forgot, hell," I said. "You did that on purpose!"

"You're okay," he grinned, "just turn the wheel slowly to the right and you'll be able to follow the train."

Back on course, I was following the train track easily when Sherry reached up from his compartment below and tweaked out the hair on my leg. "Don't do that," I yelled. "This is serious stuff." And that was the extent of my first flying lesson.

After Benshit's protocol pullback, the crew became much closer and we started going to West Palm Beach, about 90 miles away, on weekends when we were off duty. Little Joe, Waide, and Rum were not party types, so there were usually seven of us. We would take a train to West Palm and rent two convertibles. The officers and noncoms usually didn't hang together, so we devised a system of keeping track of the location of the cars. If one of us needed a car, we would leave a message at the front desk. The driver of each car was required to call the hotel for messages, every two hours, on the hour. If you wanted a car, you left a message at the desk, then waited in your room for a call. This method worked very well and, surprisingly, there was never any conflict in reserving a car.

When we arrived in town, we'd pick up our cars, then drive to the liquor store to stock up our rooms. That done, we would head for our favorite watering hole. Our hotel of choice was the centrally located George Washington. The only problem was that most of the guests were elderly people who quietly sat around the lobby all day. When we burst into this library-like atmosphere, carrying our bottles of booze and talking loudly, we got stony stares of annoyance from the regulars. Once, when we were checking in, the hotel manager told us that he highly valued our patronage, but could we try to hold it down just a bit. We agreed that we would and tried to contain our exuberance until we were in our rooms.

I usually paired up with Red, Bill, or Sherry. For whatever reason, it was rare for more than two of us to hang out together on any given evening out.

Red liked to drink, so we usually went bar-hopping. By evening, we would be deep enough in our cups that female companionship wasn't a possibility. Besides, as tough and outgoing as Red was with guys, he was very shy around the ladies.

One evening, Red and I got back to the base late and he had a pint of whiskey concealed in his jacket. He decided we needed a nightcap, but we had no ice and no chaser. We tried the Rec Room, but the soda machine was empty. "Tell you what," I said; "why don't we go over to the mess hall, get some coffee, and pour a shot into our cups."

"Damn good idea," said Red.

The mess hall was closed, but we saw the mess sergeant in the kitchen and walked over to him. "Hi, Sarge," I said. "Mind if we get a couple cups of coffee?"

"Help yourself. There's clean cups over there."

Red and I filled our cups three quarters full with hot coffee, went out into the dining room, and sat down at what the Army called a table but was really a wooden picnic table with a solid top.

Red pulled the whiskey from his jacket and poured some into our cups. We lit cigarettes and sipped our coffee and booze. After a few minutes, the mess sergeant walked past us, then stopped and came back. He picked up Red's cup and sniffed. "You're drinkin' liquor!" He grabbed both cups and yelled, "Get the hell out of my mess hall 'fore I call the MP's."

Red and I went into the latrine right across from the mess hall to take a leak. As we washed our hands, I saw dozens of empty bottles on the long shelf above the basins. Everything from Vitalis and Listerine to Coke and beer bottles.

"Red, pick up as many bottles as you can carry."

"Why the hell do I want to do that?"

"Just do it and follow me."

Red started picking up the bottles, mumbling, "You're losing your fuckin' mind, Norm."

Walking outside, we stood across from the mess hall and I began pelting the door with the bottles. Red started laughing like hell and joined me. The mess sergeant ran to the door, but whenever he tried to open it, we unloaded a new barrage of bottles. He went back inside and soon returned with a lieutenant. We threw our last bottles and ran like hell for our barracks.

Jumping into bed with our clothes on, we pulled the blankets over our heads. In a few minutes, two MP's came in flashing lights at every bunk. Guys were covering their eyes and yelling, "What the hell is this?"

Then the MP's left.

For weeks afterward, Red and I were afraid we'd be recognized if we returned to that mess hall, so we walked half a mile to another one for our meals. But it was worth the inconvenience. Every time we recalled the incident . . . we would double over with laughter.

Bill was a fun guy to hang out with. He had a wonderful half-laugh, half-giggle that was disarming, and everybody liked him. He enjoyed being in the company of girls, but that's as far as it went. There was a steady back home, and he was faithful to her. Whenever we went to Avon Park, he always brought his expensive-looking camera along and introduced us as photographers for *Stars and Stripes*. Naturally, every patriotic American girl wanted her photo in *Stars and Stripes*, so Bill would shoot photos in a variety of poses and his subjects would be delighted to spend some time with us. He neglected to mention that his camera was never loaded with film.

Several weeks before we were scheduled to leave Avon Park, Bill came to me for advice. "Norm, I want to get engaged before we ship out. I know I can't get leave to do it, but I've gotta get to Lowell to give my girl this ring . . . even if I have to go AWOL." He showed me a beautiful engagement ring he had bought in Sebring.

"Bill, there's gotta be a way to swing this without you going AWOL and really getting your ass in all kinds of trouble. Let's go talk with Daddy and see if he has any ideas."

Daddy's idea was for Bill to take off for three days without telling anyone he was leaving. "I'm pretty sure we can round up someone to take your place on the plane while you're gone. If you get caught, we're all shit out of luck, but I know how important this is to you and it's damn well worth the gamble. So do it."

I could see Bill choking up when he thanked Daddy. He left for Massachusetts the next morning and all of us, with the exception of Benshit, sweated his return. Three days later, we delightedly welcomed him back with back-pounding, ribaldry, and congratulations on his engagement. He said that they'd had a wonderful time and he was grateful to all of us for making it possible. Little did his fiancée know about all the teamwork that went into it!

One evening around six o'clock, Daddy came by our barracks and said he'd been asked to help on a training mission to check out copilots on night landing. He needed a radio operator and an engineer to complete the crew and, if Red and I were free, he would like us to fly with him. We said we'd be glad to go along, and he told us to meet him at the hardstand at 8:00 P.M.

When we arrived, we were surprised to find that a colonel was flying with us. He was not our CO, but a command pilot who was going to grade the copilots on their landings.

When we were airborne, the door to the bomb bay was left open, because the copilots sat in the radio room as they waited to be called to the cockpit for their turns. I could lean over and see when Benshit took his turn at landing. It took three attempts before he could land the plane. On the first two, he bounced so hard he was forced to take off again. In all fairness, some of the other copilots bounced damned hard, too, but Benshit was without a doubt the worst.

The next day, Daddy sent Benshit off on an errand before we boarded the plane. He gathered the crew around and said, "I have a question to put to you guys. To be perfectly honest with you, I don't like the way Benedict lands the plane. We tested out ten copilots last night, and he was one of them. It's not just because he had some very rough landings last night. I'm not happy with some of the landings he's made in the daytime, and I'm sure you couldn't help noticing. For my part, I'd rather he didn't land the plane again, period. Day or night. But, I leave that decision up to you. Whatever you say, I'll go along with it."

The vote was unanimous. None of us wanted Benshit landing the plane. I don't know if Daddy told him that he wasn't going to land any more, or just didn't offer him the opportunity. When we were airborne, Benshit was frequently at the controls, but he never landed our plane again.

As we moved into the final weeks of our transition training, we were all getting a little edgy about our upcoming move to a combat zone. I think that if we had known just where we were headed, we might have been more accepting, but speculating back and forth between fighting the Japanese and the Germans was unsettling.

Then there was another blow: the crew's weekend trips to West Palm Beach were broken up, because both the officers and the noncoms were now scheduled for Saturday training sessions. And, with the exception of the two waist gunners, none of us attended the same classes. Pilots had their own group, as did navigators, bombardiers, engineers, radio operators, ball-turret gunners, and tail gunners.

I was lucky that radio-operator classes were early morning, and I began going into West Palm alone afterward. I would usually be able to get into town around 3 P.M. Then they changed the rules on us: until we shipped out, radio operators would have classes all day on Saturdays.

One Saturday night, before the change in the class schedule, I ended up at a nightclub that featured strippers. Three were scheduled to perform that night. The first came out and danced with fans; the second held two bouquets of long white feathers. Their performances were artful and professional, with no hint of being vulgar. They were young and pretty and, even though the audience was largely comprised of guys in uniform, there were no catcalls. Just long and loud applause.

"And now," the MC proclaimed, "the act you've all been waiting for. Fresh from a sparkling engagement in Atlantic City and a triumphant tour of the United States, we are pleased to present the talented. The enchanting. The exciting. The breathtakingly lovely . . . LaVerne LaBelle!"

LaVerne LaBelle was strikingly beautiful, with shoulder-length light blonde hair and a body that was indeed "breathtakingly lovely." She danced with light blue transparent veils, so gracefully that she seemed to be floating on air. She was being eaten up by the eyes of uniforms lonely for wives and girlfriends.

After leaving the club, I found a waffle house-type restaurant, and it was full of military guys with their dates. The smell of coffee and pastry wafted through the air as people came out of the doors, and I suddenly realized that I was hungry. I couldn't see an open seat in the place, but I went in anyway, just as a single sailor got up at the end of the counter. I quickly walked over and sat down.

I ordered coffee and a doughnut. As I lit a cigarette to enjoy with my refill, I glanced over at a booth to my right where two women were sitting. One of the women was in her forties, and the other one—was her. It was LaVerne LaBelle. I recognized her even though she had covered her pale blonde hair with a white kerchief and removed her makeup. She was still impossibly beautiful. They were both smoking and drinking coffee. It was hard as hell to keep from staring, but I forced myself to concentrate on the baked goods in a glass case behind the counter.

A young Air Force sergeant came in, gunner's wings displayed on his shirt, and stood at the end of the counter waiting for a seat. When he noticed that one side of LaVerne's booth was open, he removed his cap, went over and asked, "Do you mind if I sit here, ma'am?"

LaVerne looked up and said, "We're having a private conversation."

"Sorry," the gunner said sheepishly and moved back to the counter. After a couple of minutes, he seemed to decide it wasn't worth the wait, and he left.

I was embarrassed for the gunner, and the more I thought about it, the angrier I became. The kid wasn't being fresh, he wasn't drunk. What was her problem?

I stubbed out my cigarette and stepped over to their booth. "I just want to thank you for being so nice to that gunner who asked to sit here. In a few weeks, he's gonna be overseas. Putting his life on the line. Protecting your freedom to make money off other guys in uniform, who pay to see you perform. Congratulations. You're very patriotic."

As I turned away, LaVerne reached out and took my hand.

"Wait a second," she said. "Give me a chance to apologize. I was rude and I deserve everything you said. I've had a very tiring day and I spoke before I thought. Sit down. Please. Sit down and talk to me for a minute." She truly did seem sorry, and my anger melted away almost instantly.

As I eased into the other side of the booth, I felt as if I was drowning in her large, blue eyes. The older woman got up. "I'm whipped," she said. "Gotta get some shuteye. See you tomorrow, LaVerne." Then she left.

We talked for a while. She asked me where I was from. How long I'd been in the Air Force. What was my position on the plane. If I had a girl back home.

I answered, "Memphis. About sixteen months. Radio operator/gunner." And, "No."

She was from Texas. Twenty-four years old. Had gone to New York to study ballet, but ran out of money and turned to stripping. Then, out of the blue, she asked, "Are you hungry?"

"I can always eat," I laughed.

Her next question blew my mind. "How'd you like to come over to my place and I'll fix you some breakfast?"

My knees felt weak and my head was swimming, but I managed to say, "That sounds great."

Her apartment was in a unit that the nightclub leased for its performers. LaVerne turned on a record player, and I sat in the living room and listened to *Stardust, Deep Purple, String of Pearls,* and other hit songs while she cooked bacon, eggs, toast, and coffee. Why had no breakfast in memory ever tasted so good before?

I did the dishes and she dried. Then she asked if I would like to take a shower. When I came out of the bathroom, she was in bed, motioning for me to join her. How can I explain what happened next? I can't. There were lingering kisses and soft, flowing hair. There was the fragrance of perfume and there was smooth, velvety skin. There was softness and warmth and wetness. There were drumrolls and violins. Thunder and muted trombones. And finally, after the entire world had exploded into a million flashes of colored light—we both lay there in each other's arms and giggled like a couple of kids necking in a hayloft.

We woke up around noon, and I no longer felt like a bumpkin. We ate pimiento cheese sandwiches with sliced tomatoes and drank cold buttermilk. LaVerne had some errands to run before she went to the club, and I had to get back to the base.

We kissed good-bye in the living room. "You'll be back in town next weekend?" she asked.

"Nothing could keep me away," I said.

"Will you call me?"

"Will a bee make honey? I have your number here and at the club. I'll call you on Thursday."

I don't know why I took a taxi to the train station. I could have easily floated there. In fact, I could have found thermals and glided all the way to Avon Park.

Never in my life has a week passed so slowly. Every hour dragged along maddeningly. Finally, it was Thursday and I called LaVerne. Her voice set my heart pounding again.

"Will you be in tomorrow night?"

"Yes, I will."

"Meet me at the club and after the show we can walk home together."

The train to West Palm seemed to be traveling at half speed, and we appeared to linger forever at every stop. I arrived at the club early enough to get an up-front table again. At one point, LaVerne peeked through the curtain and I waved.

The first two strippers danced and then LaVerne came out. All at once, I felt uncomfortable that hundreds of people were watching her body. But my pangs of jealousy disappeared when I remembered last weekend.

I met her in the lobby after she had changed into street clothes. This time she wore a hint of makeup and her lips were glossy red. Her eyes sparkled as she came over and kissed me. This time we didn't stop at the waffle house. We went straight to her apartment and postponed breakfast until later.

On Saturday, we ate lunch out. Afterward, we went for a stroll in a park. LaVerne wore white shorts and a floral patterned blouse. Uniforms were everywhere, some with dates, some not. I don't think anyone recognized LaVerne, but I don't believe anyone we passed failed to notice her either.

When she went to work that evening, I stayed in the apartment and read and listened to the radio. I would pick her up at the club later. The news from England was not good. Buzz bombs were leveling parts of London. In fact, the war was not going well in either theater.

I knew that our love affair had no future. But, for now, I was too ecstatic about the present to think about the future. LaVerne was the focal point of my life, and everything else was blotted out.

We made a date for the next weekend, and LaVerne walked a few blocks with me before we kissed good-bye.

This time, on the way to the station, I didn't feel nearly so buoyant. I had a sneaky feeling that we might be shipping out in a couple of weeks. When I got back to my barracks, my misgivings turned out to be true. We were indeed being moved to parts unknown in two weeks. And then, to make matters even worse, I was informed that there would be a radio operator's training session all day on Saturday.

I was determined to spend one last weekend with LaVerne even if I had to go AWOL. I ran into a radio operator friend from another crew and was telling him how upset I was with the new Saturday training schedule. He said, "Ya know, Norm, that thing is gonna be such a damn zoo. They're holding it in a hangar. If you aren't there, nobody will ever know."

"Yeah," I said, "but when they call roll, I'm dead meat."

He said, "Hell, if they call your name, I'll answer for you. Who'll know the difference?"

"Just don't forget to listen for my name," I cautioned.

"Don't give it a thought. I guarantee, if your name is called, I'll sound off loud and clear. So go on to Palm and enjoy yourself."

My penultimate week at Avon Park was so frenetic, I didn't have much time to clock-watch, so it passed more quickly than the week before. I caught the late afternoon train to West Palm and tried to read a book, but after I finished each page, I didn't remember what I'd read. I scooted down in my seat, put my head against the window, and dozed off. I woke up when a conductor called out, "West Palm Beach. Everybody off for West Palm Beach."

When I picked LaVerne up at the club, she immediately sensed my mood. "Are you all right?" she asked.

"I didn't realize it was that obvious," I said.

"What's wrong?"

"We're shipping out next week. This will be my last pass to West Palm."

"We knew it had to come. Let's don't allow it to spoil our weekend. We won't even talk about it right now. Okay?"

"I'll try my best," I said.

Funnily enough, I'd never danced with LaVerne. I hadn't asked, because even though I didn't dance badly, I felt I'd be self-conscious with a professional. When we got to the apartment that night, she mixed a couple of drinks and we sat close together on the couch sipping and smoking. Then she asked me to dance. We pulled back the carpet and, to my surprise, I felt very comfortable with her. She put her head on my chest and moved so smoothly, I couldn't make a misstep. We danced only to waltzes. Slow, sentimental stuff. After a while, she took my hand and led me into the bedroom.

Now it was she who looked a little sad, but we never spoke of it.

This time our lovemaking was slower, as if we were trying to savor every second. Trying to commit each precious caress to memory.

On Saturday, I woke up before LaVerne and couldn't get back to sleep. I got out of bed slowly and closed the bedroom door as I went out. I put on a pot of coffee and opened the drapes in the living room. I was greeted by bright sunshine. I promised myself that I would be cheerful when she woke up. I poured myself a cup of coffee and lit a Camel.

She came in wearing a pink gown and a smile.

"I'm sorry. Did I wake you?"

"No, the aroma of the coffee and cigarette did."

I poured her a cup and lit her cigarette.

"What would you like to do today?" she asked.

"I really don't care, just so we're together."

"Why don't we borrow my friend Nikki's car and go for a drive?"

"Sounds good to me."

Nikki lived just around the corner. She was a cute brunette in her early twenties, with a short haircut and a nice figure. She worked as a bartender in another nightclub where LaVerne said the patrons tipped very generously. Her car was a fire engine-red Chrysler convertible.

LaVerne asked me to drive and we cruised around for a while, top down, enjoying the air and the sun. Then she suggested we go to a Cuban restaurant she liked, just outside the city limits. It was a very popular spot, but, since it was afternoon, we had no problem being seated. I'd never eaten Cuban food before, so LaVerne ordered for us and I was pleased with her selection.

After the meal, I walked LaVerne over to the club and then roamed around the area. Alone, I could think about the finality of these last few hours and I felt depressed and empty. I wallowed in my own pity for a while, then forced myself to shelve my bad thoughts so I could put on a happy face for LaVerne. I went back into the club and nursed my drinks carefully. The last thing I wanted to do was get crocked on our final night together.

Again, that night, our lovemaking was slow and tender. Afterward, neither of us was sleepy, so we brought coffee to the bed, smoked, and talked softly. LaVerne asked me what I wanted to do when the war was over.

"I'll go back to school and study journalism," I said. "How about you?"

"Well, I've been stashing away as much money as I can. When this whole thing is over, I'd like to go back to Texas and open a ballet school."

Finally, we stood in her living room for the last time and kissed good-bye. Then she took a gift-wrapped package from a bookshelf and handed it to me. "Don't open it until you get back to the base."

"I'm embarrassed," I said. "I didn't get anything for you."

"Its nothing, really. Just a keepsake to bring you good luck."

Back at Avon, I headed for the PX to buy cigarettes and brought LaVerne's gift with me to open along the way. I tore the wrapping off and took out a lacy pink bra. I brought it to my face and smelled her delicious perfume. After that, every time I flew, I hung my lucky charm from the lamp over my radio table. The guys tried to pin me down as to where I had gotten it, but I always dodged the question.

I never thought that I would get back to West Palm again, but one morning Daddy suggested that our crew go to dinner there that night as a sort of farewell salute to Avon Park. We ate at a very nice restaurant and there were toasts all around.

All evening, I fought against the urge to call LaVerne. I knew that if I did, it would simply be another good-bye, and I was still dealing with the sadness of the last one. I didn't call, but I was so torn by making the decision, I became depressed and drank too much. I was definitely not the life of the party.

Three days later we shipped out to Camp Kilmer, New Jersey.

Chapter Eight

QUEEN LIZ

T wo days before we boarded a train from Avon Park, Florida to Camp Kilmer, New Jersey, we were issued .45-caliber automatics and holsters. We had used the gun on the firing range and Red really liked the heft and the feel of it, so the next day he wrapped it in newspapers, packed it in a box, took it to the post office, and sent it home.

I said, "Red, you can't even imagine what kind of friggin' trouble you're getting yourself into. We're not talking about a few days in the guardhouse. We're talking long-term jail sentence for stealing Government property. Are you out of your cotton-picking mind?"

"When we get overseas, I'll say somebody stole the gun on the ship and they'll issue me a new one."

"Really? If you think they'll buy that crock of shit, you're pretty damned dumb."

Red had had enough of this conversation. "Yeah? Well, we'll hafta wait and see then, won't we?"

I shouldn't have been surprised, because I knew that Red led a charmed life. When we got to England, he told his story and was issued a new .45. Nobody chewed his ass out. Nobody questioned him. Amazing.

The train trip was rather uneventful for the first hour. Some guys played cards; some wrote letters, most recalled wild escapades in West Palm Beach and laughed at each others' accounts of drunken antics and close calls with MP's.

Then we pulled off on a siding and were told we'd be there for about fifteen minutes, so we all piled off the train to stretch our legs. Around a hundred feet from the tracks was a citrus processing plant and the loading dock was filled with crates of oranges. A pretty young woman came out on the dock, smiling and waving to us. Someone yelled, "How about an orange?" She opened a crate, took out a large navel orange, and held it out. The guy ran up and claimed his orange. He was soon followed by others, and she opened another crate. Then, some greedy nutcase picked up a whole crate and brought it back to the train, and that set off a bunch of copycats, who proceeded to empty the dock.

The young woman's generous gesture had set off a mass pillaging, and she was no longer smiling. She began to scream for the guys to return the crates, but that was never going to happen. I'm sure that, ultimately, Uncle Sam was billed, and paid, for the stolen fruit.

We were scheduled to be at Camp Kilmer for four days. I expected we would use this time to pack our duffel bags, write final letters home, and drink beer at the PX. The camp commander had other ideas. He decided that the noncoms would pull work detail until we shipped out. We were all aircrew members. There wasn't a man among us who was below a buck sergeant in rank. Sergeants don't do work detail. Enlisted men, who are stationed at a camp as permanent party, do work detail. What kind of a shithead would assign menial jobs to NCO's three days before they left for a war zone? A real creep, that's who. A CO who would never set foot outside the United States, that's who. Every NCO in our group was beyond pissed.

On the day we arrived, it was late afternoon and we escaped any work assignment. The second day, we were part of a group selected to police the area. It reminded me of basic training, when we did that job while a sergeant yelled, "Let's get it done fast. All I want to see is assholes and elbows!"

The second day, a lieutenant who was making the assignments asked if anyone knew how to drive Army trucks. Red quickly raised one hand and, dammit, pointed to me with the other. Before I could object, the lieutenant said, "Good. Check out two trucks over at the pool and pick up the garbage cans at every mess hall. Then take 'em to the dump. And you'll need four guys to help load the trucks."

"Got 'em right here, Lieutenant," Red said, pointing to Little Joe, Bill, Waide, and Rum.

"Okay, give the sergeant your names and get going."

When we got out of earshot, I said, "Red, you've really lost your marbles this time. I can't drive one of those damned trucks. Can you?"

"Naw, but we can learn in a few minutes. Ain't nothing to it."

The other guys complained about hauling garbage. Red said, "You don't have to put your damn hands in it. Just load the cans on the truck. It's better than some of the other crap we coulda got stuck with. And we won't have nobody riding herd on us. We'll take it easy and make this job last all day."

Learning to drive the truck took more than a "few minutes." The damned thing had a zillion gears and we bucked backward and forward until I thought my eyeballs would pop out. Finally, we were able to move in the desired direction, although we never did master the clutch to the point where the trucks didn't jerk forward like a bronco after every stop.

We dawdled along on our garbage route, took over an hour for lunch, and stopped at the PX for a while. By the time we picked up at the last mess hall, it was getting dark. We had been told where the dump was located, but we couldn't find it. Every soldier we stopped on the road and asked for directions, turned out to be a transient like us.

By now, it was very dark. We stopped for a conference and Red said, "It's dark and cold and I'm getting hungry, let's get rid of this shit."

"Where do you suggest we get rid of it?" I asked.

"Hell, why not right here?"

"We don't even know where we are, Red."

Red pointed into the darkness, "I'm gonna back up and shine my headlights out there. Maybe this is the dump."

His headlights showed nothing but space. We walked over to the shoulder and, testing with our feet, found that the ground sloped sharply downward. How far down, and what was at the bottom, was anybody's guess.

"I say we back up to the edge and dump the cans right here," said Red.

"What if this isn't the dump, Red?" I asked.

"Who gives a shit. We're leavin' tomorrow."

"He's right," said Bill. "Let's get rid of the garbage and get the hell out of here."

Little Joe, Waide, and Rum agreed.

"Just hop on the trucks and kick 'em out," said Red. "If you think we're gonna take these fuckin' cans back to every mess hall, you're crazier'n hell. Kick 'em out."

We backed the trucks to the edge of the road, dragged the cans to the tailgate, and began booting them out into the darkness. They made one hell of a noise rolling down the hill. The guys laughed like hell when the clanging cans bumped together as they fell. I was having trouble finding the humor in all this. I had a bad feeling that this escapade wasn't going to be very funny when it backfired on us.

The next morning there were notices on every barracks' bulletin board calling an assembly at 8 A.M. We lined up in two formations, commissioned officers on one side, noncommissioned officers facing them on the other side. A colonel, flanked by a lieutenant and a master sergeant, appeared, looking as if the shit-on-a-shingle, or SOS, he ate for breakfast had disagreed with him terribly. SOS was dried beef in cream sauce poured over toast.

"Last night," he said, "garbage cans were dumped down the hill near the parade ground and ended up covering the entire garden area, which is a showplace for this camp. I'm holding every god-damned one of you responsible for this vandalism and as soon as you're dismissed, you're going down there and clean this mess up. When you're finished, I better not see one fucking piece of paper left on the ground."

I looked over at Red; he had a smirk on his face. I was surprised that they didn't identify our crew, because our names were on yesterday's roster for garbage pickup.

The colonel looked over at the noncoms' formation and pointed his finger at us. "That means every single one of you birds. And if I see anybody screwing off, you can give your soul to God, because your ass belongs to me."

One of the officers said to the colonel, "I don't think that's fair, sir. Why do all the noncoms have to suffer because a few jerks scattered garbage around? And how do we know that officers weren't involved?"

"We don't. But the noncoms are going to clean it up."

Then, a lot of the other officers started chiming in, defending their men. "That's not fair, Colonel!" "We're going overseas today. What kind of a sendoff is this?" "My men weren't involved; we were all together last night."

The colonel said, "I don't want to hear any more about it. You heard my orders. Dismissed!" Then he spun around and left.

We started walking toward the garden "showplace," while the officers stood around, still complaining. One of them said, "This is bullshit. Let's go help the guys clean it up." Almost all of the officers agreed and came over to join us. I looked back and saw Benshit heading toward his barracks. Actually, with so many helping, it didn't take long to clean up. Red kept poking me in the ribs, trying to make me see the humor of it all. As I looked over the sea of scrap-pickers, I couldn't help laughing. Maybe we had a hand in promoting New Jersey as the "Garden State."

We left Camp Kilmer by train late in the afternoon. Because we were on the East Coast, it was obvious that we were going to England, but security was so tight, there were only rumors about our destination. We were warned that every letter we wrote would be censored, and that any speculation would result in the letter being destroyed. This was in keeping with the pervasive slogan: "A slip of the lip can sink a ship."

Until we reached New York Harbor, we had no idea we were going to cross the Atlantic on the *Queen Elizabeth*. This former Cunard luxury liner, along with her sister ship, the *Queen Mary*, was in New York just after World War II started, and it was decided to use them as troopships. To someone who'd never been on anything larger than a rowboat with an outboard motor, the *Queen Liz* looked like a tall building, floating horizontally on the water in a long metal trough. Once luxuriously appointed vessels, enjoyed by the world's wealthiest travelers, the pair of *Queens* had been taken to Sydney and converted to carry Australian and New Zealand troops to Great Britain. Now, they also ferried American GI's across the pond. Each ship could accommodate over fifteen thousand passengers and more often than not, because of their speed, they traveled without convoy or escort.

Though the *Queen Liz*'s hull was now painted a drab warship gray, no attempt was made to dull the appearance of the interior of the ship, and evidence of her former splendor could be seen everywhere. Red and I were in the same "stateroom," once a cabin intended for two that now slept eighteen men in three-tiered bunks. Even with so many guys sharing the room, the quarters didn't feel cramped. And the bathroom was quite large. Taking a bath at least kept you clean, but it wasn't very satisfying. When you got out of the tub, your skin felt sticky because the bath water was only partially desalinated. We left New York Harbor that afternoon, and the *Queen*'s powerful engines drove the huge hull through the water so smoothly, it was hard to believe we were aboard a ship. I got my first look at the Statue of Liberty as the *Queen* moved out to sea, and I had a sobering thought: would I ever again set eyes on this lady holding aloft the torch of Liberty?

We'd been given standing orders that we were never to go up on deck without a lifejacket. The next day, I put on my jacket and went topside for some air. Just as I stepped onto the deck, the engines were silenced and the ship came slowly to a stop. I asked one of the British sailors what was going on.

"Our radar has spotted a sub off to starboard, a few miles ahead of us, and we stopped our engines so they won't know we're here."

"That doesn't sound good. What happens next?"

"Oh, we just sit here until we're aligned with them, then we start our engines and take off."

"But won't they give chase and torpedo us?"

"There's no danger of that, mate. We'll outrun 'um. We can go thirty-five knots. They can't do better than twenty-two. It's no contest."

Fortunately, he was right. In about twenty minutes, the engines began their steady hum again and the ship moved ahead at top speed. It was good to have that kind of assurance.

The biggest source of entertainment on the ship was gambling.

Poker, blackjack, and shooting craps were the favorite games, and the most popular spot was a former ballroom, now called the "Warrant Officers' Room." The room could hold several hundred people, and it was filled with GI's twenty-four hours a day. Benshit said he'd won $2,000 at blackjack. Knowing how much Red liked playing poker, I was surprised that he didn't gamble. "I don't like the setup," he said. "Too damned many people."

There was also the totally unexpected and pleasant diversion created by the presence of one Sgt. Joe Louis, the heavyweight boxing champion of the world. Joe, who was black, was on board with two sparring partners, and they staged exhibition matches for us in a ring erected in what had been a large ballroom before the *Queen* was converted into a troopship. I wondered whether the sparring partners, who were also black, were selected for their special skills or because the United States Armed Forces were still segregated. As a boxing fan, I had always admired Joe, and it was a great thrill to watch him perform. It was obvious that he was pulling his punches when sparring, but once in a while he wasn't able to slow his momentum in time and the force of the blow registered clearly on his sparring partner's face.

Besides his prowess in the ring, Joe was a real class act as a person. Unaffected by his celebrity, he would stop to chat with anyone on the ship. One day, when he wasn't surrounded by the usual multitude, Red and I went over to talk with the "Brown Bomber." When Red asked about technique, Joe told him to assume a fighting stance and Red put up his fists and rose onto his toes. Joe shook his head, "You don't want to get up on your toes, 'cause then you're off balance. Set back on your heels and punch, and you'll have a lot more power." Both of us left with Joe's autograph, but when we were shot down on the Berlin mission, whoever went through our belongings back at the base must have pocketed them. We never saw the prized autographs again.

With more than fifteen thousand military to feed, it was necessary to serve each soldier just two meals per day. Of course, no one
was going to go hungry, because there was an ample supply of C
rations available. In order to avoid overcrowding in the mess hall,
we were issued color-coded meal tickets, to be presented at the
door before entering. Each color represented a two-hour serving
period. If you missed the time frame when your ticket was valid,
you couldn't enter the mess hall until your color came up again . . .
hours later. A lot of guys became so involved with gambling, they
often lost track of time and missed their scheduled meal.

Red was not happy with the serving-by-ticket system. "Hell, I
ain't always hungry when my color comes up. Besides, who wants
to be clock-watching all day?"

On the second day of our voyage, we had eaten breakfast quite
early and around noon, Red came over and said, "Let's go get
some lunch."

"We can't get in the mess hall now, Red. Our color don't come
up again until five o'clock."

Red grinned, "Sure we can," and reached inside his jacket to pull
out huge wads of tickets in every color issued.

"How in the hell did you manage to get those?"

"What difference does it make? I got 'em, don't I? C'mon, I'm
buyin.'"

Damned if our "procurement officer" hadn't done it again.

Most of the time, the food was hardly worth the effort. The best
you could say was that it was hot. The first time I saw corned beef
on the menu, I was salivating over the prospect of good old-fash-
ioned deli beef on rye bread, slathered with mustard. Was I ever
disappointed. The beef was cut in huge slabs, fire-engine red in
color, and so coarse and grainy in texture that it looked like the
meat had been scored with a branding iron. Never mind that it was
so tough, you couldn't chew it to the point where you felt you

might digest it. At least with C rations, you knew what to expect. No surprises. Meat and bean combinations could be heated in the can or eaten cold, chocolate and soluble coffee were as potable as could be expected, and hard candies and caramels provided a familiar dessert.

Six days later, we docked in the harbor at Glasgow, Scotland. A crowd of people waited on the shore cheering our arrival, and a squad of Scottish bagpipers welcomed us with their mournful dirge. I knew that the bagpipe inherently produced a constant, somber drone, but I'd heard livelier tunes played on the instrument before. Too bad. As a bunch of men, most of whom were teenagers who probably had never traveled more than five hundred miles from home before . . . we could have used some cheering up.

A guy standing beside me at the ship's rail turned toward me and pointed at the bagpipers, resplendent in their towering hats, tartan knee-length pleated kilts, and boots, and said, "When the Queen comes to Scotland, they have a parade for her and, afterward, she inspects the troops."

"Is that right?"

"Yeah. Know how she inspects 'em?"

"No, I don't."

"She stops in front of each soldier and puts her cane between his feet."

"What does that tell her?"

"Well, she has a small mirror attached to the end of her cane."

"You're fulla shit."

"Naw, it's true. Ask any one of those bagpipers. They'll tell ya."

"Right. If you believe these guys are sissies because they're wearing skirts, you're nuts. Why do you think they're called Ladies from Hell? I'll get somebody I don't like to ask 'em."

In a few minutes, we were told to disembark, crew by crew. As I walked down the gangplank, I was cheered by the sight of pretty

Red Cross girls waiting on shore to hand out coffee and doughnuts. Then I saw the guys digging into their pockets to pay for them. It wasn't the twenty cents; it was the principle. What a letdown.

We were herded onto a train and, after an hour's ride, arrived at our bivouac for the night, an exclusive high school for girls. The school must have been closed for the duration of the war, and there was not one girl in sight. But we enjoyed their comfortable beds and the unaccustomed privacy of the toilets, each stall delicately equipped with its own door.

The next morning, after a breakfast of porridge, sausage, potatoes, and coffee, we piled onto Army trucks for the completion of our trip to the 447th Bomb Group airfield in Rattlesden, England.

We arrived in Rattlesden in the afternoon and were ferried from the train station to the base by Army trucks. The area was totally agricultural and reminded me of the many farms that surrounded Memphis. It was a clear day, the sky a beautiful shade of blue, marred only by an occasional B-17 returning home after a training flight or a mission. It didn't dawn on me at the time that many of the planes I saw were partially disabled and that's why they were limping back alone. I wrote to my mother that night, "It's so quiet and peaceful here, it's hard to believe there's a war going on. I hope to get a pass soon to visit my great-uncle." I didn't mention where I was, but the reference to my great-uncle, who lived in London, would give her my approximate location.

Our quarters were Nissen huts, made of corrugated iron sheeting, formed into a semicircular shape and bolted down to a concrete floor. It looked exactly like an immense culvert pipe, sliced in half, with the cut side placed down. Our cots were quite comfortable because we were issued three square pillows, or "biscuits," to cover them. At one end of the hut was a small pile of coke briquettes for use in the small stove that stood in the center of the hut. Unfortunately, the stove was missing a few critical parts, which were necessary for us to fire it up. It stood on two front legs, the back end being held up by four bricks; the door on the front was also missing; and there was no stovepipe to carry away smoke.

Red looked at me. "With this iron top and concrete floor it's gonna be cold as a well-digger's ass in here tonight. We cain't sleep in this place without any heat. I'm gonna see if I can get a replacement for this stove."

In a few minutes he was back. "They don't have no stoves. Said a shipment's on the way. We'll freeze our butts off before that happens."

"I guess we're screwed, Red. Nothing we can do about it."

"The hell there ain't. Go over to Quartermaster and check out a screwdriver, some pliers, and a hammer. I'll put on my coveralls."

"You can't fix this stove without parts."

"Don't worry about it, Norm. Just do what I said."

I didn't know what he was up to, but I didn't argue. This was a helluva challenge, even for Red, but he'd been right too many times before.

When I came back with the tools, he threw them into his empty duffel bag and asked for my bag. When I handed it to him, he looked at his watch and said, "I know it's chow time, but don't go yet. Just wait here for me. I'll be back in a little while."

By the time I'd smoked a couple of cigarettes, Red was back.

This time both duffel bags were full. First, he unloaded stovepipes, then two stove legs, and, finally, a door. He had swiped the parts from other huts while the guys were at chow.

"Red. . . ."

"Don't say nothin'! I got these way over on the other side of the base. Every piece came from a different stove. Nobody's coming way over here to look for a missing part."

"But what about the tools? They're checked out in my name. How long before they put two and two together and come looking for me?"

"Damn! Don't you have nothin' better to do than worry? Ain't nobody gonna come looking for you."

In a few minutes, Red had the legs and the door bolted on and the stovepipes in place. We put newspapers on the grate, filled the stove with briquettes, squirted lighter fluid on the coal, and tossed in a match. It was roaring away as we headed for the mess hall. When we got back, the rest of the crew were squatting around the stove enjoying the wonderful warmth it was putting out.

"You got a new stove," Little Joe said.

"Yeah," Red answered. "They had only one left." Damned if he didn't come through again. And, as usual, he was right . . . no one ever did come looking for me.

There's an old saying in the military: When a guy says he wasn't scared in combat, he's either lying—or he was too fucking stupid to be scared. To me, fear under fire was less traumatic than the hours before a mission, when your imagination ran wild with petrifying scenarios of what might be waiting for you "over there." I would guess that most of the guys who asked to be removed from flying status didn't do so immediately after returning from a mission, but in the intervening time before the next mission. That hellish period when your mind would conjure up images of colliding with another plane in the tight formations we flew; of your plane taking a direct hit by flak and exploding in mid-air; of bailing out with a defective chute that wouldn't open and watching the earth come up to meet you; or of helplessly holding a wounded buddy in your arms and watching him die in the sub-zero altitude.

Asking to be grounded was not a simple decision. You would lose your rank and your self-esteem at the same time and be assigned to the most demeaning jobs available. And you would bear the disgrace of your decision forever. Yet I doubt that there were many who, at some point, didn't consider this option. I know

I did, but it was always: this is my last mission. If I get back from this one, then I'll quit.

Between missions, everyone was on edge, and our reactions to this suspense were varied. Some would sit on their cots holding sotto-voce conversations, usually two guys, exchanging confidences and fears, discussing the odds of their survival. Others would constantly write letters to family and girlfriends; not many to wives, because most of us were too young to have reached that point in a relationship. And some wrote letters to loved ones, beginning with, "If you receive this letter. . . ."

Tensions sometimes caused us to act irrationally. I returned to our Nissen hut one afternoon to find Bill standing in the center of the hut swinging a two-bladed ax. Little Joe, Red, and three guys from another crew were standing out of range, watching him silently. It was obvious that he was not trying to strike anyone. His face fixed in deep concentration, he swung the ax in one direction with the force you would use to chop down a tree, then he reversed and wielded it in the opposite direction. I said, "Bill, put the ax down before you hurt yourself."

He didn't react at all. It was as if he had suddenly been struck deaf. I asked again, and there was still no indication that he'd heard me. At the end of every arc, his arms would end up so far around one side of his body, he would have to pause momentarily to bring the ax back the other way. I waited until he had completed an arc, then stepped in quickly and snatched the ax from his hands. I thought he would be angry with me, but he just stared at me blankly for a few seconds, then turned and walked outside. I asked the others in the hut if Bill had been in an argument with anyone, and the answer was negative. I took the ax to the Quartermaster and was told that someone had checked it out and not returned it. The person who signed out for it was not Bill. After about an hour, Bill reappeared, and there was not the slightest indication that he remembered the incident. He interacted as genially as always with everyone in the hut, and it seemed pointless to make mention of his strange interlude. He hadn't threatened anyone, and we weren't qualified to analyze his strange actions.

Though Red and I were close and talked about many issues in our lives, we never discussed probabilities of our early demise. I'm sure he felt, as I did, that our thoughts on this subject were off limits, and we didn't invade each other's privacy. Instead, we followed the pub crowd for the warm dark beer, the fish and chips wrapped in newspaper and sprinkled with vinegar, and the Scotch whiskey rationed out at a single shot per patron, about four times an hour.

No matter what mood you were in when you entered the pub, after a few beers you would join in with the ribaldry of the other GI's and, for a few hours, forget about tomorrow. The locals, who stopped by every night for a several pints of mild or bitter, had grown accustomed to our boisterous behavior and treated us like their kids. They were curious about the United States, and they listened intently to our stories about home, vowing to come and see us one day. These were the same farmers who looked up from the fields to watch our B-17's take off early in the morning to bomb Germany and other Axis targets and prayed for our safe return. We found it very easy to bond with these good people, who spoke the same language as we did . . . after a fashion.

During our first two weeks in Rattlesden, our crew made daily practice flights over England. We went up after all the combat crews had taken off on missions and landed before they were scheduled to return to base so we wouldn't get in their way.

When I was in radio school, we were advised that the British were first-class radio operators and could send, and receive, Morse code as fast as an expert typist. We were cautioned that it would be best if we sent no faster than we could receive, because responses to our messages would be returned to us at exactly the same speed as we dispatched them. The first time I radioed in for a fix on our position, I had forgotten this bit of advice and tapped out my request at about forty words a minute, when I could receive only at the rate of twenty-five. Suddenly, my radio crackled: brrrt, brrrt, brrrt, as forty words per minute came rushing through my headset . . . and I couldn't copy a single sentence of it. I quickly called back with an apology, that I hadn't intended to send that fast, couldn't receive that fast, and would appreciate a response of about twenty-five words a minute. I got back an immediate Roger, Wilco, at twenty-five words a minute, and I never made that mistake again.

One morning, I attended a class for radio operators in a one-room building not far from the flight line. We were seated in chairs, and the instructor was handing out some material, when a tremendous explosion rocked the building and pieces of plaster came raining down on us. The instructor yelled, "Hit the deck! Hit the deck!" Most of us managed to get our heads under his wooden table. We stayed put for a minute, then got up and went outside. We saw fire trucks going by, and one of the firemen called out, "Plane exploded on a hardstand."

The instructor tried to resume our class, but after a few minutes he realized that we weren't going to get much out of what he was saying, and even he didn't seem too interested in continuing, so he dismissed us. I walked down to the flight line and all I could see was smoke and molten metal. Thirteen men had died in the explosion, and no one could explain what had caused it. Later, I learned that one of the dead was an aircrew member who had been in my barracks in Avon Park. He didn't need to be at the hardstand that morning, but he was an armorer/gunner and was interested in seeing how the bombs were loaded. He was a nice, quiet kid whom I saw every day for almost a year. Before we left for Camp Kilmer, he'd introduced me to his eighteen-year-old bride, a cute little blonde just out of high school. It was hard to believe that he had just vanished. Evaporated. Nothing left to bury.

The 447th required that all replacements fly their first two missions with experienced crews who had completed maybe ten or more missions. For my first two missions, I was assigned to Lt. Hayden Hughes's crew, and what an adventure that turned out to be. His crew had completed twenty-two missions and were only three away from going home. These were ten battle-hardened flyers, close to the end of their tour and jittery as hell. They spoke with each other in quiet tones; there was none of the usual joking and kidding around. They were all deadly serious.

My first mission was to Brunswick, Germany, and our target was an aircraft plant. One of the waist gunners, Roger Hess, came into the radio room after we took off and tried to ease my anxiety over my first mission. He was a very likeable kid from North Carolina, and I felt we would have become pals if he hadn't been heading back to the States soon. I had no idea that within four days, we were both fated for a calamitous event that would bond us together as lifelong friends.

After Roger went back into the waist compartment, the ball-turret gunner came into the radio room, nodded in my direction, then sat behind my chair and opened a bible. He turned to a place marked by a slip of paper and began to read. We were still several miles from the coast of France when I heard the door behind me close. He had returned to the waist without ever saying a word, but I was a bit calmer just knowing that he had prayed for us.

At briefing that morning, we had been advised that clouds could be expected over the target and we were probably going to have to bomb by instrument. Our planes were loaded with general-purpose and incendiary bombs, and we would be 21,000 feet over the target.

As predicted, the target was cloud-covered, and we dropped our bombs on another aircraft plant on the other side of Brunswick. This is where I was introduced to flak. As I heard the ping of fragments hitting the aluminum "skin" of the plane, small holes appeared in the radio room. At the first sign of flak, the intercom began to crackle with the voices of our crew members calling out when they observed bursts. The German radar was very effective, and the thinking was that if you saw a burst of flak near the tail, and then another near the nose . . . the next shot would hit the middle of your plane and blow you out of the sky. The crew began to yell warnings like, "Watch it, Hayden, we're bracketed. Move the damn plane!" The pilot wasn't supposed to get out of formation, but he did manage to rock the plane a bit without straying too far. Though the flak was fairly heavy, we undoubtedly benefited from the inclement weather. All of our planes returned to base.

I ran into Roger in the mess hall the next morning, and we ate breakfast together. He congratulated me on my first mission and said that I had done well. "Just because we weren't hit bad, didn't run across any German fighters, and didn't lose any planes, don't consider yesterday a milk run. There aren't any milk runs. A raid where only one plane is lost might be considered a milk run by the top brass, but if it's your plane that goes down, and if it's your ass that gets blown away . . . that ain't no milk run."

Our second mission was a long one. We were going to bomb an aircraft plant in Friedrichshafen, Germany, which was situated on the shores of Lake Constance. On the other side of the lake was Switzerland, and if you had mechanical problems and were forced to land in Switzerland, you were interned there for the duration. As on my first mission, Roger came in to talk for a while, after he left, the ball-turret gunner appeared, this time without even a nod, and solemnly sat down behind me to pray.

It was a helluva long mission, well over twelve hours roundtrip.

I was glad I had eaten breakfast, especially since crews going on missions were served fresh eggs rather than powdered reconstituted ones. We were flying at 26,000 feet as we approached the target. Apparently the Germans had been notified of our arrival too late, because the smoke screen they set off at the target was not yet thick enough to obscure the aircraft plant and the bombing results were good.

When we landed at Rattlesden, we were greeted by the usual "Any hot news?" Meaning did we sight any of our planes going down; did we see any chutes coming out of the doomed planes; did we notice any partially disabled planes limping back alone, etc.

Afterward, because of the length of our mission, we were each rewarded with a bottle of Scotch. I had asked for a pass to London the week before, and as I left the conference room, a sergeant on the administrative staff handed me the pass, effective that evening. I thought about grabbing a bite to eat, taking a shower, and heading for London that night, but after having a sandwich and a large gulp out of my bottle, I realized that I was bone-tired. I decided it would be smarter to shower, sip a bit more of my booze, hit the sack, then leave fresh in the morning.

Chapter Nine

GERMANY: A DESCENT INTO HELL

I was falling through the sky feet-first now, and I watched the fragments of my B-17 until they disappeared from view. It was hard to believe that the *Mississippi Lady* was no more, her graceful wings torn asunder, her throbbing, powerful engines silent forever, violated by the long, probing anti-aircraft guns that sent flak tearing through her fuselage, ripping her apart.

When I jerked the pull-ring on my chute, the unbuckled left side flew up and hit me under the chin, knocking me out. When I came to, I was surrounded by a thick white mist. There was no feeling of motion, and I figured I was dead. I pondered the horrible boredom of going through eternity enveloped in this moist white fluff.

As I began to pray aloud, I recoiled in surprise at what I first believed to be the booming voice of someone else. Then, I realized that the shouting was coming from my own throat. The sudden change from being on a burning plane, with its engines roaring as it tore through the sky, to the ethereal quiet of this new, white, white world in which I now floated was so shocking, so breath-taking, that I was completely frozen.

Then my face began to sting where I had suffered powder burns from my exploding ammo. I touched my face and it hurt like hell. I didn't have to be a scientist to realize that the dead feel no pain. When I burst out into the open and saw land beneath me, I remembered that at our briefing that morning, we were told to expect cumulus clouds at 14,000 feet over the target.

I was floating 14,000 feet over Berlin, but I was alive!

For the past several days, I had been having nightmares about being shot down and captured by the Germans. In keeping with my plan for survival, I reached up and pulled my dog tags from my neck, the newly issued tags with the telltale "H" pressed into them. The "H" was the United States Armed Services designation for Hebrew, which meant that I was Jewish. I felt that disclosing my religion to the Nazis could be suicidal, so I threw the tags as far away as I could. Wounded and defenseless, I drifted toward the ground, toward a welcoming committee of hate-filled civilians who were hell-bent on killing me.

Flying has always been a surreal experience for me. As a plane rolls swiftly down the runway on takeoff, your speed is visible. You look through the windows and see objects on the ground flashing past: people, vehicles, trees, and houses. But once you're airborne, once you're far above the earth, there is no visual movement to relate to and you feel as if you are literally hanging in space. There is no sense of motion.

It is a similar sensation coming down to earth in a parachute. I had bailed out of my burning plane from a height of 28,000 feet, but since there was nothing close by to give me a feeling of speed, I felt as if I was simply floating. Intellectually, I knew that I was moving rapidly toward the earth, but my senses were incapable of confirming this.

Then, as I came closer to the ground, my perceptions quickly began to change. I could see that I was moving toward a stand of trees and, recalling my brief instruction in guiding a parachute, I reached out with both hands and pulled on one of the cords attached to my chute. This did indeed move me in an opposite direction from the trees, but I felt a sudden acceleration and, looking up at my chute, I saw that half of it had collapsed, so I immediately released my hold on the cords. The chute reinflated, but I was descending much faster than before. Then, suddenly, I was no longer moving and floating toward the earth. The earth was flying up to meet me, and I slammed into it with such a crushing impact that I felt as if I had been swallowed by it.

Momentarily unconscious, I was quickly brought back to reality by many hands jerking me to my feet. Had I not been supported, I would not have been able to stand. I had landed first on my right knee, where I had taken a piece of shrapnel. I was bleeding from wounds in my arm, body, and face, which was also burning from the explosion of the shells in my gun.

Looking around, I realized that I had landed in the backyard of a large house. I was surrounded by three women and two men armed with garden hoes and rakes, and they began beating me about the head and back with the wooden handles. They were angrily shouting at me in German, but their words came out in torrents and, with my meager knowledge of the language, I was able to understand little of what they said.

Then one of the men broke away, ran over to a toolshed, and returned with a length of rope, which he tied tightly around my neck. He threw the loose end of the rope over a tree limb, and then they all took hold and began to pull. Frantically grasping the rope just above the noose with both hands, I was standing on tiptoe when I heard the sound of a motorcycle and saw a soldier roar into the yard and jump off his bike. "Nein," he shouted as he rushed over and snatched the rope from their hands.

My captors were still hell-bent on hanging me, however, and began to argue loudly with him. The soldier spoke slowly and more distinctly than my would-be executioners, and I was able to understand when he told them that first he would search me, and if he found a gun, they could hang me as a spy. Otherwise, he would have to take me in for interrogation. He quickly determined that I was unarmed, then, seating me behind him on the motorcycle, he gunned the machine and spirited me away. He didn't bother to bind my hands, and I held on to him tightly to keep from falling off. Having just saved me from a lynching, he apparently felt that I was eager to put distance between myself and the civilian mob and, since I was obviously weakened by my wounds, he appeared to have no fear of my attacking him.

We drove for about fifteen minutes, until we arrived at a small command post in an old house in the suburbs of the city. Taken inside, I was ushered into the office of a German major who appeared to be in his sixties. He had probably been a reserve officer who had been called back into service and stationed at this outpost, which was a processing point for POW's.

He seemed really eager to converse with me, but I tried to make it clear that I spoke no German. "Can you speak in German?" he asked.

"No," I answered. "Only English."

"French?"

"I speak some Spanish," I said.

"Nein," he said in disappointment.

Then an orderly entered and, from what I could gather, suggested bringing in someone who had lived in Milwaukee before the war. The major agreed and dispatched the soldier to fetch the person.

Meanwhile, he continued trying to converse with me. He

obviously considered the English and Americans to be worthy foes, and was trying to impart that the Russians were subhuman. Seated behind his desk, he raised his index finger and inclined his head forward to assure my attention. There was a cup on his desk, and an empty plate with a fork lying beside it. Picking up the fork, he pretended to take food from the plate; bring it to his lips; take it into his mouth; then slowly chew and swallow.

Again, he pointed his index finger at me. "Americanish essen so," he said.

Then he reached for the cup and carefully picked it up between thumb and forefinger, curling his pinkie as he brought it to his mouth and delicately sipped. "Englander essen so."

I almost jumped out of my chair when he leaped up, rushed around to the front of his desk shouting, "Rooskie! Rooskie!" Then the major got down on all fours, placed his face close to the floor, began snorting like a pig, and said, "Rooskie essen so. Nicht mann. Animal! Animal!"

Before he could continue, the door opened and the orderly brought in an old man who appeared to be in his eighties. Now the major became even more excited. He shook hands with the old man and turned to me, saying, "Milwaukee. Milwaukee."

The old man, smiling broadly, came over to me, saying "Hallo, meester." Pointing to himself, he continued, "Me Milwaukee. United State."

"Hello," I answered. "When were you in Milwaukee?"

The major beamed. We were conversing. He ordered the "interpreter" to ask me my name. The old man nodded and said, "Was ist deine namen?"

I made believe I didn't understand. The major was getting annoyed. Now he shouted at the old man to ask me my name in English, not German. I guess he hadn't spent as much time in Milwaukee as he'd led people to believe, because he now turned back to me and, with a nervous tic at one side of his mouth, said, "Hallo, Meester. Was ist deine namen?"

I shrugged my shoulders and looked confused. This was too much for the major, who began shouting imprecations at the "interpreter," grabbed his arm, and escorted him to the door. He then had a heated conversation with one of his aides and dispatched him on a mission, the purpose of which I could not understand, other than that he wanted something to take place and he wanted it to happen fast: "Schnell!"

Then he took a German/English dictionary from a shelf, sat down at his desk, and began leafing through it. Occasionally he would glance over at me as if he were about to speak, then he thought better of it and went back to his browsing. Soon a soldier came into the office carrying a medic's kit and began to examine my badly burned face. Then he opened the case, took out a jar containing some kind of white powder, and began to dust it onto my face by tapping the jar with his forefinger. My face stung as the powder adhered to my weeping flesh. Although bloody holes in my uniform clearly indicated that I had been injured and I had visible shrapnel wounds to my jaw and temple, the medic made no attempt to give me further treatment.

Shortly after he left, there was a knock at the door and the dispatched aide returned, beaming, with an officious-looking lieutenant in tow. The officer clicked his heels and saluted the major smartly. They had a brief conversation, and then the lieutenant came over to me and said: "Stand." He stared into my eyes with obvious contempt. "For you der Var iss ofer."

Then he handed me a pad and ordered me to write down my name, rank, and serial number. According to the rules of the Geneva Convention, which the U.S. and Germany had both signed in 1929 and which entered into force in 1931, this was the only information I was legally obligated to disclose, so I did as I was told. The major then began to dictate questions for the lieutenant to ask me.

"Why do you come to bomb our glorious Berlin?"

"I didn't come to bomb Berlin."

"What did you come to bomb?"

I did not respond to this question.

"You come to bomb untersea boats?"

Submarines sounded like a good target. "Yes," I responded.

"Where are your dog tags?"

Of course I had jerked my dog tags from around my neck as I descended in my chute and thrown them away. I hoped they had fallen where they would never be found.

"I don't have any," I said. "The chain broke and I lost them when I bailed out of my plane."

"Hah! Without identification, we can shoot you for a spy."

"I'm sure you can," I replied, "but I'm not a spy."

Then he unbuttoned the jacket to my heated suit and found the inside pocket that held my escape kit. The kit contained maps, a compass, and counterfeit German money.

This was obviously the first time he had seen an American escape kit. He put the maps and compass on the desk. Then, when he pulled out the currency, he and the major both began to laugh. "Zis money is worth nossing. You hear? Nossing. You could not spend it in Germany. It iss only paper."

Then, his fingers discovered the wires that ran through my flight suit, like an electric blanket, to conduct heat to my body. He had a serious discussion about these wires with the major and then asked me to remove my jacket and pants. Using a penknife, he exposed some of the wires, then grasped them tightly in his hands and pulled. The wires tore loose, taking with them large pieces of cloth, some of which had already been burned, and shredding my suit. After he'd ripped out all of the wires, satisfied that there was no more contraband, he handed my clothing back to me. I got dressed, but my insulated suit had been reduced to rags.

When I bailed out, the last thing on my mind was the shoes I wore, and this is something that I lived to regret for many months to come. In my confusion, I forgot my durable GI shoes as I jumped from the burning plane, and though my fleece-lined flying boots were warm and cozy on the plane, they were not designed for walking. The boots were covered with the thinnest sliver of flexible leather, and within three weeks they disintegrated and I was barefoot.

I hadn't really had time to think of my fellow crew members until the Germans finally completed their body search and interrogation, then more or less ignored me. The major and the lieutenant had apparently gone to lunch, and my single guard spoke no English and seemed disinclined to try to converse with me. Left to my own thoughts, it suddenly dawned on me that I was probably the sole survivor from my crew. I thought I couldn't feel more miserable about my situation, but this sad realization made my despair deeper than before.

Soon, a sergeant I had not seen before appeared and growled, "Raus," a contraction of Heraus, meaning "Out." This was a command that I would soon become very familiar with.

My right knee had become very swollen from the piece of shrapnel that had penetrated my patella, and when I stood up I found that I could put very little weight on that leg. I struggled painfully to keep up with the sergeant as he made his way outside the command post.

As we walked up the road, I could see several German guards coming toward us, escorting a group of five men who appeared to be American soldiers. When they came closer, I was overjoyed to recognize them as part of my crew.

Red was the first to yell a greeting. "Norm! I thought you were dead. You're so damned slow, I just knew you never made it out of the plane." Red was supporting Rum, whose legs were so rubbery they were practically useless. The front of Rum's flying suit was soaked in blood and he looked ghastly. I later learned that he had taken a 20-millimeter shell in his shoulder. That is a very large caliber bullet, and I was surprised that he had survived such a severe injury at all.

I didn't know what to say to Rum and was afraid to touch him anywhere, so I just reached out and gently ran my hand across his head. It was shocking to see the face I remembered as always being wreathed in a smile, now twisted into a mask of excruciating pain. I thought about the medical kit that burned up on the plane and how the morphine it contained would have brought some relief to him. The Germans had given him no medical treatment at all.

Waide had a piece of cloth covering both his eyes and was being led along by Daddy. I was shocked, assuming that he had been completely blinded. Fortunately, he had lost only one eye from a fragment of flak that had ricocheted off his machine gun. I didn't ask why both eyes had been covered by the makeshift bandage; I was just grateful that he was still sighted.

Daddy grinned broadly and squeezed my hand. "I was really worried about you, Norm. The rest of us came down fairly close together and we couldn't figure out what happened to you. We lost Landis and Longteig. Rum believes that Bill and Joe were wounded and never made it off the plane."

I asked Waide how he was doing, and he said, "Not so good." In my imagination, I often envisioned how we might be wounded in combat, but in my mind I had never even thought of the peril of blindness. Waide was a very lucky guy.

Benshit was walking alone, helping no one, which was no surprise to me. He was apparently uninjured, and his face bore its customary smirk. He evinced no sign that he was pleased to see me alive.

A military truck pulled up beside us, and our guards herded us aboard. We were driven for less than an hour over some very bumpy roads. The truck had no seats, and the hard floorboards conducted every jolt right up to my knee. I could only imagine what this terrible ride was doing to Rum and Waide.

Finally, we turned off into a small airport and drove around it until we came to a one-story building from which German soldiers were coming and going. The truck pulled up in front, and we made our way inside.

A sergeant, sitting at a desk, was handed a sheaf of papers by one of our guards and called out our names. Then we were led down a tile-floored hallway with four barred cells on the left and windows on the right. At the end of the hallway there was a latrine with a single commode. Each cell contained a wooden cot, fashioned at a permanently reclining twenty-degree angle. They were constructed of very rough wood and had no mattress or cover.

Rum and Waide were each put into a cell, but the doors were left open. We were able to go into their cells and give them water, which was all we had to offer them. At least we could sit on the edge of the cot and talk with them. Daddy and Red had on jackets, which they removed and balled into "pillows," forming at least some cushion against the hard wood.

A guard, stationed at the entrance to the hallway, spoke a little English, and we asked him about getting medical aid for our wounded crew members, pointing out the gravity of their condition. He said that Rum and Waide would be going to a military hospital in the morning. I began to wonder if Rum was going to make it through the night, he had lost so much blood. He was intermittently moaning from the pain.

Waide began to yell for the guard, who turned and called to the sergeant at the desk. The sergeant went into Waide's cell, and we were all startled to hear Waide berate him because he had received no medical help. "According to the Geneva Convention, which the United States and Germany have both signed, you are obligated to give us medical attention, and I demand to see a doctor right now."

The sergeant understood most of this, because he said, "Yah, Morgen in Krankenhaus. Morgen." Then he left.

The guard translated, "Tomorrow, you will see doctor in hospital."

Waide was far from appeased, but his further complaints fell on deaf ears.

It was now late afternoon, and we wondered if they were ever going to give us any food. None of us had eaten since about five A.M. What they eventually brought in was not what we were expecting. Each of us was given a cup of what they called "Kaffee." It was ersatz, of course, and tasted like no coffee I had ever drunk before. I called it Black, Burned, and Bewildered, because of its color, its flavor, and my inability to even remotely compare it to anything I had ever consumed before. We were also given one slice of black bread each. I've been a lover of pumpernickel bread all my life, but I wouldn't give you a nickel for a whole loaf of this pump. Contrary to the coffee we drank, which was at least a hot liquid, this bread had no taste at all. It was dark and heavy, coarse-textured, and had not the slightest flavor of wheat. We later learned that one of the main ingredients was sawdust and that it couldn't be eaten for twenty-four hours after baking, because it was poisonous until then.

We each took a small bite out of our slice, then laughed at this ridiculous excuse for bread, and placed the remainder on the windowsill. We didn't know that a single slice of bread would become our morning and evening meal, along with a cup of imitation coffee or tea, and that we would soon wait eagerly for it.

Daddy, Benshit, Red, and I were ordered to sleep on the tile floor in front of the cells. I lay down beside Red and, surprisingly, I quickly fell into a deep sleep filled with the ghastly events of that morning, only this time it was like an out-of-body experience and I had a view from above the entire air battle. Many planes were on fire and twirling out of control in death dives, others were exploding in mid-air; crews were bailing out, many with their chutes ablaze, while German fighters sprayed them with machine-gun fire. Some of our group were dropping their bombs on other B-17's below them. It was a horrible nightmare, but I don't recall waking up once during the night.

The next morning I woke up slowly, trying to remember where I was. I tried to open my eyes, but they remained shut. I had some-times experienced terrifying dreams when I felt as though I was awake but couldn't open my eyes or move my limbs, and I thought this was one of those. Then I heard German soldiers talking out-side, and I moved my hands and feet. Now I knew that I was wide awake . . . and I panicked. I was totally blind!

Reaching out, I felt Red's arm and latched on to it with a death grip. "Red!" I screamed. "Red, I'm blind! I'm blind!"

"Shut up, fool. You ain't no such thing. Matter's got your eyes sealed shut. Let go my arm so I can get some water."

I felt a wet cloth being gently wiped across my eyelid. At first, nothing happened. Then I saw a tiny glimmer of light as a part of my eyelid became unsealed. "Red, I can see. I can see light now."

"I told you it was just matter. Now, lay still so I can get your other eye open."

To my delight, both eyes were now unstuck. My facial burns had caused a drainage of fluid during the night that sealed my eyes shut. I was immensely relieved to know that my sight was not impaired. Even looking through the grimy windows of the jail, the sky and the sunshine were wonderful.

The guards brought us each a cup of hot liquid that they pre-posterously called "tea." It wasn't Lipton's, that's for sure. It was some sort of mint-flavored water, and it burned as it went down your throat. They also gave each of us another slice of the black bread. Suddenly, the bread was not nearly as bad as we had thought. Not only did we eat every morsel of the morning's ration of bread, we also gobbled up every crumb from the slices we had made fun of the day before.

Rum and Waide had gone through a rough night. Rum was in a lot of pain and would periodically groan. His eyes were glassy and he seemed to be running a fever. He refused anything except a little water.

Waide drank some of the tea but wouldn't eat any of the bread. He complained about the discomfort of the wooden cot and said that every bone in his body was aching. He wanted to go to the latrine, and I led him down the hallway. I was glad that he didn't mention his blindness, because I wouldn't have known how to handle the subject.

Shortly after I brought Waide back to his cell, a guard told us we would soon be leaving for an interrogation center in Frankfurt am Main. We asked about medical treatment for Rum and Waide and were told that transportation was on its way to take them to a hospital.

We all went in to say good-bye to them. It was hard to leave them so grievously wounded, but we had no choice. We wished them well and told them that we'd all be together again soon.

As it turned out, Rum's injuries were so severe that he was ultimately repatriated to the U.S. in exchange for a German POW who was also gravely hurt and held by the American military. Waide, after his eye was removed and he was released from the hospital, actually ended up in the same POW camp as Red and me, but he was in a different compound and we were not aware of this until we returned to the U.S.

When a large truck pulled up in front of the jail, the guards motioned us out of the building. When Daddy, Benshit, Red, and

I climbed on the truck, we saw that there were already about twenty American POW's on board. They were all Air Force, but none from our bomb group. All had been shot down on the Berlin raid the day before.

We were driven to a train station and remained on the truck until the train pulled in and all passengers had disembarked. The guards seemed jittery as they formed a phalanx around the truck and ordered us to board the last car. We wondered if they were afraid that we might try to escape, but their real concern was that we might be recognized as American airmen and attacked by the civilians on the platform.

Because the U.S. Air Force had no dress code for combat crews, we were a pretty nondescript bunch, but some German civilians on the platform did recognize us and the word spread quickly through the crowd. Our guards hustled us on board the train, shouting, "Schnell! Mach Schnell," and slammed the doors shut against the rising roar of the enraged throng. The train slowly pulled out of the station, and it was none too soon for us, because the mob began pelting the windows with rocks, garbage, and any other objects they could lay their hands on.

Chapter Ten

Frankfurt am Main

The rest of our train ride to Frankfurt am Main, the Luft-waffe interrogation center for downed Allied airmen, was uneventful. In fact, whenever the train stopped at depots along the way, we looked so nondescript through our car's dirty windows that people waiting on the platforms would wave to us, believing we were German soldiers. We waved back enthusiastically, enjoying the delightful irony of the situation.

By the time we arrived that evening, my right knee, the one that had taken a piece of shrapnel, had become so swollen and painful that I could put almost no weight on it. The truck ride from the train to the interrogation center was agonizing, and I bit my lip with every bump. Descending from the truck was an ordeal and, by the time I reached the ground, Daddy, Benshit, and Red had already entered the building. As I hopped on one leg to follow, a guard yelled, "Helf your Kamerad!"

I looked behind me and saw a guy leaning against the back of the truck, obviously unable to move forward. He appeared to have been shot in both legs, and his pants were ripped and soaked with blood. Though there were others who had no trouble walking, the guard chose me to "Helf," apparently to enjoy watching us struggle together. I went back to the truck, put my arm around the guy's back, and lifted him, then gritted my teeth as I was forced to put more weight on my injured knee. The pain was unbearable, but somehow we made it. We were inside a large room filled with POW's waiting to be registered. My companion asked if I could take him across the room, where he placed his back against the wall and slid down to the floor. He looked up at me, forcing a smile, "Thanks, pardner." I tapped his shoulder a couple of times and hopped away.

The processing seemed to take forever, but finally I was "enrolled" and followed those in front of me into another large room where we were strip-searched. After I dressed, I was escorted to solitary, a six-by-eight-foot cell with: no lights; no toilet; no water; and no window. The heavy wooden door locked from the outside. At the door, I was handed a cup, a small bowl, and a spoon. Then I was locked inside.

The bed was made of rough wood with 4 x 4's for the head and foot posts and 1 x 8's for the sides. The "mattress" was a burlap bag filled with a few handfuls of straw so that when you lay on it, the straw slipped between the five narrow wooden slats and you ended up lying on the slats, with their edges pressing into your back. The only space to move around was the couple of feet at the foot of the bed.

All of the cells opened on a long hallway with a three-stall latrine at the end. The stalls had no doors. In order to go to the latrine, you had to pound on your cell door and yell for the guard. When he finally opened your door, he would curse you for disturbing him and lead you down the hallway. It was rare that you encountered another POW there, because the guards didn't want you to talk with anyone else and usually permitted only one POW on relief call at a time. If you did happen to be there when another POW was allowed in, any conversation heard by the guard while you were in the latrine would be reprimanded by an angry shout or a punch.

The first time I asked to go to the latrine, I was escorted by a guard who remained outside in the hallway. As I sat on the commode, I was puzzled by many brown streaks on both sides of the stall and on the wall behind. They were short, straight, and separate, with no one line touching another. All too soon, I learned the reason for these strange markings. When I looked around for a toilet paper dispenser, I discovered that there was none. From that day forward, I learned to pocket any scrap of paper I could find, newspaper, cigarette wrappers, or even leaves, as a substitute for tissue. There was a cold-water washbasin, but no soap. I washed my hands, trying not to think about germs, then dried them on my pants.

Our daily ration consisted of a half slice of black bread, morning and evening, along with the now-familiar cup of ersatz coffee or tea. At noon, we received a small bowl of soup containing either dehydrated cabbage or some kind of grain. The system of distribution was that one guard unlocked and opened your door, and another guard followed pushing a rolling cart, handing out the bread and hot liquid. The unlocking guard would then go back and secure the door of the prisoner who had already received his ration, then go forward again to unlock the next door.

One morning, my door was opened and I handed out my cup to be filled with tea. As the guard reached back for my slice of bread, his comrade called out to him and they had a conversation outside my cell. The next thing I knew, my door was being locked again and I still hadn't received my bread ration. I began pounding on my door and yelling for the guard. After a minute, the guard unlocked my door again and shouted, "Was ist los?" I told him that I had gotten no bread. He said that he'd given me my bread, "Yah. Brot." I insisted that he hadn't, so he came into my cell and patted me down, then searched my bed and looked underneath it. Finally, still showing doubt that I was telling the truth, he gave in and brought me a slice, then slammed the door in my face.

After I had eaten every crumb, I lay down on my straw mattress and pondered how important a piece of black bread had become to me. It was hard to believe that I could get so upset and shamelessly pound on a door and yell for a tasteless piece of bread that we had laughed at and carelessly tossed on a windowsill only a few days earlier.

I was interrogated daily by German officers who spoke fluent English. Several of them had, at one time, lived in the United States. Each session was varied in its approach. Usually, I was questioned by a single officer, but sometimes they used the good cop–bad cop approach. A couple of times, I was slapped around by the "bad cop."

The first time I was brought in for questioning, I didn't know what to expect. I was taken into an office where a smiling Hauptmann, a captain, sat behind a desk. He rose and extended his hand. He spoke with hardly a trace of an accent. "Good morning, Sergeant Bussel. Please have a seat. How are you today?"

"Fine," I nodded.

"Good. I hope you are not too uncomfortable here. You see, we are very tight for space because so many American flyers are being shot down lately."

On his desk was a bottle of Scotch whiskey, two shot glasses, a pack of Camel cigarettes, and a lighter. He took a cigarette out of the pack and lit it, blowing smoke in my direction.

"Would you like a cigarette?" he asked pushing the pack toward me.

Camels happened to be the brand I smoked. I drew a breath and could almost feel myself taking a deep drag on a cigarette, the calming smoke flowing softly into my lungs. As I exhaled, it was everything I could do to avoid pursing my lips as I imagined blowing the smoke gently out of my mouth.

"No, thank you," I said. "I don't smoke."

"Then maybe a drink. This is very good Scotch whiskey," he said as he poured a drink for himself, then paused with the bottle tilted over the second glass as he waited for my answer.

I couldn't keep from licking my lips. I could just feel the golden liquid rolling over my tongue, the delicious warmth as it coursed its way to my stomach, the sense of release that rose to my head.

"Thank you, no. I don't drink either," I lied. The finality of my words seemed to hang in the air as he enjoyably sipped the whiskey from his glass.

He spoke as amiably as if we were discussing a sporting event. "You were shot down while bombing Berlin on April 29. You were flying a B-17, right?"

"Sir, I can only give you my name, rank, and serial number," I said.

"Yes, I have that right here." He patted a stack of papers on his desk. "So tell me, how many of your crew were lost that day?"

"I can't answer that, sir."

The captain soon grew tired of the game and called a guard to return me to my cell.

I've often heard that people who are facing death sometimes find their whole lives flashing through their minds. I didn't have that sensation when I jumped. Had I not been so deprived of oxygen . . . maybe that would have happened. But being locked in a tiny, dark cell twenty-four hours a day did evoke thoughts of my past, which I had the leisure to review in my mind . . . very slowly.

To control the worsening claustrophobia, I tried to hypnotize myself into believing that I was being transported to enjoyable times in my past, but I couldn't achieve that control over my mind. At times, I did manage to lie quietly in my bed and let words, or thoughts, course through my head. I tried to avoid too much concentration on any single image, because then I would be drawn away from my reflective state. My stream of consciousness brought forth snippets of events, places, and people, many of them long forgotten.

Kennebec, Penobscot, and Androscoggin: rivers in Maine. (Seventh-grade geography.)

"Paon-cil." (Tenth-grade algebra witch.) "Drop your paon-cil on the floor during the test and you may leave the class . . . because you're getting an F."

"Name four epic poems, Norman."

"Beowulf."

"Yes."

"Cynewulf."

"Yes."

"Beowulf, Cynewulf. . . ."

"Yessss."

"Beowulf, Cynewulf . . . I don't know . . . Werewolf and the Big Bad Wolf!" (Eleventh-grade English.)

Dancing with first adolescent love. One year younger than I. Five years more mature. My chewing gum caught in her hair. Biting through each strand to free gum before song ended . . . and I died. (Peabody Hotel.)

"You're going to have a baby? Why do you want to embarrass me? I'm a senior in high school, for God's sake!" (My mother's revelation of my expected sibling.)

"Norman doesn't have a kidney problem." Mrs. Carr. "He said he keeps going to the bathroom because if he stands very still, a little mouse comes and walks over his shoe." (First grade.)

"Out of the night that covers me." (Memorization of *Invictus*, age fourteen. Juvenile bravado, but those words gave comfort in solitary.)

"Do you always kiss with your mouth closed?" (At fifteen, I didn't understand why I would want to kiss with my mouth open. Hell, I wouldn't even take a sip out of someone else's glass.)

At times, my ability to escape by mental transport would fail and I was doomed to endure the terror of perpetual darkness. Unable to see the walls, I imagined they were coming together to crush me, and I would extend my arms to prove to myself that they were not. I could only lie on my back in bed. If I turned on my side, my hip would push apart the slats and I would fall through. The same with lying on my stomach: my knees and elbows would poke through.

Breathing became a terrifying problem. The darkness seemed to have taken on a heaviness. I perceived that I was lying in a huge vat of motor oil, and with each breath I felt that I was trying to draw into my lungs something that defied inhalation. I would gasp and feel that I would lose consciousness. I wanted to yell for help but, engulfed in this sea of oil, who would hear my screams?

Not that I was in the mood for it, but the guards would not permit you to sing or whistle in your cell. They would pound on your door and yell, "Ist verboten!" Yet there was one guard who drove me absolutely insane by walking the hallway every night whistling the same tune, never a variation, and keeping time by stamping heavily with his foot on the downbeat. When he tired of whistling, he would sing, "Pom, pa pa pa, pom pom, pom pa, pom pa, pom pa pom. Pom, pa pa pa, pom pom, pom pa, pom pa pom." It was a French song called *Auprès de ma Blonde*. The beat pounded and pounded in my head, and even when the guard went off duty I could still feel it throbbing there. I can still feel it today.

I was interrogated several more times by different Luftwaffe officers, each one using a slightly different tactic. The last officer I saw threatened me with a firing squad because I had no identification, but offered leniency for information. By now, this threat had become trite and I no longer believed they would carry it through. I repeated that I was obligated to give only my name, rank, and serial number, and I was not summoned again.

After twelve days, I was released from solitary and brought into a room where about twenty other POW's were gathered. Among them were Daddy, Benshit, and Red. Everyone was talking non-stop after the long silence, surprised at the sound of our own voices. That afternoon, we were to be shipped to Luftwaffe POW camps, commissioned officers to one camp and noncommissioned officers to another. We were all garrulous, and the topics of our conversation shifted continuously. Out of the blue, Benshit comes up with, "You know, the Germans are assholes, but some of their ideas aren't all bad. I was thinking just the other day about the times I played gin with Sherry and wondered, why am I playing cards with this Jew?"

Red and Daddy stared at him in silence while I fought back my overwhelming desire to slug this bigoted rat. To smack him for anti-Semitic remarks in this venue could prove disastrous for me, but I vowed to look him up when we returned home and seriously mess him up. For now, I could be happy with the mere fact we wouldn't be in the same POW camp.

Chapter Eleven

LUFT IV

S talag Luft IV, Kriegsgefangenenlager der Luftwaffe (Prisoner of War Camp of the Air Force), a German POW camp
for captured U.S. Army Air Forces noncoms, was located
just outside the town of Grosstychow in East Prussia, near the
Baltic Sea. It was opened in May 1944. Red and I were in the first
contingent of sixty-five men to arrive at the camp. It wasn't long
before we shortened the German word for POW, Kriegsgefan-
genen, to Kriegie, which is what we began to call ourselves.

The site of the camp was an isolated, forested area and nothing
was visible beyond the trees. Comprised of four "Lagers," or compounds, each section was separated from the others, and from the
outside world, by two barbed-wire fences, which ran parallel to
each other and were about twelve feet apart. The fences were ten
feet high, and the space between them was patrolled by rifle-toting
guards. Just outside the compounds were appropriately spaced

guard towers, made of logs, manned by a sentry with a large searchlight and a mounted machine gun.

Inside each compound, about twenty feet from the first fence, was a warning rail, made of three-foot-high tree limbs driven into the ground and topped with a continuous line of one-by-four planks. Our bulletin board offered an endless list of actions that were Verboten, and touching the warning rail was one of them. Every violation listed was pretty tame, yet most carried the standard threat that every violator would be "Shot Without Warning." The phrase was used so interminably that we all took it with a grain of salt. Everyone agreed that the Nazis were fucking butchers, but who would shoot a man down in cold blood for such a trivial infraction? We soon found out.

Each compound held ten barracks, ten rooms to a barracks, with each room holding between sixteen and twenty-four men. In the center of each compound was a parade ground, where POWs gathered for roll calls each day, and an in-ground, concrete "swimming pool," which we presumed was for use by a bucket brigade in case of fire, because we were warned of dire consequences if we dipped so much as a toe into the water. Five barracks were situated on either side of the compound, with their entrances facing the pool.

Everyone entering the camp had to pass through the Vorlager, which housed the administration building; quarters for the guards and their officers; warehouses; and what was called the "Krankenhaus," or hospital. The hospital was a joke, because it had the barest of equipment and almost no medicines. Every new POW was processed through the administration building: searched, fingerprinted, and photographed. We were issued German POW dog tags, a square piece of metal, perforated at the center, with the same personal statistics imprinted above and below the perf. In the event that the wearer perished, the tag could be bent back and forth until it separated, with one half left on the body and the other held with his records.

Because the Germans were sending every able-bodied soldier to the front, POW camp guards and personnel were dredged up from the bottom of the barrel. They were usually older men, often World War I vets, in their late forties or early fifties; or guys who probably scored barely enough on their IQ tests to pass even the minimum standards.

Processing us in at the administration building was taking forever, since this procedure was being handled by these cretins. Getting bored, Red stood by a window, looking out and whistling. One of the guards turned and said, "Nicht pfeifen."

I stepped over to Red and said, "The guard told you not to whistle."

"He wasn't talkin' to me. Besides, how the hell do you know what he said?"

The guard turned and this time spoke louder, "Nicht pfeifen!"

"Red, you better cut it out."

"Oh, bullshit!"

"Okay. Don't say I didn't tell you."

Red continued to whistle, and the guard came up behind him and smacked him hard in the back of the head. Holding his hand over the spot where he was hit, Red turned to me.

"Son of a bitch! You understand this shit?"

"A little."

He came over and stood beside me. "Knowin' the lingo could be real helpful to us in this joint, huh?"

"Maybe, but I don't want to rush it. I need to understand the idioms a little better first."

"Yeah, they are pretty stupid, ain't they?" said Red.

Red and I were assigned to the same room in Barracks 1. Each room was furnished with eight double-decker bunks; a wooden table and a bench; a stove, for which we were rationed three small coal briquettes a day (which lasted about an hour); a one-gallon capacity aluminum water pitcher; and a tin bucket to carry boiled potatoes from the Kuche, or kitchen, to the room. Our bunks came with five wooden slats to support a "mattress" made of a material we Southerners called croker sack, a rough burlap, like what produce companies used to ship a hundred pounds of potatoes to my father's store. It was the same as before: the mattress was filled with straw, which would quickly settle between the slats, leaving you to sleep on the bare slats covered only by a thin layer of burlap.

All rooms faced a hallway that ran the length of the barracks. At the end of the hallway was a so-called "washroom," an empty room that had no water and no washbasins. Across the hall was a pit latrine, for night use only. This was simply a wall-to-wall box, topped by planks that had four holes, about the size of a toilet seat opening, cut into them. BYOP (bring your own paper). Daytime latrines were spotted around the compound.

The latrines were pumped out once a week by a contraption we quickly dubbed The Super Dooper Shit Scooper. Constructed from a metal tank, equipped with a large hose, atop a wagon with rubber tires that was pulled by two draft horses, the Scooper was driven by a Russian POW, an officer who had lost a leg in combat. There were a few Russian POW's in our camp. They were assigned to the worst jobs, horribly mistreated by the Germans, ostensibly because the Kremlin had not signed the Geneva Conventions; in reality, it was because they hated the "Rooskies" a helluva lot more than they hated the Americans, as my first interaction with a German officer had clearly indicated. Protruding from the top of the tank was a lidded, funnel-like gadget, containing a hand pump, used to pull all the air from the tank. Then a match was lit and stuck into a small opening near the funnel. There was a very loud explosion, followed by the revolting sucking sound of human waste being forced into the tank. This procedure had to be repeated several times. The hose through which this excrement flowed was inserted into the pit and removed by the same Russian POW . . . with his bare hands.

Several times a day, we were required to stand roll call, which the Germans called Appell, on the parade ground of our compound. At our first roll call, we didn't know what to expect. We were told by a German sergeant to form platoons and line up in a column of fives. Then we waited . . . a commonality shared by every military organization in the world. Finally there was a stir at the gate leading to our compound and the sergeant shouted in German, "Achtung!" This was a word we all understood, but the rest of his commands were also in German, which was a loss until we all caught on through daily repetition. "The lieutenant comes. Eyes right."

When we turned our heads toward the gate, we saw an officer on a bicycle coming toward us. His lifeless left arm was suspended from a leather braid, attached to a coiled spring, which was then joined to a leather band around his wrist. As he rode across the uneven field, the spring permitted his arm to bounce up and down with each bump he rolled over. He had trouble keeping his balance, and the bike wobbled so badly that he was constantly turning the handlebars to keep from falling on his ass. To guys our age, anyone over forty was ancient, but this man had to be seventy. We quickly dubbed him The Wheel.

Getting off his bike, der Alte stood before the formation and gave the order for "At ease." He had brought an interpreter with him and, as he spoke in a croaking voice, his words were translated.

"I am the second in command at Stalag Luft IV, and I want to explain the conditions of the camp. First, you were shipped here six weeks before we were prepared to receive you, and we do not have sufficient food on hand. For this reason, you will have to subsist on half-rations until more supplies are delivered. You will also receive food parcels from the International Red Cross, but we do not know when they will arrive.

"Next, you will obey the guards at all times. It doesn't matter what your rank is. A German private is superior to any POW in this camp. To disobey the command of a guard is cause for a court-martial.

"Every day, you will be responsible to read the notices on the bulletin board in front of your barracks. Every notice is by order of the Camp Kommandant. If you fail to follow exactly any of these orders, you will be subject to court-martial, or you could be shot without warning." That was our indoctrination.

We were called to attention again as The Wheel turned, lit a cigarette, mounted his bicycle, and, with the cigarette dangling from his lips and his dead arm dangling from the spring, rode unsteadily back to the gate.

I found it laughable that The Wheel said we had arrived earlier than expected, therefore we would subsist on half-rations until more supplies were delivered. Our daily diet consisted of half a slice of black bread, which contained sawdust as an ingredient, along with a cup of ersatz coffee or tea at morning and night. The only redeeming factor about the "coffee" and "tea" was the warm water it was made with. Otherwise, neither tasted like any beverage I had ever swallowed before. What were we waiting for? A fresh shipment of sawdust, so they could bake more bread?

At noon, we were given either dehydrated cabbage soup, which was flavorless and caused severe diarrhea, or a barley soup that was afloat with bugs. At first, we carefully extracted the bugs. Then, someone came forth with the wisdom that bugs contained protein, which was rare in our diet, and we stopped fishing them out. On luckier days, we received a boiled potato. And once in a great while, the soup contained a few grams of stringy mystery meat, probably from a horse that had keeled over and died. The dried cabbage came in large bags and had to be reconstituted with water, by boiling. Was that so hard to come by? Was it taking a long time to breed more bugs for the barley?

I stayed in this camp for almost a year, and our rations never increased by so much as a crumb, which makes me believe that The Wheel was referring to Red Cross parcels as half our ration. It was around July when the Krauts told us that the first Red Cross parcels had arrived. We always suspected that they had been in the warehouse at Stalag Luft IV before we even set foot into the camp, because the Krauts were notorious for stealing the parcels for their own use. The parcels were paid for and packaged by the United States Army and shipped into Germany via the Red Cross.

If each POW had received one parcel per week, as intended by our government, we could have survived nicely, but that was rare. Most of the time, packages were shared by two, three, or four Kriegies, except for the times when the Germans told us, "No Red Cross packages this week. The shipment was bombed by your Kamerads."

The parcels were designed to give us a balanced diet, and without them, those of us who were long-term POW's would not have survived. Each parcel contained canned tuna, corned beef, liver paté, Spam, crackers, instant coffee, Klim powdered milk, prunes, raisins, sugar, jam, and chocolate D-bars. Another important inclusion that not only satisfied our addiction, but also became the medium of exchange for buying parcel products from our buddies or bartering with guards, was . . . American cigarettes. Then there was the smallest item in the box, but arguably one of the most vital to our health: sour-tasting ascorbic acid tablets, Vitamin C. We ate these because they were something else to chew on, unaware that they were good for us and prevented scurvy.

Probably the best deal we ever made with our American cigarettes was the bribing of a German guard to smuggle in the components to build a crystal radio receiver. Overnight, we had access to the British Broadcasting System radio news programs. Sure, certain subjects were censored, but now we knew with certainty that the Yanks were coming! And, among other things . . . they were coming for us. It was such a damned thrill to know that the Allies were winning this stinking war. And, of course, we all went wild when we heard about D-Day. We figured that we could be liberated before winter set in. It was a blessing that we didn't know it would be ten long months before we were set free.

Next, there was the problem of distributing the news every day. We decided that writing the news on paper and passing out a copy to each barracks was just too risky. If the Krauts got hold of a copy, the jig was up. Several Kriegies memorized a single, condensed record of each day's news, then went to each barracks with a verbal report. Following that, the written copy was destroyed. We didn't know who operated the radio, or what barracks it was hidden in. And we didn't want to know.

Our wounds were left untreated, and there was no medication available for any kind of illness. Most debilitating were our stomach problems. A gastroenterology intern would have had a field day among us. Everyone had watery stools almost daily, and because the Germans did not see fit to supply us with toilet tissue, we hoarded whatever bits of newspaper or scrap paper we came across. The harshness of the paper further compounded our physical deterioration.

The shrapnel wound in my face had become infected and swollen to the point that, when I walked, it jiggled like a woman's breast, about a C-cup. One day at roll call, a German doctor came into our compound and peered at each of us as we stood at attention. He couldn't miss my exposed "breast" and pulled me out of the formation, motioning for me to follow him. We entered the Vorlager and went inside the small hospital. He brought me into a room, seated me, and called in his orderly. After examining my face, he turned to the orderly and said, "Schneiden." I recognized the word, which means to cut, and waited for the shot of Novocain to anesthetize the spot before he made an incision. The orderly handed him a scalpel . . . no shot. He simply sliced open my face, while the orderly held a towel to catch all the pus and corruption that came gushing out. The pain was unbelievable, and I couldn't keep from screaming out. He looked down at me in disgust and left the room. He hadn't said a word to me during the whole procedure. The orderly bandaged my face and I returned to my compound. Four days later, my face was just as swollen as before.

Within weeks, our bodies were covered with malnutrition sores and lice. Our constant scratching made the lesions worse and drove us nuts. God knows how many illnesses we fought off simply because we had the will to live. I had no desire to put myself in the hands of the Kraut doctor again, and neither did most of my friends. Our body weight dropped dramatically and soon the effort of just walking around the compound was enough to make most of us faint. At first, we would go to a fallen buddy and help him to his feet. We soon came to a tacit agreement that we were all expending too much energy in this process and it was better to let the stricken person lie there until he came to on his own.

The first time I saw Old Joe, I hated him just as I did all the German guards. That wasn't his real name, but we gave most of the guards nicknames which we felt were appropriate. Most of them were simply referred to as "goons." Whenever a guard entered our barracks, there would be cries of "Goons up," to warn everyone of his presence.

Old Joe was about fifty-five, a World War I veteran, and a typical German master sergeant, right down to his Hitlerian mustache. Our POW camp had just been completed, and since we were the first prisoners to arrive there, our guards were highly suspicious of us. Most of them had never seen an American before. Old Joe solemnly observed us as he patrolled the compound, hands clasped behind his back.

One morning, walking near my barracks, I suddenly felt dizzy and fell to the ground. It was a cold day, and when I revived, I was covered with my blanket. When I was able to get back to my room, I asked who had been kind enough to cover me. I was shocked and humiliated to learn that Old Joe had come into my barracks and asked for my blanket. I was embarrassed because I didn't want his damned compassion. I crawled into bed, pulling the blanket over my head so no one would see my humiliation.

I was the only one in my room with a smattering of German, so I was able to understand Old Joe when he came into our barracks the next morning and spoke to me.

"How are you feeling?"

"I am better. I would like to know why you covered me yesterday."

He hesitated a moment. "Because I have a son your age and you look very much like him. He was captured by the Americans and is in a POW camp in Texas." Then he smiled for the first time. "How would you like to change places with him?"

I responded to his joke, "Any time you can arrange it, I am ready."

I flatly refused to have anything more to do with Joe. I told my friends that the less we spoke to the guards, the better. They persisted, however, and I finally agreed that I'd try to elicit news about the fighting. I soon found out that Joe's only knowledge of the war came from Goebbels's propaganda, and that was worthless.

Afterward, I tried avoiding Joe, but each day he would stop by my room to talk. Then he began to bring me little gifts. The first time this happened, I didn't realize what he was doing. He was leaving, as usual, with his hands clasped behind his back, when an onion fell to the floor. I thought he had dropped it accidentally, but my room-mates felt it was deliberate. They were right. Some days, he would leave behind a cigarette or a box of matches. All precious items. I was angered by his gifts, but my buddies told me I was being foolish. He asked nothing in return, but I felt guilty nevertheless.

One day as I sat in the window of my room, Joe was walking outside the barracks and, seeing me, he came over. As we spoke, he turned his head and, noticing some activity in the nearest guard tower, suddenly went pale and hurried away.

I didn't see him for more than a week, and I didn't dare ask any of the other guards about him. Then, one day, he appeared in my room and I could see the concern in his eyes.

"A tower guard took my picture while I was speaking with you at the window, and I was threatened with court-martial. It was lucky that you were in the shade and they could not identify you. I told my superiors that a POW had asked me a question and I didn't even remember who he was. Because I fought in the first World War and have a good record, they have let me off with a warning. Next time it will not go so easy. From now on, I will have to be very careful and talk with you only inside the barracks."

Despite his fear and my admonitions, he continued to bring me gifts. I worried that eventually both of us would be caught.

Finally, there was one thing we could be thankful for . . . the weather. Summer had arrived, and those of us who had no shoes, or clothing to speak of, were grateful for the warm days. We wandered around the compound in our GI undershorts and tried to devise ways to amuse ourselves. Some of the Kriegies were very inventive. Before long, tiny sailboats began to appear in the swimming pool, and races were held with cigarettes bet on the outcome.

Those of us who lacked the skill to build a sailboat soon dreamed up less complex ways of amusement. One of the most popular, for guys who were not craftsmen, was fly racing. The warm weather brought an invasion of immense houseflies, and the screenless windows in our barracks were an open invitation for them to harass us. Then some genius came up with a substitute for the Sport of Kings: the Sport of Wings. First, you wrote your initials on a scrap of paper, then you rolled it into a conical shape. Next, you placed your hand on the table, little finger down, thumb up, and waited for a fly. When your prey lit on the table, you swiftly scooped it up and closed your hand. Then, you carefully removed it from your fist, and even more carefully inserted the pointed end of the paper into the fly's anus. When all contestants were ready, their charges were released into the air, each clearly visible by its paper tail, and the trainer of the first to reach the opposite end of the room . . . won the cigarette pool. Judges were stationed at the finish line to resolve close contests.

Tin cans from our Red Cross parcels became the material for numerous inventions, one of the most useful being a device for boiling water. Constructed from several tin cans, the tiny stove had an opening to insert twigs for fuel. Then there was a tunnel with a small paddle wheel, which was propelled by a hand-turned crank that worked as a bellows to blow on the flame and bring the heat to high intensity. This became a thriving business for the craftsmen, who were able to produce and sell them for cigarettes. Now we were able boil water quickly for our powdered coffee whenever we wished. The stoves were very efficient and were clocked at bringing water to a boil in two minutes.

Some of the guys had managed to conceal their small pocket knives during strip searches and were now using them to carve yo-yos and other objets d'art. It was fascinating to watch one fellow's daily progress as he carved a chain from a long wooden mop handle. It took infinite patience to cut into this hard wood and it was amazing to see a beautiful chain protruding from the remainder of the handle.

Every day, we would find copies of German newspapers lying around the compound, probably by intent, because I'm sure the Krauts wanted to expose us to Goebbels's propaganda. I found it easier to read the newspapers than to understand the spoken word, since I had more time to piece together the printed matter. Most of the articles about the war were ludicrous: New York City Bombed into Rubble; or Victorious Against England. Members of the United States Air Corps were labeled Terrorfliegers (terror fliers), or Luftgangsters (air gangsters), giving tacit approval for civilians to lynch captured American airmen. Pictures of downed bomber crews appeared regularly in the German press.

Then there were the rabidly racist caricatures of Neger Terrorfliegers (Negro terror fliers), which depicted a flying-helmeted black man with a very broad nose; mouth stretched wide by thick, wet lips contorted in a savage leer; exposing big teeth, between which protruded a swollen tongue oozing droplets of saliva. It reminded me of a brand of oysters that my father sold in his store, the label showing the head of a black savage holding an oyster between his thumb and forefinger, suspended over his mouth, a mouth just as the one described above, and which the processor still dared, in the early forties of the South, to call . . . Nigger Head Oysters.

Of course, the United States Air Corps was segregated during World War II and there were no black bomber pilots. The only black USAAC pilots were the Tuskegee Airmen, a group which Eleanor Roosevelt, along with some black leaders, pressured the president to form, and they flew fighter planes.

The powder burns inflicted on my face had transmogrified into thick scabs, mostly on my forehead and around my eyes. Along the edges, the scabs were beginning to curl and flake off. My friends kept urging me, "Why don't you pick those damn scabs off. You look like something out of a horror movie." But I resisted the temptation, because I'd heard that could lead to scarring. The scabs also kept the infection out, or at least helped. Instead, I spent a lot of time in the sun and the scabs slowly came off, leaving the skin beneath discolored. As I tanned, the shades of my skin blended and, fortunately, I was left without a single cicatrix.

With the advent of warm weather, American POW thoughts turned to baseball. We used a bunch of old socks, tied tightly together, for a ball, and found a fairly straight tree limb that we debarked and made into a bat. One day, we were playing ball in front of my barracks. The next batter took a powerful swing, connected squarely with the ball, and sent it flying past the center fielder. It continued to roll until it came to a stop just a few inches beyond the warning rail.

A guard tower was just outside the fence and the guard on duty had been watching us play. The fielder walked toward the guard rail, stopped a few feet from it, and looked up at the guard. Motioning at the ball, he asked the guard, "Okay?" I might have imagined it, but I thought the German gave him a slight nod. Even if he didn't, there was no goddamned question that the fielder wasn't trying to escape. Feeling that he'd been given authorization, the guy got down on his knees and reached under the rail for the ball. The guard quickly unslung his rifle from his shoulder, aimed, and fired two rounds into the fielder's back.

We stood there looking at our dead buddy in stunned silence. Soon, others who had heard the shots came over, and we must have had fifty Kriegies gathered around, all protesting loudly. Another rule on the bulletin board cautioned that POW's who formed groups of more than three were subject to the old standby of being "Shot Without Warning," which we now knew they would happily do. Again, the guard aimed his rifle and fired several shots just inches from our feet. We all turned and slowly walked away. Not one of us ran. In a while, two guards came with a wheelbarrow, loaded the fielder into it, and carted him out of the compound. I wondered how his death would be reported to his family.

This callous killing brought home to all of us that the Germans were not making idle threats with their postings on the bulletin board. And the guards had proved that they derived a sadistic pleasure from using us for target practice. One would think that, in the future, we'd give the Krauts no further opportunity to shoot us and all would be well, but only three weeks later we lost another buddy just as needlessly. Our problem was that we tried to rationalize the Germans' behavior, instead of accepting that they were not rational people.

One caveat, near the bottom of the commandant's list, forbade us to step from our barracks windows into the compound. We'd all been guilty of this infraction, myself included, because it seemed such an innocuous thing to do. In the first place, we were simply stepping into the compound where other Kriegies were already moving about. We were stepping into an area where we were permitted to be. We weren't anywhere near the fence. The reason we took this shortcut was that our energy level was so low, we didn't want to waste the extra steps walking to the front door. I had just entered the compound, by stepping through a window in my room. I was lucky that a sentry hadn't seen me.

I was sitting in the sun with some friends and we were facing the side of our barracks, when a guy in the end room came through a window and onto the grass. A sentry, patrolling between the fences, spotted him and brought his rifle down to a firing position. He got off one shot that penetrated the guy's right arm, halfway between the shoulder and elbow, continued through his body, then exited his left arm at the same spot. The kid was dead before he hit the ground. The sentry replaced his rifle into a marching position, right hand holding the butt, and casually continued his patrol. That was the last time anyone stepped through a window.

These cold-blooded murders deepened our hatred of the Krauts, but if they were trying to control us by fear . . . they had failed. We became more cautious, but were just as defiant of their rules. One thing this tragedy did make clear was that the sentries and tower guards were different from the guards who walked within our compound. The former were trained marksmen, uncompromising killers, with orders to shoot down instantly any POW who violated the rules. There was no consideration of the degree, or intent, of an infraction. They were executioners, and their job was to Shoot Without Warning.

What we didn't know until later, when some of us began conversing with the guards, was that the camp Kommandant, Lt. Col. Aribert Bombach, had lost his family during an American bombing raid. His hatred for Americans had obviously taken him over the edge, and we often saw him in the Vorlager screaming at tower guards and sentries. I can only guess that they had missed opportunities to fire at us.

Every few days, the guards in the towers would test-fire their machine guns into the surrounding forest. Since we never knew when this exercise would begin, we always overreacted, because explosions and gunfire were the last sounds we remembered on the day when our own combat experience had abruptly ended. Shortly after the Kriegie who stepped through the barracks window was killed, the guards began test-firing their weapons inside the compound. They fired into the ground, into the space between the warning rail and the barbed-wire fences. Fortunately, none of us was ever hit during this irresponsible and unnecessary show of force, but we all expected a bullet to ricochet off a rock one day and kill a Kriegie.

In the event of an air raid, we were allowed one minute to return to our barracks before being "Shot Without Warning." There was never a real air raid, but the Krauts would set off the air-raid sirens as a drill and would fire on anyone outside the barracks after the passage of a minute. One day, a POW inside his barracks was holding a cup of coffee, when it was shattered in his hand by a machine gun bullet.

It was rare for us to hear the sound of aircraft in our camp, but one sunny and cloudless day, we were all brought running into the compound by the high-pitched whine of fighter plane engines screaming through the sky. We weren't prepared for the excitement of a USAAF P-51 fighter hot on the tail of a German Messerschmitt 109. A dogfight . . . right before our eyes! No longer were we in a POW camp; we were at our high school football game and our defensive back was chasing our opponent's end, who was racing for the end zone. Then our back overtook their end, stripped him of the ball, and recovered it inches from the end zone.

There was no barbed wire, no guards, no nothing, only the thrill of seeing our fighter chasing theirs. Three or four times the planes circled in the sky, with the P-51 pilot trying to close the distance so he could effectively fire at the German. Then, in a burst of speed, the P-51 came into range and you could see the flashes of its machine gun fire. The Me 109 slowed down, then went into a steep dive. Seconds later, a huge cloud of black smoke drifted upward from the trees. And what did we do? The same thing any schoolboy would do at a football game, after a great play. We cheered and whooped and clapped our hands . . . and the tower guards began firing into the compound. Back in our barracks, walking down the hallway, some guy grumbled, "Poor fuckin' losers!" That broke the tension and we all laughed like hell.

During our roll calls, when The Wheel or some other German officer arrived to take the report, the Sergeant of the Guard, right hand raised stiffly toward the Himmel in salute, would greet the brass with "Sieg Heil!" (Hail Victory!). On July 21, 1944, we were surprised when The Wheel approached our formation, saluted, and both he and the sergeant loudly shouted, "Heil Hitler!" The words burst from their lips as if each had been stuck in the ass with a bayonet. The entire procedure that day was so highly charged, we knew that some change was in the works and that, whatever it was, it did not bode well for us. That evening, when our reporter came by to recite the news from the BBC, we learned of an assassination attempt on Hitler the day before, by several of his senior military leaders. Unfortunately, the attempt had failed, but orders had filtered down that der Führer would be acknowledged by his troops at every military ceremony. So the Master Race continued its program of mutual masturbation.

Lest I create the impression that all POWs were angelic souls, strong of character, honest to a fault, delightful company, and filled with caring for their buddies, it must be realized that we were a cross-section of America: from diverse backgrounds, religions, and cultures. Just because we fought together, became POWs together, and suffered the same deprivations, did not imply that we were, every single one, honorable men . . . any more than every police officer, every Congressman, every lawyer, every doctor, or every clergyman must be presumed an honorable man.

Everybody in my room was a classy guy, except for one. He didn't let it be known that he'd been a Golden Gloves fighter. We picked this up later from a Kriegie in another barracks who came from the boxer's hometown and said that this creep had been a bully even when they were in grade school together. One day, this tough smacked a quiet kid in our room for no real reason. The rest of us pulled him off and told him unequivocally that the next time he hit anyone in our room he could plan to take on all of us. He never socked anybody else in our room, but he was constantly getting into brawls with guys from other barracks.

Then there was the guy who stole a loaf of bread. We hadn't gotten any Red Cross parcels yet, and everybody was starving on our meager rations. In our room, we took turns in slicing our bread allotment, with a different guy doing the honors every day. Every slicer did his best to cut the bread evenly, and nobody quibbled about the size of each slice. One day, just as we were divvying up our bread, the guards came through our barracks, yelling "Raus! Raus! Appell!" Roll call.

We left our bread on the table and when we returned, as expected, it was untouched. Then we heard loud, angry voices from the room next door. Minutes later, two guys from that room appeared. "Somebody stole a loaf of bread from our room. We aren't accusing anybody, but we need to search every room in the barracks. It's gotta be here, because we were all at roll call."

One of our guys said, "Sure, go ahead. You got a right to look for your bread."

When they were finished, one of them said, "I'm sorry we bothered you guys. Thanks."

After we ate, several of us wandered over to their room out of curiosity. They'd searched the entire barracks to no avail. Two guys were going through their umpteenth inspection, when one pulled back the blanket on a bed and said, "Here!" The loaf hadn't been visible beneath the blanket, because it had been forced down between two slats. The kid who slept in that bed ran for the door, but was tackled before he made it. He started to cry and apologize and all of his roommates wanted to beat on him, but after a few blows his abjection and wailing seemed to hold them back, but they still wanted blood. They were totally enraged and demanding the most severe punishment for him. Unable to come to a quick decision, one suggested they hold a "kangaroo court," and the others quickly agreed. They dispatched two guys to inform all other rooms in the barracks that a court would be convened in the washroom in half an hour.

The event drew a crowd, with some Kriegies overflowing into the hallway. The guys from the thief's room brought him in, stood him in a corner, and took over the officiating. One presented the case to the attendees, who would all vote on the malefactor's fate. "The worst crime a POW can commit against his buddies is to steal their food. We're barely stayin' alive on what the Krauts are giving us, and stealing a loaf of bread could mean the difference between life and death. How goddam lowdown can you get—to take bread out of your brother's mouth when you're both starvin'? We can't afford to have rats like that living among us. We need to set an example right now. I vote that we give him the death penalty by hanging!"

I was not nearly as astonished that one imbecile would suggest the death penalty, as I was that the majority in the room were yelling "Yeah!" "Yeah!" "Give him the death penalty!" "Hang his thievin' ass!" The accused stood in the corner wiping his nose on his sleeve and shivering while the rest of us were perspiring. I saw him look up at the high rafters in the room, and I knew exactly what he was thinking.

Then several calmer heads moved up to the front of the room and began to speak. One said, "Before we get really carried away here, I want you to stop for a minute and think. We're considering hanging another POW by the neck until dead for the crime of stealing a loaf of bread. It's not even a good loaf of bread. It's made with sawdust. Now I know even a slice of shit like that is important to us, because the fucking Germans aren't giving us much else. But the guys in your room wouldn't have died if you hadn't found that bread. Somebody would've been hungrier tonight, but you wouldn't die. C'mon guys, think about it. Are you really going to kill a guy over a fucking loaf of bread?"

A few others spoke up, some more eloquently, some less, but all made the point, quite clearly, that the punishment was way too severe for the crime. I made my way to the front of the room. "I just want to say that when this process was suggested, the person in your room who brought it up called it a kangaroo court. I wonder if everybody here knows the definition of the words 'kangaroo court.' A kangaroo court is a mock court, which means that it's run by people who aren't authorized to judge someone else. It also means that any verdict you reach here is illegal, because it wasn't made by using the principles of the law, in a court of law. What it boils down to is this: if you hang this guy, you'll have violated the rules we have to live by as members of the U.S. Air Force, and there ain't a chance in hell that you won't be court-martialed when you get home. And let me say this: I'm not a lawyer, but I wouldn't bet a Kraut Pfennig that you won't be charged with Murder One.

"Now, I'm not saying that this creep doesn't deserve punishment. But I think it would be much more in keeping with his crime if we . . . say . . . give him the silent treatment for the next ninety days. And not just the guys in our barracks. Spread the word around the compound, and if you see someone talking to him, go over and clue him in."

There was some grumbling from up front, but most of the others started backing off and then somebody said that the silent treatment sounded good to him, and before long others agreed, and when a vote was taken, it passed. I've never again looked at a loaf of bread in the same way.

With the exception of the former Golden Glover, whom we convinced that in the future it would be bad for his health to use anyone in our room for a punching bag, the rest of my roommates were great guys. In addition to the irrepressible Red, I became really close friends with George Hamby and Roger Hess, the fellow from North Carolina I had met back at our air base in England.

George Hamby was in a different bomb group than Red and me, but we were shot down on the same Berlin mission. The day I met George, his face, hair, hands, and much of what was left of his flying suit were dirty with smudges of grease from an oil line that had burst on his plane. One pants leg had been torn away, exposing his leg, with a deep cut from the knee down. He had also been hit in the neck by shrapnel. A sleeve of his jacket was rolled up to his elbow, to keep it from touching a hole in his wrist, where he'd been hit by a

German fighter-plane bullet. The wound in his wrist where the bullet had entered was small, but on the side where it emerged, the erupted skin was raised about an inch and was red and inflamed. The Germans had given him no medical treatment, and he was lucky that the bullet had not hit an artery passing through, or that he didn't succumb to a deadly infection in the camp.

George had the thinnest wisp of a mustache and his facial hair was very light, probably because he was one eighth Seminole. There was a vacantness about his eyes, which made you feel that, though he seemed to be listening to what you were saying, he wasn't fully comprehending. It was the same empty look we all wore during those first astonishing days after our capture, when our minds refused to grasp the suddenness of our transition from combatant to captive. Now, after having been POWs for almost three weeks, that initial stunned reaction had largely faded and we were adjusting to our new role as survivors. Not so with George. He hadn't been able to shake off the shock of being wounded, losing his plane, and bailing out into the waiting, hostile hands of German soldiers. He was in the same traumatic state he had fallen into on Day One.

Almost every hour, George would come to me and say, "Norm, my heart isn't beating."

"Well, George, if your heart isn't beating, how are you able to stand here and talk to me?" Then I would take his hand and bring it up to the side of his neck. "Just feel your pulse. It's throbbing strong as hell, isn't it? You're absolutely fine. Stop worrying. If you want something to worry about, concentrate on when we're getting out of this shithole."

George and I, along with many others, shared the nightly problem of "lock-up." Promptly at eight P.M., the lights were turned off. The shuttered windows didn't bother us much while the lights were on, but as soon as the Germans doused them, the darkness took on a palpable density. The shutters were closed tightly, and our room would become engulfed in a stygian blackness that I and many others found unbearable. After solitary, I became so claustrophobic, I found it hard to breathe at night in my room. I was unable to take a full breath and felt I would suffocate. It felt as if the room had suddenly been filled, floor to ceiling, with thick axle grease, clogging your ears and nose, shutting out sound, cutting off your breath. I would sit on my bunk and fight the dizziness that overcame me. George could not be still and would leave the room to walk up and down the long hallway until daybreak. The single door at the front of the barracks was locked, but no one would have gone out anyway, because police dogs roamed the compound at night. At the first sign of daylight, George would come back into the room and stumble into his bunk, exhausted, eyes puffy from lack of sleep.

My other close bunkmate, Roger Hess, was also in the 708th Bomb Squad. I flew my first two missions with his crew. We were both on that ill-fated Berlin mission that downed my plane, but his crew would've been on their twenty-fifth mission, which was what they needed to complete their tour, so I had assumed that they were all safely back in the States until I saw him at the camp.

It was a week after my arrival at Stalag Luft IV when I saw a small group of new POWs being brought from the Vorlager into our compound, and I walked toward the gate to see if anyone I knew was among them. My attention was drawn to a Kriegie who was limping badly . . . it was Roger. I ran over to greet him. "Dammit, man, I thought you guys had made it home."

Roger looked at me in amazement. "I thought you were *dead*, Norm. We were just off your left wing when I saw your plane get hit and catch fire. You were able to keep up your speed and altitude and I watched until you blew up . . . and not a single chute came out."

"I was the last one to bail, just a few seconds before she

exploded. We lost our navigator, bombardier, and ball-turret and tail gunners. But what in hell happened to you?"

"Let's go sit down on the grass," Roger said.

"We salvoed our bombs over the target," he told me, "and made our turn to head home, when we took a direct flak hit in the radio room. It wasn't a minute later, we took two more hits; another in the radio room that knocked me down; and then one inside the waist that broke the plane in half. The tail section fell free and was spinning down like a damn maple leaf, and I was in it. My partner's head was blown off and it was rolling around in the tail with me. It didn't feel real. It was like a dream. I tried to reach the open end of the tail so I could hang out far enough to use my chute, but centrifugal force kept pulling me back. Finally, my feet made contact with something I got a toehold on, and I shoved hard as hell. I got my hands on the broken edge of the tail, but my left shoe was caught, wedged so tight, I couldn't budge it. I tried to pull loose, but no way. I knew I was getting damn close to the ground, so I had no choice but to pull my chute. It jerked me out so hard, I must have torn something in my hip and back. I can't hardly put any weight on it."

I sat there spellbound and horrified. I was afraid to ask, but I had to know. "What happened to the others?"

"They're all dead, Norm. I'm the only one that got out."

I thought about my own survivor guilt for the four crewmates I'd lost. What in God's name was going through Roger's mind? He had lost nine buddies who were supposed to be going home with him in a matter of hours. He was the only one spared. How was he going to live with that? We talked every day, but we never rehashed that mission again. It was too painful. Roger was always quiet and controlled, but I wondered what kind of emotional tempest was surging inside him.

Most of the guards who walked among us inside the compound

were fairly innocuous; middle-aged farmer-types who, after they saw that the "Terrorfliegers" were not as vicious as Goebbels had portrayed us, tried to be pleasant. We had little conversation with them, however, because they spoke no English.

Then there was Sgt. Hans Schmidt, whom we called "Big Stoop." I think his foremost qualification as a POW camp guard was his unbridled viciousness. Perhaps he had been hand-picked by the camp Kommandant. Standing about six-foot-seven and close to three hundred pounds, he was a former professional wrestler. A brooding hulk of a man, he skulked around the compound holding a leather belt with a large buckle, making eye contact with no one but watching everything. We quickly learned to stay well out of his extended reach, because he delighted in inflicting pain on POWs. Without warning, he would sneak up behind you and smash his belt buckle into your head; clap both his hands to your ears at once, bursting your eardrums; or fell you with a single blow from his huge paw.

A few of the guards were still suspicious of us and, though they would say "Guten Morgen" or "Guten Abend," they still watched us warily. We referred to all the guards as "goons," and there were goons we particularly liked to insult, without their knowing it, of course. Roger Hess and I used a language that the Krauts wouldn't understand: Pig Latin. When a goon we didn't like approached, we'd greet him with, "Guten Morgen, othermay uckerfay! Ucksay imay ickday! Oc-kay uckersay! Eetway itshay!" We smiled warmly through our curses. Then we'd try to restrain our laughter until the goon was out of sight.

There were also guards we called "ferrets," because they could understand English and were constantly trying to eavesdrop on us. We avoided having conversations anywhere within earshot of them.

One day, Roge and I decided to provoke a ferret by continuing our discourse even though we knew we could be overheard. But we would talk in Pig Latin. We were standing with our backs to the steps leading into our barracks when a ferret came up behind us and stopped in the doorway. We continued talking animatedly and, after a few minutes, the ferret left the compound and went into the Vorlager. He was soon back at the gate with another guard and was pointing in our direction. This guard, obviously a ferret too, casually ambled over and positioned himself behind us in the doorway. Roge and I raised our voices so our gobbledygook could be clearly heard. Before long, this new linguist returned to the Vorlager, where the first ferret was waiting, and shook his head negatively.

After perplexing two more ferrets, we finally called off our little game when the fucking Kommandant himself appeared and began berating the cluster of confused ferrets. It was time to turn off the gas before the pot boiled over. Roge took off in one direction and I in another.

Whenever an opportunity came along to make the Krauts' lives miserable, we took it. Some civilian carpenters were brought into our compound one day, and Red and I watched them come through the gate, each showing his photo ID to the guard. As the workers passed in front of us, one tried to replace his card in his back pocket, which already held a handkerchief. The card fell out of his pocket and onto the grass. I quickly scooped it up and hid it in my shirt, but not fast enough to escape Red's eagle eye.

"What the hell do you think you're gonna do with that? You can't get out of here with it. You don't look nothing like that damned Kraut. Now who's lookin' for trouble?"

"I have no intention of trying to get out with it. Let's go inside the barracks." I headed for the night latrine and, when we got there, Red looked over my shoulder as I dropped the Kraut's ID into the shit.

"Now, what's that gonna getcha?" asked Red.

"What do you think's going to happen when that Kraut gets ready to leave at five o'clock?"

"They won't let him out," said Red.

"Exactly. And that's when we're going to have some fun watching him try to talk his way out of here."

At five P.M., the carpenters began filing through the gate, except for this one poor dolt, who stood there searching through every pocket in his clothing. At first, he was indignant at not being allowed out, which just pissed off the guard. Next, he tried earnest entreaty, but the guard just stopped listening to him and, likely, told him to move away, because he soon retreated about thirty feet from the gate and sat on the ground.

Red and I let some of the guys in our barracks in on the caper, and we all stood around joking and guessing what was in store for the dummkopf.

Nobody ever came back to retrieve him, and when the guards who patrolled at night came into the compound with their snarling canines, he took refuge in our barracks. Looking miserable, he slouched down on the floor just inside our doorway and waited. Finally, the Sergeant of the Guard appeared at our barracks with two other guards and a copy of the guy's ID. When they were satisfied that he was the missing civilian, they took the contrite carpenter away, smothering him with a shitload of imprecations. When the work crew came back the next day, he wasn't with them.

Whenever new POWs arrived at our camp, the word spread quickly and we waited near the gate, searching each face in hope of seeing someone we knew. Whenever a Kriegie yelled out a greeting, you turned to see who had found a kindred soul from his Bomb Group or from his hometown. No matter whom you spoke to, the first question was, inevitably, "How long you been down?" The newcomers were always in awe of those of us who'd been POWs for several months. I tried to allay the new guys' apprehensions about what was in store for them by saying that conditions were not good, but bearable, and that they'd make it just fine. My little white lies even made me feel a bit better.

Around the middle of July 1944, other American POWs and some British were brought in by ship from Stalag Luft VI at Hydekrug in East Prussia. A Luft IV captain was in charge of the guards assigned to march the newcomers from the harbor to our camp, a distance of about three kilometers. Obviously, the captain had planned beforehand to brutalize these incoming Kriegies, who were already debilitated from two days spent in the filthy holds of two coal freighters. These POWs were forced to run the entire distance to the camp. Those who fell were clubbed with rifle butts. Others were bayoneted in the buttocks and set upon by guard dogs.

We stood by the gate as each new group entered our compound, prepared to offer help to those who had been savaged by the guards, simply because they were too ill to run. None of the wounded was provided with medical attention.

Every night, I would sit on my bunk in the dark, fighting a panic attack and believe that I was losing my mind. My own "lock-up" was starting to get the best of me.

For weeks, I played a mind game with myself. Each day I would think about what body part I would sacrifice to be released from prison camp. I started out by giving up a toe each day. Then I gave up my ears, one at a time, and tried to envision how I might look without these protuberances. I was so engrossed with my pretense that I half-expected someone to ask, "What the hell happened to your ears?"

Then came each finger of my left hand. Left leg. Right leg. Left arm. Little finger, ring finger, middle finger of my right hand. I couldn't stand the thought of losing my one remaining eye, the other rendered useless by the swelling in my jaw, so I gave up the index finger on my right hand, then my thumb. Finally, I closed my eyes one night and looked at myself in an imaginary mirror. Horrified by what I "saw," I decided that life in this state wasn't worth living. So I reclaimed all of my missing body parts; "watched" them flying through the air and reattaching at the point of their amputations; then seriously questioned my sanity for engaging in this bizarre delusion in the first place.

It was noon on October 2, 1944, and I was in my barracks having lunch, a boiled potato, with my roommates: Red, Vito, Nick, John, and Roge. A piece of potato went down the wrong way and I began choking.

Red said, "Careful, Norm. Watch out for the bones."

Roge looked up from his spud. "You okay?"

"Yeah," I said, a little dazed. "I just thought of something. Today's my twenty-first birthday."

Vito was crestfallen. "Damn, Norm! Why didn't you tell us? We'd have prepared something a lot fancier than a fucking boiled Kartoffel."

"You're old enough to vote now," Nick grinned. "And buy a drink without worrying about ID."

John said, "Norm, I'll tell ya what. You got screwed out of your birthday lunch and that's not fair, so we want to make it up to you. We'll buy you one gift, anything you want. And don't worry about the price. You're only twenty-one once in your life, and we want to make this a memorable occasion. Ford V-8 convertible? Fine. A night with Miss America? Just say the word. Take your time, and remember, the sky's the limit."

I thought about it for a couple of minutes, then said, "You know what I'd really like?"

"What?" they all chimed in.

"I'd like to go home in the morning."

Silence. Then Vito said, "Norm, that can be arranged. A little bit touchy, but we can manage it. I just want you to think about a couple of things before we go to work on the details. When you're back home, warm; showered; shaved; clean clothes; eating a nice, thick juicy steak smothered in onions, with French fries on the side; sipping from a large glass of dry red wine; eating a three-inch-high piece of creamy cheesecake and washing it down with strong, real coffee; smoking an expensive Cuban cigar while you lay back in an easy chair and relax; how are you gonna feel when you remember us?

"We'll still be here freezing our asses off; scratching at lice; eating our half-slice of black bread and picking sawdust out of our teeth. Trotting to the latrine before the dehydrated cabbage soup we ate for lunch runs down our legs. If you feel you can live with yourself, knowing that your buddies are still back here barely surviving . . . then we'll get started right now and you'll leave for home in the morning."

I put my elbows on the table, bent my head into my arms and between loud, mock sobs, said, "No! No! I can't leave you guys here to suffer by yourselves. Forget the trip tomorrow. I'm stayin.' I wouldn't leave my buddies for anything in the world."

Still "sobbing," I jumped up and hugged everybody at the table. When I got to Red, he said, "Stop, fool! You crazy?"

Everyone was "thrilled" with my decision. At dinner that night, after we had eaten our black bread and mint tea, I was asked to leave the room for a minute. When I returned, Roge had made a candle from tightly twisted paper, and he lit it and stuck it into a piece of bread while everyone sang Happy Birthday. I never knew who sacrificed the half-slice of bread, but I was beyond touched.

Chapter Twelve

THE WINTER OF OUR DISCONTENT

The European winter of 1944–45 turned out to be one of the coldest of that century. Our coal ration of three small briquettes a day burned up so quickly, you had to stand right up against the stove to feel even a bit of warmth before the fire was reduced to only embers. At night, our aluminum water pitchers would freeze to solid ice in our rooms. Many of us had bailed out of our planes wearing only flight suits and flying boots. My flight suit had been ripped apart when the interrogator jerked out the insulated wires while searching me. Like an electric blanket, the wires transmitted heat to your body while on the plane, but once you were no longer plugged in, the suit's thin material provided almost no warmth.

My flying boots had disintegrated. I stood roll calls in my bare feet, often in the snow. At Thanksgiving, some light hobnailed shoes were brought in by the Salvation Army, a wonderful gift, but by then we'd already had several snowfalls.

The most popular food on our menu, and the only one that tasted exactly as it did at home, was the plain boiled potato. On the days that spuds were served, if "served" is the appropriate word to use for something transported from kitchen to barracks in a water bucket, a POW was dispatched from each room to pick up the hot Kartoffeln. The allotment was one potato to a person, and they were all medium-sized, so you just reached into the bucket and pulled one out. There was never an extra.

I was bringing back our potatoes one day, and I saw a guard posting a notice on the bulletin board, so I stopped to read it. We were advised that our barracks and several others were being placed under quarantine because a contagious, unnamed illness threatened to spread throughout the camp. We would be moving out of our barracks that evening, into "temporary quarters."

An hour later, we heard hammering and we went outside to see carpenters nailing together small prefabricated huts: our temporary quarters. Each hut would house eight men, who would sleep on straw that had been thrown down on the wooden floor. Poles were driven into the ground and a new barbed wire fence was strung up around us, with a locked gate, and we were ordered inside. Red and I moved into the same hut.

Within our enclosure was a shed with a padlocked front door and also a side opening, covered by a shutter that was secured with a smaller lock. Red said, "Wonder what's in that shed?"

"I don't know, but I bet you're going to find out."

"I sure in hell am. Keep an eye out for the goons while I check it out."

The four huts in our area were sandwiched between two barracks, so we weren't visible to the tower guards, and a goon would have to approach from either end to observe us. Red came back wearing the familiar grin that foretold an acquisition.

"Guess what? I can see through a little crack and that damn shed's fulla potatoes."

"That's nice. It's also got a big lock on the door."

"I know. You can't get through the door. But you know that opening on the side? The screws that fasten the hasp to the wood . . . they're all rustier'n hell. I bet I can pry 'em out with just my fingers."

"Okay, but you have to wait till dark, Red. I don't want to be responsible for your getting caught in broad daylight."

"Awright. You get another guy from our hut to be lookout at one end, and you can come with me to the other."

I didn't think it was dark enough, but Red was impatient and never listened to me about these sorts of things anyway, so we carried out our caper early. He pulled the screws out easily and we reached through and took out eight potatoes each. Then he pushed the screws back in and, since there was no pressure on them, they held fine. We scooted back to our hut and gave each guy two potatoes. The we sat down on the straw, rubbed the dirt off on our pants, and ate them like apples. Agreed, they were much tastier boiled, but they filled our bellies. What more can a guy ask? We repeated this mission every night during the quarantine.

We'd been in the huts a little over a week when a fierce storm blew in one night. There was thunder, lightning, and wind so strong that we thought our hut was going to blow away. Then there was a blinding lightning flash and an ear-blasting crack, and we heard screams from a nearby hut. We ran over and saw that the hut had taken a direct hit, the walls were split apart, the roof was lying on the ground, and the large nails that had held the hut together had been melted by the intense heat of the lightning bolt. There was the nauseating odor of cremated flesh. We pulled five guys out of the wreckage, mostly unharmed except for being in shock. The other three were dead. It was dawn before guards bothered to come over and investigate. That afternoon we were allowed to move back into our barracks.

The two or more daily roll calls might have been comical if we hadn't been standing them in sub-freezing temperatures. We never knew how long it would take to get a count, because the guards were all mathematically challenged. At our first roll call, in May 1944, there were only sixty-five of us and the count was easy. But with the steady influx of new Kriegies, the camp filled quickly and in ten months our number swelled to more than ten thousand.

You would think that in a country with one of the most efficient armies in the world, some of that efficiency would trickle down to even dumb assholes like our guards. The problem was that they had us line up in rows five guys deep, but then they had no fixed number for the width of the formation, which could be thirty-two, forty-nine, fifty-seven, or anywhere they chose to cut off the formation. If anyone was misaligned by so much as half a head, the guard would motion for him to move over and by the time the POW did, the guard had forgotten how many he'd counted and would have to start all over.

But that was just the beginning. After the Kraut counters came up with the number of rows, they had to multiply that number by five, and that exercise was far beyond their cerebral capability. So they would go back and count loudly again. And again. And again. "Eins, Zwei, Drei, Vier, Funf, Sechs, Sieeeeben. . . ." I don't remember the total ever coming out right on the first try. Often we stood roll call for twenty, thirty minutes, or more. Along with our existing physical travails, the last thing we needed was to add the torturous pain of frostbite, an injury that would continue to afflict us for a lifetime.

Initially, we were issued one very thin blanket and, since our low caloric diet didn't help generate any body heat, we were shivering constantly. Some guys doubled up with a buddy to stay a bit warmer. The narrow bunks and the weight of two people often caused the thin slats to break and both guys would end up on the floor. I was more comfortable toughing it out alone.

With the frigid weather, even the lice got cold and dug in deeper for warmth. It wasn't enough that the cold had made my skin thin as parchment, but with the constant itching and scratching my whole body became a bloody mess. Although the water pumps in the compound never froze, who in hell was going to stand outside and wash?

Then there was the rude awakening when the bodily function that I had looked forward to as an enjoyable stress reliever in July became a most unwelcome nocturnal surprise in the bone-chilling cold of winter. The occasional summer wet dream that I, still somnolent, smiled about and quickly went back to sleep soon after, now fully awakened me in the winter as the warm ejaculate, immediately turning cold, spread its viscid moisture to harden and stiffen the hair on my abdomen, while I lay there shivering.

One morning we were having our usual breakfast of black bread and abominable brew, when everyone suddenly went silent. I looked up and saw a guy standing in the doorway. He said that he had been assigned to our room, but we just stared at him. Nobody uttered a word. We were rendered speechless by his sartorial elegance. Spotlessly attired in a long greatcoat, expensive-looking suit, starched shirt, fashionable necktie, polished shoes, all topped off by a black derby hat, we didn't know what the hell to say. My first thought was that he'd been sent to spy on us, but even the Germans weren't stupid enough to think we'd fall for that. We had been warned in England to watch out for an American POW who had thrown in with the Germans and was helping them extract information from other POWs.

The new Kriegie's name was Nick Vargo, from Cleveland, and for a couple of days we had very little to say to him until we were convinced, by the burns on his face and his knowledge of American sports, that he was a genuine POW. Nick had been shot down over Belgium and picked up by resistance fighters, who outfitted him as a civilian and moved him from place to place, until one day their panel truck was pulled over on the highway by SS troops and he was captured. I hated to think what had happened to his benefactors.

Nick was an engineer/gunner with the 445th Bomb Group, flying out of England, and was acquainted with a famous Oscar-winning actor in his squadron, a B-24 pilot by the name of Major James Maitland Stewart, better known to the world as Jimmy Stewart. Nick reminded me of Stewart because he also was a tall, soft-spoken, easy-going guy. Nick remains a dear friend today, and we still laugh about the time when everyone in our barracks suspected that he was a spy.

Once a month, the Germans doled out a single razor blade to each room in a barracks. With more than twenty guys trying to get a shave from the same blade, we drew names out of a bucket to decide the order of use. I was usually lucky enough to hit within the top ten shavers, while my roommate, John Glass, invariably ended up in the high teens. The irony was, John's facial hair was the texture of steel wool, the toughest whiskers in our room. Each successive guy tried to sharpen the blade by rubbing it back and forth on the inside of his coffee cup, but this process soon reached the point of diminishing returns. Every month, John would beg me to shave him. "Norm, I just can't do this to myself. You gotta shave me." So we'd wait for the noon cup of hot beverage, I'd lather his face with a sliver of saved soap, dip the razor into the fast-cooling liquid, and listen to him scream as I brutalized his face with the very dull blade.

As the temperature continued to fall, so did our spirits. It was getting dark a little after four P.M. and, even during daylight hours, we ventured outside less and less. Sitting around in our room for long periods fostered group conversations, and topics ranged from school to sports, booze to broads; but no matter where we began, we invariably ended up with food. Guys who had probably never watched their mothers cook were now remembering their favorite dishes and trying to figure out the ingredients that these recipes required. Some of the ethnic and regional dishes brought roars of laughter from guys who'd never eaten them, or maybe never even heard of them. A kid from New York salivated as he spoke about his mom's battered and deep-fried squid; while one from Mississippi mooned over cornbread, turnip greens with smoked ham hocks, and a side of black-eyed peas.

Many of us spent a lot of time in the sack. I knew nothing about self-hypnosis, but often I could pull my thin blanket over my head, achieve a trancelike state, and transport my mind back to 1099 North Parkway, Memphis, Tennessee. I would visualize every member of my family and project what each one was doing at that hour. Waking up afterward was not so great, because I felt more homesick than ever. Some of my friends, charged with anxiety, were unable to even sit and they paced up and down the hallway with the expressionless look of caged animals. We were all going stir-crazy. John Glass was from Pennsylvania and, at twenty-eight, the oldest guy in our room. He was also the only one who was married. He spoke constantly about his wife Margie, and I could sense his longing and the fear that he might not make it back. One evening, just before lights out, someone was teasing John and he became upset. He took off his GI belt, wrapped the end around his fist, and announced, "I'm warning you that I'm gonna be swinging my belt around and if you're not in your bunk, you're probably gonna get hit." When the lights went out, you could hear the hum of the belt as it flew through the air and I winced at the heavy sound of the buckle whenever it struck a bedpost. Nobody moved, scared to egg him on any further, and after about five minutes, John climbed into his bunk and went to sleep. John was an inveterate joker and I never knew him to get angry when he was the butt of a joke. I suspect that he was particularly depressed that night, maybe thinking about Margie, and had just gone over the edge. When he awoke the next morning, his disposition was as if nothing had happened.

Trying to raise a Kriegie out of his despondency was no easy task, especially when you were hanging on the ropes yourself. But I think we all tried, because if a buddy's melancholy was that obvious to you, you were likely just a notch above him on the sad scale, and felt a bit superior . . . with maybe a little schadenfreude thrown in to boot.

I guess it had to happen. Looking at the menacing barbed wire fences every day, it must have crossed every POW's mind that there was a quick way to end this mental anguish. It certainly occurred to me. The terrible consequences of deep depression were brought home to us very harshly one day. Red and I were out for a short walk and noticed a guy from the next barracks who had been looking crazed for weeks. He was only thirty feet in front of us when he suddenly stopped, looked up at the tower guard, screamed something unintelligible, then leaped over the warning rail and onto the fence. Within seconds, he was dead. Caught on the barbed wire by one sleeve of his jacket, his bullet-riddled body suspended, he had escaped the fence that confined him—by becoming a part of it.

Chapter Thirteen

CHRISTMAS

I t is said there are no atheists in foxholes. I doubt that there are many atheists in POW camps either. At Stalag Luft IV, we were fortunate, after a few months, to have three clergymen sent to our camp: Reverend Anthony Jackson, Isle of Guernsey; Reverend T.J.E. Lynch, Aldershot, Hawts, England; and Reverend G. Rex Morgan, South Wales, England. Lynch and Morgan were both captains, and chaplains in the British Army, who had become POWs. It didn't seem to matter what your religion was. We were all seeking some kind of faith to cling to, and whenever one of the ministers came into our compound to hold a service, almost everyone attended.

I was particularly impressed by Reverend Jackson, a British civilian who was interned in Germany after the Nazis took the Isle of Guernsey in July 1940. This was the only British territory captured by Germany during World War II. He was later offered release in a swap for a German who had been detained in England under similar circumstances. By this time, Allied troops were being captured by the Germans and sent to POW camps.

Rev. Jackson said that when he first heard the news, he was elated at the prospect of returning home to his wife and eight-year-old daughter. Then he began to think about the POWs who were arriving daily and the thousands more who might be captured in the future. That's when he realized that this could be a rare opportunity to serve POWs, in desperate circumstances, who would be in great need of spiritual guidance. It was the ultimate "opportunity" to do God's work—be a true indicator of his faith.

To POWs, who dreamed constantly of their liberation, Rev. Jackson's sacrifice was so incredible that in our eyes he had practically achieved sainthood. When he held services in our compound, we hung on his every word with an intensity that I have not experienced since.

I will never forget one particular crisis that Rev. Jackson helped me get through. In mid-summer of 1944, a notice appeared on the bulletin board of my compound announcing that at next morning's roll call, all POWs would assemble in the center of the compound in two formations: Christians to the right and Jews to the left.

I spoke with several others who I knew were Jewish, and they all planned to assemble in the left formation. Because I had thrown away my dog tags, I couldn't be identified as Jewish, but I knew I would feel a deep sense of guilt if I didn't stand with the other Jewish POWs. When I presented the problem to some of my Christian friends, every one said that I'd be crazy—standing to the left would be taking a chance on being executed.

Rev. Jackson held a service that day; afterward, I asked to speak with him privately. When I presented my dilemma to him, he put his hand on my shoulder and said, "Look, I can understand that you will feel guilty if you don't stand with the other Jewish POWs.

But the Germans don't know you're Jewish and, frankly, we don't know what they intend to do. If you can show me how your action will benefit one single person, I would say, yes, go ahead and stand in the left formation. But we both know that your doing so will help no one other than the Germans, and they're the last people on earth you want to help. Outwit the Germans. Stay alive. That's my advice to you."

Oddly enough, I heard very little discussion in our barracks about the Germans' plan to segregate Jews the next day. There was no talk of a plot to disrupt this scheduled action as there had sometimes been with other German edicts. I was somewhat puzzled by this unaccustomed passivity.

The next morning, everyone assembled in the center of the compound, Christians on the right and Jews on the left. I looked across at the Jewish POWs and I was riddled with guilt. A German captain approached the formation where I stood and asked, "How many here are Jews yet? If you are Jews, you must to move links . . . left." The officer's question seemed to be the catalyst that upset everyone in the Christian formation and immediately prompted some grumbling questions from the POWs within the ranks:

"Are we gonna let these assholes get away with this shit?"

"We're all in the U.S. Air Force, what gives these goons the fuckin' right to split us up?"

"If we let these bastards pull Jews out today, whose turn will it be tomorrow? Catholics? Baptists?"

Then, as if by an agreed-upon plan, all the men in the right formation walked over and blended into the left. The captain asked us repeatedly to separate again, but no one moved.

The captain, a lieutenant, and two sergeants, one of whom was Old Joe, walked over to the gate to confer. After a few minutes they came back, asked the guards to do a roll call, then dismissed us.

When I saw Old Joe later, I asked him what had happened. He

said the officers didn't think it was worth forcing the issue. The orders had come from Berlin but were signed by a minor official. With the military situation being so critical and the isolation of our camp, he doubted that anything further would be heard about this issue from the High Command. He wouldn't speculate on the possibility that the Jewish POWs might be executed, but his eyes seemed to indicate that this could be the plan.

A few weeks before Christmas, we sent word to the Camp Kommandant asking permission to practice Christmas carols and march around the compound singing on Christmas Eve. At first, he refused, but after several requests, he finally relented and told us we could use the "Kuche" where our cabbage soup was prepared, for rehearsal. We could go there for an hour each afternoon, but only in the presence of three guards.

We tried to ignore the three guards, all English-speaking, who were there to ensure that we weren't making escape plans. They laughed and made jokes at our "religious foolishness." But after a few days, a very strange thing happened. Either the guards had some religion in their upbringing, or our sincerity finally got through to them. Whatever the reason, they began taking off their caps when they came into the kitchen where we were rehearsing.

The afternoon before Christmas Eve, we assembled for our last rehearsal. To our amazement, one guard stood watch at the door while the other two joined us in singing! We asked no questions, and their obvious joy in participating was equaled by our delight in their "conversion."

The guard at the door was so intent on our rendition of *O Come All Ye Faithful* that he didn't see someone approaching until the door burst open and a German sergeant stood there. It was Old Joe. He looked very severe, and we could see the panic on the faces of the guards. Then Old Joe grinned and said, "Go ahead. I will watch the door."

For many days, we had been hoarding the meager rations from

our Red Cross parcels for one big blast of a dinner. Each room in our barracks, decorated with whatever scraps we could scrounge, presented a festive appearance. We had made up our minds that for this one night, we wouldn't go to bed with empty stomachs, but the anticipated gorging was somewhat disappointing. Because our stomachs were so shrunken, we were unable to consume nearly what we expected, and much of the "feast" was left over for Christmas Day.

The Germans, after much negotiating, had grudgingly agreed to let us walk within the compound that Christmas Eve and sing Christmas carols. After so many months of seeing the night sky only through a tiny crack in our tightly closed window shutters, the view was breathtaking. Someone had talked a guard into giving us a couple of candles in exchange for a package of Lucky Strikes from a Red Cross Parcel, and they flickered cheerfully at the beginning of our procession.

Then we began to sing Christmas carols, and I was astonished at the strength, the sheer power of the words: Joyful! And Triumphant!, Peace on Earth, Let Nothing You Dismay. We even sneaked in *My Country, 'Tis of Thee . . . Let Freedom Ring.* "Let Freedom Ring!" How inspiring these words suddenly became.

Our voices soared upward, toward the star-studded sky, lifting over the ugly barbed wire fences, past the menacing guard towers bristling with guns, over the snow-covered earth, far above the dense woods, lightly, effortlessly . . . to freedom. **Freedom.** *FREEDOM!* I thought my chest would burst with the sheer joy of it.

And then I knew, knew positively, that some day . . . some of us would return home. Oh, I wasn't so naïve as to believe that all of us would make it. I wasn't even very confident that I might be one of the lucky ones, but it no longer seemed so hopeless. As it turned out, there were still more difficult months ahead: evacuations, forced marches, cramped boxcar rides, cold, abuse, and hunger . . . always hunger.

Chapter Fourteen

NUREMBERG:
ON LESS THAN TEN CALORIES A DAY

Toward the end of January 1945, we began to hear rumors from some guards of our imminent evacuation. Old Joe, ever our source of information, confirmed that the rumors going around were very likely true. It was obvious that the Germans did not want us to be liberated, and the Russians were advancing rapidly. Perhaps Hitler saw POWs as a hole card to be used for bargaining with the Allies as his troops continued to retreat on every front.

Early in February, the order came to leave Stalag Luft IV. The guards told us that some would be going to a camp in Nuremberg by train, and others would travel on foot with no announced destination. The plan was to fill the boxcars first, and then all who remained would march.

Packing for the move was easy. Whatever clothing we owned,

we wore on our backs. It was bitterly cold, and the GI overcoats that the U.S. government had sent in via the Salvation Army were a godsend. Carrying food was not a problem: we had none. At best, some of us had a few crackers or part of a chocolate D-Bar from a Red Cross parcel, or maybe a stolen raw potato.

The guards in the towers still watched us as we marched out of the camp, but the ten thousand POWs who were the commerce of Stalag Luft IV were flowing through the gate. I glanced back at the grim scene behind me: the barbed-wire fences; the drab barracks with their doors hanging open; the parade ground where we stood roll call in the snow; the spots where some of our guys were recklessly, remorselessly, Shot Without Warning. At that moment, if I'd been given the choice, I would have been delighted to set the whole camp on fire and watch it burn slowly to the ground.

When we arrived at the depot in Grossetychow, I was expecting to find the same kind of passenger train that brought us to Luft IV in May. Instead, waiting on the rails were the "40 Hommes-8 Chevaux" boxcars that my father saw when he was in the U.S. Army and fought against the Germans during World War I. The cars were tiny compared to American boxcars, yet seventy-eight men were crammed into our car. I found out later that these were the same type of cars used to transport Jews and other enemies of the Third Reich to concentration camps.

There were enough boxcars to hold about three thousand men, including some of the walking wounded. My lager was selected to board first, and by the time we had climbed onto the train, most of the cars were full. The rest of the camp went on an 86-day forced march, with the sole intention of keeping them from being liberated. Dr. Leslie Caplan, an Air Force flight surgeon who accompanied 2,600 of these men on the march, details the experience in his medical journal:

"Our sanitation approached medieval standards. The inevitable result was disease, suffering and death. Dysentery overwhelmed us. The sad spectacle of a soldier relieving himself right on a village street was so common that it excited no comment from German villagers."

At the front and rear of each boxcar, on opposite sides, was a three-foot window with no pane, strung over with barbed wire. I was very fortunate to be one of the first to get on the train, because I went right over to the front window. Red was right beside me. Just being unable to move an inch without touching someone else was enough to trigger my claustrophobia, but being able to put my face into the barbed wire for a breath of fresh—although frigid—air was some relief. I soon found out that I was able to sleep while standing. Surrounded by other POWs, whose bodies were only inches from mine, I couldn't have fallen if I'd tried.

Just before we departed from Stalag Luft IV, the Salvation Army had shipped in a small number of books. As we left our barracks, I picked up one to read on the train. I was not familiar with the book: *The Robe* (1942), by Lloyd C. Douglas, but I remembered that the author had written the best seller *Magnificent Obsession*.

The Robe turned out to be one of the most moving novels I had ever read. The book is about a young Roman officer, Marcellus, who angers a prince and is ordered to serve in Gaza. While there, it falls to Marcellus to officiate at the crucifixion of Jesus, who he believes to have been wrongly convicted. Later, he wins Jesus' robe in a dice game and ultimately discovers a faith that sustains him until his death. Although it was an inspirational Christian story and did not reflect my core beliefs, I found it to be very uplifting at a time when I needed to be uplifted more than ever.

The sun, shining through the boxcar window, reflected the barbed wire onto the pages of the book and onto my head as well, giving me my own crown of thorns. All of the time I had been a POW, I never completely believed that I would survive this ordeal and return home. Maybe some of us would survive, but I was never convinced that I would be one of them. After I finished *The Robe,* I felt a sense of spiritual release and was certain that I would be liberated soon.

If I thought I had suffered before, the ensuing trip would make many previous hardships seem insignificant. The cramped conditions made me feel that I could not draw a full breath, and I constantly fought the panic of imagined suffocation. We had no food or water for three days. Our toilet was a water bucket hung from a hook in the ceiling. The Germans would not permit us to empty the bucket until the train stopped. Then it refilled very quickly, sloshing its foul contents all over everyone. The stench was overwhelming, and soon every one of us reeked of the same odor as the swinging bucket.

When someone died on one of the cars, the deceased was not taken off until the next stop. There was no room for the corpse to lie flat on the floor, so it lay across the feet of those around it. I never found out how many died on the trip; but had the Germans not been so utterly ruthless, I doubt that a single POW would have perished.

I remembered my boxcar ride from Scott Field, Illinois to gunnery school in Laredo, Texas. At the time I thought it was such a primitive way to transport troops. How I would have welcomed one of those boxcars now, with its kitchen car serving three all-you-can-eat hot meals a day; a latrine car with real toilet seats and washbasins; and bunks with clean sheets and mattresses.

Back at Stalag Luft IV, if anyone had told me that one day I would look back with longing at my hard, wooden-slat-bottomed bunk with the potato sack "mattress," I would have told them that they had taken leave of their senses. But oh, how I would have loved to be out of that cramped, smelly boxcar, lying asleep in that bunk at this moment, maybe having a special dream. Yes, many of my dreams were nightmares, but I was sometimes fortunate to have pleasant scenarios. One of my favorite dreams found me in clean pajamas, propped up in a hospital bed with blindingly white sheets, being served breakfast by a beautiful nurse who would later bring me a cigarette to smoke with my second cup of real coffee. In another, I would be seated at a family dinner, gluttonously inhaling the wonderful delicacies that my grandma and my mom kept heaping on the table. But my most blissful and recurring dream always found me in LaVerne's bed, making love or giggling together afterward over the decibel level of the recent sounds of our uncontrollable pleasure. When I woke up from this dream, I always wondered if my sheepish look was showing.

Since troops and war matériel took precedence over our POW train, we were constantly being sidetracked. One of our most terrifying experiences took place in a marshaling yard in Berlin. We were on a siding while another train passed, when the air raid sirens began their fearful wail. This meant that Allied planes were coming to bomb and strafe, and rail yards were a favorite target.

It was just dusk and through the small, barbed-wire-covered window, we could see the guards who had been patrolling beside our cars racing for the air-raid shelters. Then I saw Old Joe run up to our car and unlock the door so that we would not be trapped inside a sitting target. Before he could slide it back, a German officer dashed up, shouting for him to lock the door and go to the shelter. Joe argued so strongly that the officer drew his pistol and threatened to shoot him if he didn't obey. Old Joe locked the door and looked despairingly up at us as he walked to the safety of the shelter.

The American fighter planes didn't know there were American POWs on the train, and they unloaded on us with a fury. The bombing lasted only minutes, but it seemed like hours to me. We were very lucky that our boxcar wasn't hit, but several others were that were filled with men, and the train station was damaged and burning.

It was dark when we got under way again, and we traveled for less than an hour before pulling off on another siding. There was no moon, but through the window I saw tiny glimmers of light coming from the edges of blackout drapes in a nearby house. I heard the guards talking about dinner and watched some of them moving toward the house, which seemed to be a mess hall stop for troops passing through. A slight breeze carried the tantalizing odor of food, and my empty stomach ached.

I was standing there trying to inhale the smell when I heard tapping at the window. At first I could see nothing; then I made out a dim form beside the car. I didn't know who was there, or why, until I heard Old Joe's voice.

"I am holding something outside the window," he whispered. "Take it, but be careful you don't cut your hands."

I reached through the barbed wire and felt a loaf of bread, which Joe had speared on his bayonet! He passed up three loaves, then vanished into the darkness. Red and I tore the bread into small chunks, then handed it to others for distribution. I doubt many pieces ever reached those at the other end of the car. I chewed my small portion slowly, making it last as long as I could.

The next afternoon, about an hour before we arrived at the POW camp in Nuremberg, we were stopped on a siding when the doors to our car slid open and the guards shoved two large aluminum pitchers of water on board. It was the first water they had given us since we left Luft IV, and we took turns gulping down the cold liquid. After we drank the water, everyone began to complain of the strange "perfumed" taste. Then, someone saw the soap suds in the bottom of the pitchers. It was water the Germans had washed in, then poured into the pitchers and served to us. It wasn't long before everyone on our car began to have severe stomach cramps and diarrhea, and the swinging bucket was full again.

The next stop was Nuremberg. A group of strange guards yelled us out of the boxcars and into formation, then began a head count. It was then that I realized our old guards weren't coming with us. They were lined up about fifty feet away, facing us.

I was looking around for Old Joe when a buddy poked me with his elbow and nodded, "There he is in the second row."

Our old guards were about to board the train again and Old Joe had been trying to get my attention. He was looking in my direction. Suddenly, he pulled a red bandanna from his pocket and began waving it vigorously. When he knew that I saw him, he gazed steadily at me for a long moment, then blew his nose into the handkerchief, turned, and got on the train. I never saw him again.

This time I wasn't ashamed of the tears rolling down my cheeks or the sudden lump in my throat. In this hated land that had spawned the worst genocide in history, I had just said goodbye to someone who truly cared about me and had risked his own life to provide me and my fellow prisoners food and information. And he was a German!

Chapter Fifteen

ESCAPE

The camp at Nuremberg was only three kilometers from the city. Although the Allies were aware that the camp housed POWs, they still rained bombs on the city daily. While they carefully targeted the city proper, it was almost impossible to avoid an occasional bomb landing in our camp. Being so close to a prime target for air attacks by United States and British bombers was an ironic twist for guys who only a short while ago had been flying those same kinds of planes on raids over the very same targets. As we looked up at the bombers moving swiftly across the sky, each one of us could visualize his own position on one of the planes and know exactly what he would be doing at that very moment. And who among us did not fantasize, more than two decades before the television series *Star Trek* was a glimmer in its creator's mind, how marvelous it would feel if he could be "beamed up" to one of the planes and return safely to his old air base. When the planes came too close to our camp, we shook our fists at our comrades on high and cursed at them to avoid dropping their deadly cargo onto our camp, but every one of us wished them well, and just seeing them overhead gave us a feeling of hope that soon the Germans would be crushed and we would be free.

The timing of the raids was so consistent, you could almost set your watch by them—if the German guards hadn't already confiscated your watch. The Eighth Air Force would attack around eight in the morning; the 15th around noon; and British Mosquitoes would descend on us at night. The Mosquitoes, made of plywood, were so fast that the Germans rarely had time to douse the lights. It would have made little difference anyway, because they dropped flares that lit up the area like a football field. There was no place to take cover. A concrete culvert bordered the camp on one side, but it was very deep and about twenty feet across. If a bomb landed anywhere in the culvert, the odds were great that anyone inside would perish. So we stood outside and watched the bombs fall. In the eerie artificial light, it appeared that every falling bomb was headed straight for you.

It was February 1945. The Master Race was losing fast, and Hitler was desperately moving Allied POWs around, like pawns on a chessboard, to prevent their liberation. While the camps had been segregated before according to rank, nationality, and branch of service, Nuremberg became a catchall for all POWs still under German control, although we were still separated by allegiance. Besides American and British POWs, there were Russians, French, Italians, Belgians, Serbs, and Poles.

A U.S. Air Force colonel, the highest ranking POW in the American lager, became so enraged that the Germans didn't provide shelter for us during the bombings that he ordered the German Captain of the Guard to bring a hundred trench shovels into our compound so we could dig foxholes. It was about eleven o'clock in the morning and, out of respect for the colonel's rank, the captain had the shovels brought in by the guards. The colonel stood in front of the pile of shovels and ordered all of us to dig foxholes. Only a few guys had picked up shovels and started to dig, when a command car pulled up to the gate and a German general erupted from a rear door before his driver could get there to open it for him.

The general ran toward the colonel, screaming, "Throw down the shovels immediately! Throw them down!"

The guys who were digging stopped and turned to the colonel for his orders.

"Keep on digging," he yelled. "Everybody keep on digging."

Before anyone could scoop up another shovelful, the general pulled his Luger from its holster, raised it above his head, and warned, "I will shoot the next man who puts a shovel in the ground."

Everyone lay down his shovel except the colonel. Locking eyes with the general, jaws clenched, speaking through his teeth, he said, "We have every right to protect ourselves. You wanna shoot somebody? Then shoot me first, goddammit!" Then the colonel continued to dig furiously.

The general stared at him for a full minute, then replaced his Luger and left the compound. The colonel had scooped out a few more shovelfuls when air-raid alarms began shrieking and soon the 15th Air Force roared overhead, salvoing their bombs on the city. Waving his fist in the direction of the general's command post, the colonel continued to dig while spitting out a steady stream of expletives. Fortunately, no stray bombs landed in our camp that day.

As American troops moved steadily closer to Nuremberg, the Germans prepared to evacuate us to a POW camp in Moosburg. It was about a 68-kilometer march, and they wouldn't let us make signs identifying ourselves as POWs, so we were very likely to be mistaken, from the air, for retreating German troops and suffer the consequences. Our luck held out until the early afternoon of the first day, when three American P-51 fighters, in formation, flew over our column from the rear. It was a narrow road lined with good-sized trees, and it appeared that the planes didn't spot us. We lost sight of them as they climbed into the sun, and then we could no longer hear their engines, so we figured they were gone. Wrong assumption. They had cut their engines, silently done a 180-degree turn, then restarted and came roaring out of the sun, strafing our column mercilessly. I raced to hide behind a large tree, but suddenly I couldn't find anything larger than a sapling. Most of us reached the safety of the forest. Some did not. When we finally got back into formation, we'd been shuffled around, and that's when I became separated from Red.

Afterward, our guards seemed to give more attention to the skies than to us, and three friends asked me to escape with them. I told them it was foolish to risk getting shot when we were obviously only days away from being liberated. They decided not to try it without me, since I was the only one among us who could speak some German.

Later, the guards gave us a rest period and herded us into a pasture that was enclosed by a two-rail wooden fence. We were sitting on the grass when a platoon of soldiers, carrying only sidearms and led by an officer, came marching up the road in formation. The officer called the troops to a halt and asked one of our guards who we were. Then he gave his men an order, and in seconds they vaulted the fence and began beating us with their fists and kicking us with their hobnailed boots.

Oddly, they didn't curse or yell at us. They just methodically pounded us until their commander ordered them back into ranks. Then, just as silently, they jumped back over the fence and continued their march up the road. Their uniforms revealed that they were Hungarian SS. No one seemed to be seriously injured, but many were limping afterward. I had been kicked in the hip and it was very painful to walk. A few months earlier, I would have felt great outrage over this almost-casual beating, but the constant abuse that I had suffered left me so dispirited that I just accepted my defenselessness as a POW, realized the futility of agonizing over my lot, and simply licked my wounds and carried on, grateful that I was still alive.

Back on the road, I and others who were lame and lagging were assigned several guards who allowed us to walk more slowly and raggedly at the rear. Soon we saw a group of about twelve uniformed young men approaching us. They appeared to be in their teens. They were about five hundred feet away when our guards spotted them and frantically began herding us back into columns.

"Schnell marschieren! Los! Los!"

I asked a guard why he was so upset. "Hitler Jugend. Hitler Jugend kommen."

The boys seemed to range in age from thirteen to sixteen. As they passed, they glared at us and made obscene gestures. I didn't make eye contact with them. When they were some distance from us, they began to hoot and laugh.

When they were out of sight, I asked the guard again why he feared these kids. "Hitler Youth are very bad," he said. "If they turned us in for permitting you to walk slowly, we could be punished severely. I have even known them to report to the SS that their parents are guilty of some violation and they are arrested. And many times it is a lie. Yes."

I wondered what would happen after the war, when these kids that were in the Hitler Youth grew up and became a factor in running Germany. Would their Nazi past simply disappear? I doubted it.

That night we were bivouacked in a woods, with the perimeter secured by guards and police dogs. It rained steadily all through the night and, since we had no shelter, we were soaked to the skin by the icy water. I had kept my shoes on as protection against the wet and cold, but when the dogs were brought in to roust us out, about 5 A.M., my shoes had filled with water. My feet were so swollen that I could hardly stand.

I knew I wouldn't be able to walk very far, and I was afraid the guards would shoot or bayonet me if I fell. Faced with this possibility, I told my friends that I would escape with them. It was still very dark and, as the guards moved the POWs into formation on the road, the four of us dove into a drainage ditch and prayed that we wouldn't be spotted. Luck was on our side. Just as the first glimmer of dawn began to break, the last of the column passed us by and we were free.

Although our clothing was filthy and ragged, and we looked nothing like soldiers, we decided it would be safer to avoid towns, so we walked across farmland. A couple of times a day, we would stop at a farmhouse and I would ask for food in my fractured German. I would explain to the farmer that American troops were only a few days away and that if he would give us food, I'd write a note saying that he had helped us. He could then show the note to the Americans and he and his family would be treated well. We got enough food to keep us going and, strangely, not one farmer turned us in. At one farm we were given bread and fatback. We scraped off the salt and ate the raw fat and bread. It tasted awful, but it was caloric. I thought about trichinosis, but figured that after surviving Kraut cuisine for a year, nothing was likely to kill me.

On the afternoon of the fifth day, we came to the busy Autobahn. There was a steady stream of trucks rolling by, each one loaded with troops. I was reluctant to cross during the day, but my friends were sure that no one would recognize us as POWs. Besides, that was the direction of the American lines.

A few hundred feet from the Autobahn, we saw a huge mound

of earth, a cellar of some sort, with a heavy door secured by a large padlock. Above the door was a small, uncovered transom.

I had the guys boost me up and I climbed through the opening. The cellar was loaded with potatoes! I tossed about twenty potatoes through the transom and then struggled back out myself.

"Look," I said, "there are enough Kartoffeln inside to live on for a year. We can hide out in there until the Americans arrive and we won't have to risk getting caught. Besides, it would take a direct hit to penetrate that cellar."

Everyone else opposed the idea. They felt that we wouldn't be recognized as POWs and insisted on crossing the Autobahn before nightfall. I didn't want to stay alone, so we filled our pockets with potatoes and headed for the road.

At the first slight break in traffic, we ran across and walked into a small village. Several people were standing around talking, and a boy in his early teens sat on a bike and stared at us as we approached. Then he turned and rode up the street in the opposite direction. Within minutes, we were overtaken by two army trucks manned by Hungarian SS troops and recaptured. Taken to a small prison, we were told that we would be court-martialed and then shot.

We were herded into a large room with about twenty-five other escapees. Four of the group were English officers, formerly interned at Stalag Luft 3, the camp where the "Great Escape" took place and most of those recaptured were shot. They said, "We're not trying to scare you, Yanks, but your future doesn't look too promising. We've seen firsthand that the Krauts' threat to shoot all escapees is not an idle one."

Finally we were assigned to separate dungeon-like cells. A young Hungarian SS soldier, about eighteen, came into my cell and, in very broken English, began chatting enthusiastically about the American movies he had seen. His favorites were Westerns, and he had seen many of them. Then he decided that we should reenact a cowboy film.

He said, "You bandeet. Me shereef." Then he quick-drew his Luger and began waving it in the air.

"Where's my gun?" I asked.

He laughed, and formed his left hand into an imaginary gun. "You make finger."

He shoved the gun toward each of my hands and said, "Ring, off."

I wore two rings. One was my 1941 high school graduation ring in orange and white pearl. The other, a brown cameo depicting a knight in armor, was a bar mitzvah present from my grandmother.

I knew that my Humes High school ring could be replaced. But the gift from my grandmother had deep sentimental value and I adamantly refused to part with it.

I argued for several minutes, trying to explain that the ring was a present from my grandmother and was very important to me, but my pleas fell on deaf ears. Then he lost patience with me and pressed the muzzle of the Luger to my forehead. "Off," said the shereef.

I didn't think he would really kill me, but he was such a hyper nut case that I felt I couldn't gamble on his stability. He would have no problem explaining to his superiors that I had attacked him and he was forced to shoot me. I gave him my rings and he left, still smiling as he locked my cell.

Because Allied troops were getting close and the Germans didn't want to be caught with dead POWs on their hands, they postponed our court-martial and put us back on the road with a group of guards who marched us to Moosburg. Bavaria was comprised of mostly Catholic communities, and as we traveled through the countryside, almost every farm displayed an old bathtub, standing on end and half-buried in the ground, with a statue of the Madonna, hands clasped in prayer, standing inside.

When we reached Moosburg and entered the main compound,

we were met by an officer whose uniform I couldn't immediately identify, but was the spiffiest I had seen in Germany. The sergeant in charge of our guards stepped forward, saluted the officer smartly, and handed him a sheaf of papers to sign. They conversed amiably, but my German wasn't good enough to catch more than a smattering of what they were saying. The sergeant then saluted again, did an about-face, and marched his men briskly out of the compound.

As soon as the guards were out of sight, our four English comrades went bonkers. They rushed forward, giving bear hugs to the officer who had received us, yelling, "Reggie!! Wot the hell!"

It turned out that Reggie was an English officer from their bomb group who had been a POW for five years. The uniform had been sent to him by his family. It was customary for POWs at each camp to elect a "Man of Confidence" who, after acceptance by the Camp Kommandant, would represent them in dealing with the Germans. Reggie had been elected to that position by his fellow POW's at Moosburg, but I never knew a Man of Confidence to whom the Germans had given the authority to receive new arrivals. Reggie immediately tore up the papers ordering our court-martial and escorted us into the camp. We were all greatly relieved to be removed from the threat of a court-martial whose outcome had been preordained.

Because most of Germany was now under Allied control, Moosburg was one of the few remaining camps that had not yet been liberated, and the POW population was startlingly diverse. Each compound was designated by country of origin. The Sikhs were interesting because of their turbans and beards, but the Africans with their teeth filed to a point were absolutely shocking. I wondered if they had fought with spears.

The weather was still quite cold, and we had nothing to burn in the small stove in our barracks. One day, a guy in our room came in with a wooden plank from the side of the latrine a couple of doors away. That night, he broke the plank into small pieces and made a fire in the stove, and we enjoyed a bit of warmth.

The next day, more planks began disappearing from the latrine, and the Germans posted an order that no more wood was to be stripped from the Scheissenhaus. Obviously, the POWs were not impressed by the order, because days later all that remained were a few studs that held up the roof. It was cold in the alfresco latrine, but it did have wooden thrones to sit on, which beat squatting over a slit trench.

It was April 12, 1945 when a guard told me, "Rosenfelt ist tot." I knew the guards' pronunciation of Roosevelt, because we were frequently told by them that "Rosenfelt ist Jude." Then he said, "Jetzt ist Troimann."

At first, I didn't believe that Roosevelt was dead. It had to be more of their propaganda. And who the hell was Troimann? It took a while for me to pull Truman out of that. Later in the day, the rumor was confirmed by a BBC broadcast picked up on a POW's crystal radio receiver. All of us mourned the death of a great president, whom most of us had not been old enough to vote for, and who had died just short of seeing the victorious end to a war that had threatened the freedom of the entire world.

Toward the end of April, we began to hear the distant thudding of artillery. Each day, the booming became louder and louder.

Then, one morning, a Piper Cub with U.S. Air Force markings began to fly around the camp at low altitude. A jubilant roar rocked the camp and when the pilot waggled his wings, the sound of our voices reached a crescendo that must have carried all the way into his cockpit.

For the next two days, the pilot continued to fly around the camp and give us wing salutes. Then, a few at a time, the guards began to disappear. With each passing day, the number of guards declined.

Early on the morning of April 29, we woke up to small-arms fire and we knew that this was the day.

For the first time in months, I thought about my appearance. I had no mirror, but I could imagine that I looked like a derelict, with my ragged garments and scruffy beard. The least I could do to welcome my liberators was to shave. I dug out my razor with the blade that had become dull so long ago that it was flagellant to use it.

By this time, bullets were zinging through our barracks and most guys were lying on the floor. Right next door was a concrete-block building that looked substantial enough to deflect rifle bullets. I filled my soup bowl with cold water, took my razor and a piece of soap I had been saving, and headed for the block house. I was not the only one who had this idea. There were about a dozen others already shaving. We stood there scraping our faces and chattering away, oblivious to the occasional bullets flying through the windows.

Then, as suddenly as it began, the shooting stopped. We came out into the compound and saw American tanks and foot soldiers everywhere. And then, the biggest thrill of all, General George Patton appeared, wearing the two pearl-handled pistols that Dinah Shore had given him. He looked nine feet tall. No matter what stories I had heard about Patton's toughness and lack of patience with soldiers who were not performing to his liking, he appeared to me a man of heroic proportions.

We were hugging our liberators, accepting cigarettes, some of us laughing and crying at the same time. Then they began bringing in loaves of bread. White bread. Soft white bread. If I had closed my eyes, I could have believed I was eating cake. Soon, the C rations arrived. The same C rations that we had always griped about now became a gourmet feast.

After eating, I wanted to step outside the gate just to feel the freedom of being beyond the barbed wire, but the German soldiers

who had guarded the gates had been replaced by English troops
with orders to let no one out of the compound.

One of Patton's soldiers came over and asked, "How long you
been a POW? "

"Three hundred and sixty-six days."

"Well, what the hell are you standing here for? Why don't you
walk out of this miserable place?"

"The Brits have orders to keep us inside."

"Well, I'll be damned. They didn't put us on the gates, because
they knew we'd let you out. You stand right here. I'll be back in a
couple of minutes."

I didn't know what he had in mind, but he was back shortly carrying something wrapped in a piece of canvas. "Come with me," he
said. I followed him into a barracks, and he opened the bag and pulled
out a pair of wire cutters with powerful jaws and very long handles.

"When it gets dark, cut holes in the fucking fence, then pass this
through the wire to the guys in the next compound."

I thanked him and hid the cutters in my bunk.

Later in the day, we were deloused and showers were set up. Then
we were issued clean clothes. We were even given fresh razor blades.

After dark, I went out with some friends and we cut a large hole
in the fence. Then we passed the tool through the barbed wire to
guys in the next compound.

At dawn, we sneaked through the hole in our fence. As we
looked back, we saw similar openings in the barbed wire in every
compound. Exultant in our victory over the plans to keep us confined, we headed for the town of Moosburg, eating our C rations
as we walked.

We strolled through the streets of the town, trying to adjust to
the feel of freedom. I felt that at any minute, a German guard
would run up and grab me.

All the shops were closed. With hundreds of former POWs

roaming around, the shopkeepers were not going to risk the possibility of looting. Oddly, none of the stores seemed to have been broken into.

I was surprised by several signs advertising an American product very well known to me. The signs showed a frosted bottle of soda being poured into a glass, and the inscription was: Coca Cola . . . Eis Kalt. The signs seemed so out of place. The familiar long-tailed "C" extending beneath "oca" and the "ola." No other ad could remind me more of home, yet here in the heart of Deutschland "Coke" was being consumed by our enemy. It seemed so incongruous that both of us could enjoy the same popular American soft drink while trying to kill each other.

We came upon several Russian POWs standing in the doorway of a cellar, drinking from large cups. As we approached, they motioned for us to join them. They took us into the cellar where we saw huge wine vats with opened spigots. The floor was covered with wine. They handed us cups and indicated that we should scoop up the wine. I wasn't able to understand their explanation of why they had emptied the vats onto the floor.

Several cups of wine later, I made my way out of the cellar and knew that I needed to lie down somewhere and sleep off the unaccustomed alcohol. I left my friends and wandered up the street until I saw a four-unit apartment. The front door was ajar, and I walked into a foyer. On the left were stairs to the second floor, and I went up. There were doors to two apartments and another door at the end. I opened the unmarked door and saw steps leading to the attic. I walked up and found a large space that was used by the tenants for storage. When I spotted a mattress, I flopped down on it and immediately fell asleep.

I don't know how long I slept, but I was awakened by shouting; when I opened my eyes, I was staring into several flashlights and was surrounded by U.S. soldiers pointing rifles.

At first, they didn't recognize me as American, and a sergeant asked me in German what I was doing there.

"I was sleeping," I said. "I'm an American POW, and I was just liberated."

"I know damn well you were sleeping, but why are you sleeping in this attic?"

"I drank too much wine and I needed to rest, and this seemed like a good spot."

"Well, it ain't. We almost shot your ass. There's a couple of SS officers wandering around someplace, and we thought you were one of 'em."

"Where can I go to take a nap?"

"There's a guard post just up the road. Ask the sentry to let you in to sleep it off."

I walked a short distance and came upon the sentry. He stood outside a shed about fifteen feet square. I told him my problem, and he said, "Sure, go on in. It's dangerous walking around here without a gun. Sleep as long as you like."

The shed was completely empty, not even a chair, so I lay down on the floor and went to sleep. I must have been asleep for several hours when I was awakened by loud explosions and the flashes of a weapon going off. The room was totally dark, and I didn't know where the hell I was. The door flew open and the sentry came bursting inside, gun in one hand and flashlight in the other. Across the room from me, blinking in the light, was a GI sitting on the floor, holding a .45 automatic.

"Drop it," the sentry yelled.

The bewildered soldier sat there for a few seconds, then slowly placed his gun on the floor.

"What the shit's wrong with you?" the sentry snapped.

"I dunno, I guess I was having a nightmare and thought I was under attack."

The sentry jammed the discharged gun into his pocket and told the soldier, "You don't get this back until you leave. You could have killed this guy, you dumb bastard."

I left the shed with the sentry. "You don't have to leave," he said.

"I don't think I'll get much more sleep here tonight."

He laughed. "I believe it, but you can't go wandering around in the dark. There's a curfew and you could really get shot. Tell ya what. See that big house across the street? A bunch of tank guys are stayin' there. Go over and tell 'em I sent you, that you're a POW, and ask if they can put you up."

My knock on the door was answered by a master sergeant with shoulders so wide that they filled the doorway. He had to duck his head to step outside. He obviously wondered who the hell I was as he scowled down at my nondescript attire and shoulder-length hair.

"Yeah?" He must also have been speculating on what language he'd hear in response to his query.

"Hi, Sarge. I was just liberated from the POW camp here and the sentry said you might be able to put me up for the night."

His expression softened immediately. "You're an American POW?"

"Right. Wow, are we happy to see you guys."

"My bunch was in the battle a few miles away, but we never got to your camp personally. You're Air Force, right?"

"Yes, we flew B-17s out of England. My plane was shot down over Berlin last April."

"Damn! You've been a POW for a year?"

"Yeah, a very long year."

"I'll bet. I can't imagine what that would be like. What's your rank?"

"Tech sergeant. I was a radio operator/gunner."

"My name's Reed," he said, sticking out a hand the size of a baseball glove.

"Norman Bussel, Reed. Glad to meet you."

"What the hell are we standing here for? Come on in, Sergeant."

It was a very nice house, with carpeted living room, plush couches, large ornate chandelier over the long dining room table, draped windows, and shelves full of delicate figurines showing a woman's fine touch.

Four other tankers were sitting around the table, looking bored. When Reed introduced me as a POW, they all perked up and began asking questions.

"How did they treat you?"

"Pretty bad. No medical care; just enough food to keep us alive; no heat; no clothing. I stood roll calls in my bare feet until around Thanksgiving, and snow was on the ground by then."

"Lousy fucking bastards! The Krauts we captured weren't mistreated. Our medics patched them up and they ate the same chow that we did. They deserve the ass-kickin' we're giving 'em."

Reed said, "I bet you lost a lot of weight, huh?"

"I'm sure I did, but I don't know how much."

Reed turned to one of his men, "There's a scale upstairs. Bring it down."

When I stepped on the scale, it showed 44.5 kilograms.

Reed looked at me. "Shit, man. You barely weigh a hundred pounds. How much did you weigh before?"

"Around one sixty-five."

They all stared at me. Finally, as if he intended to fatten me up in the next ten minutes, Reed asked, "Would you like something to eat?"

Soon, the table was heaped high with everything from C rations to home-canned foods they'd found in the cellar and bread so white it almost hurt my eyes. They all sat around and watched me eat, much like I once did with a stray puppy I had found on the street. They looked disappointed at the small amount of food I was able to consume, but my stomach had shrunken and if I overate, it would all come back up.

We talked about how soon the war with Japan might be over, and they were surprised by my knowledge of the Allies' progress in the Pacific. When I told them that we had a crystal radio and had been getting news from the BBC for months, they were truly amazed.

I chatted with the tankers until Reed saw my eyelids getting heavy and said, "Look, there's nobody sleeping on the third floor, so when you're ready, go on up. There's a bathtub up there, too."

My long soak in the tub was heaven. I scooted down until the water touched my chin and I could feel the tension leaving my body. The room I chose had a large bed covered by a lovely satin spread; the sheets were clean and white, the mattress soft and inviting. I slid beneath the covers and while trying to remember the last time I had slept in a real bed, I fell asleep.

When I awoke the next morning, I didn't immediately recognize my surroundings. For a minute, I thought I was back in the States. My head was buried in a large feather pillow, and I lay there for a few minutes luxuriating in this unaccustomed pleasure. Then I remembered the food that was available to me in the kitchen, and I quickly dressed. As I headed for the stairway, I thought I heard a woman's voice and when I reached the second landing I saw a blonde, well-dressed woman, fiftyish, standing just inside the master bedroom, holding a suitcase and talking with Reed. Her face was flushed, her voice irate, and her English damned good.

"I demand that you allow me to remove my belongings from ziss room. I haff expensive lingerie here and I vant to empty all the drawers into ziss bag before your soldiers. . . ."

"Steal them?" asked Reed. "In the first place, my men don't wear bras and panties. At least not while they're on duty. In the second place, you have no business being in this house. Until we move out, this house is officially ours, not yours. Now, why don't you just leave before I lose my temper?"

"You haff taken my house without authority, and I am forced to live in a small house with my neighbor. You cannot refuse me to take out what iss mine."

"What did you expect me to do, ask the Burgermeister's permission? I'm telling you for the last time, get the hell outta here."

Reed looked up and saw me in the hallway. "Here you go," he said pointing at me. "Here's a damned good reason why you don't deserve to take anything out of this house. This is an American sergeant who was almost starved to death in your POW camp here."

"I am a civilian and I know nossing of zee camp. Where can I find your superior officer?"

Now Reed was really pissed. "He's probably up the street screwing your sister, but I wouldn't advise you to disturb him. If you think *I'm* mean, wait till you meet *him*." He walked toward the woman. "Now, scram!"

"Vait, can I take my perfume?" she asked, pointing to a large silver tray on the bureau.

"Take your damn stinkum and *leave! Now!*"

The woman quickly shoved the bottles into her bag and left.

"Civilian, shit," said Reed. "Every last one of them is a Nazi. Come on down and have some breakfast."

We were just sitting down to eat when there was a loud knock at the door. Reed went over and opened it to a wild-eyed man dressed in a suit and tie. "What do you want?" asked Reed.

"You haff insulted my vife! She hass every right to take her clothing from ziss house. Who do you think you are?"

Reed spun the man around and kicked him off the porch. "If I ever see you around here again, I'm gonna show you who I am. I'm the guy that kicked Nazi asses all over your fucking Fatherland, and I'll have a lot of fun kicking yours!"

Afterward, as I was walking through the town, I ran into my three friends from camp. I explained where I had been, and they said they had jimmied a window in an unoccupied house and spent the night.

Two sergeants from Patton's tank corps recognized us as POWs and came over to talk. One was concerned because we didn't have any guns. "You know, it's not too safe to go roaming around here unarmed."

I said, "I'm sure we're not going to be issued weapons. We're not even supposed to be out of the camp."

"Tell you what, we're leaving in half an hour for a spot where we kicked some German ass a couple of days ago. You wanna come along and look for souvenirs? I know you can find some guns laying around."

So we went with them, expecting to get on a truck. What a surprise when we walked over to three tanks.

"You guys ever been on a tank before?"

We shook our heads.

"Well, you're in for a real treat. Climb on board."

Each of my buddies got inside a tank and I rode on top with one of the tank guys. Soon we were in the middle of piles of discarded German military paraphernalia. We quickly found barracks bags and loaded them with souvenirs. One friend and I found rifles, and the other two found Lugers. All of the guns were loaded.

When we got back to town, we thanked the tankers, then set off to find a place to spend the night. We came upon an apartment building of about eight units and knocked on the front door, but no one answered. A man in his fifties came from behind the complex and said he was the superintendent. I asked if there were any vacant apartments, and he said, "Nein."

Then I said that he would have to move someone out, because we were going to spend the night. That's when he remembered that one tenant was away. He took us to an apartment that had two bedrooms, one with twin beds, another with a double bed, and a couch in the living room. I said that was fine. Then I remembered my attic nap and the search for two SS men. I told the super that we needed to see the inside of all of the other apartments.

He knocked at each apartment, but only three were occupied. In two, there were women with small children, in the other a very old man. The super had a large ring of keys and could open every unit. When I was satisfied, I asked to be shown the basement.

When we entered the basement, we were surrounded by storage rooms, each one with a tenant's apartment number. One skeleton key could open all of the doors. The light was dim and the locks were low, so he knelt to open the first door. Not knowing if someone might be hiding in the room, I cocked my rifle and pointed it at the door.

The super threw up his hands and began moaning, "Nein!! Nicht Schiessen. Nicht Schiessen."

"Look," I said, "we're Americans. We're not Germans. We don't shoot people in the back of the head."

Still trembling, he opened all of the doors for our inspection.

When we went back to the apartment, we opened a pantry and discovered jar after jar of preserved fruit. We had a loaf of bread with us, and we gorged on the delicious sweets until we were almost sick.

The next day, we went back to the camp to stash our souvenirs. The place was practically empty. British guards were still at the gates, but they were allowing everyone to come and go as they pleased. We went back to Moosburg that afternoon.

In our meandering, we came across a garage and peeked through an opening between the doors. "You know," one of the guys said, "I think that's a Duesenberg in there."

The door hinge was rusty, and one of the guys popped it open with a short-bladed knife he had picked up the day before. We opened the doors and stood there gaping at a Duesenberg Town

Car, circa 1931, in perfect condition even down to the disappearing top. We climbed in and drooled over the car, wishing we could take it home. To our surprise, the motor started, so the car had been used in living memory; but the tank registered empty.

Several of Patton's tankers stopped to look and asked why we didn't take the car and go sightseeing. I said the gas tank was almost empty.

One said, "Hell, come over to our storage area. We'll give you all the gas you want."

We followed them over and they gave us full gas cans. "Just bring the cans back."

We filled the car and she ran like a top. Then we took the cans back and drove all over town. I was reminded of being back in downtown Memphis and "dragging Main" in my friend's Chrysler convertible. Passing a small airfield, we saw POWs from our camp standing around two C-47's. We stopped and asked a pilot what was going on, and he said they had been shipping POWs to the rehab center at Camp Lucky Strike, in Le Havre, all day.

"It'll probably take several days to get everybody transferred, though, won't it?" I asked.

"Well, maybe, but the quicker we get you to Le Havre, the quicker you'll get back to the States. It's gonna be first come, first served."

I envisioned spending a few days at Le Havre, then boarding a boat for the U.S. I could be home in ten days.

Now the guys were talking about driving the Duesenberg to Paris. It was a wonderful and exciting idea.

"Hell, this is the chance of a lifetime, man, come with us. We'll really have a blast and will probably get home just as soon as everybody else."

"What are you going to use for money?" I asked.

"Cigarettes," they answered.

It was true that cigarettes were a currency accepted anywhere, but we were receiving only enough for personal consumption.

"How are you going to get enough cigarettes to finance the trip?" I asked.

"We'll sell our souvenirs to guys back at camp."

I thought about it, but didn't want to delay my return home by even one additional day. I hated to leave my bag of souvenirs back at the camp, but I didn't have time to go back and retrieve them.

"Look, you know where I stashed my souvenirs under my bunk. Sell them too and use the cigarettes you get to help with your expenses."

I told my buddies good-bye and wistfully watched them drive away, joking about what they expected to do in Paris.

The flight to Le Havre was terrifying. I watched the engines through small windows, listening for them to stall and send the plane into a dive to earth. My palms were dripping with sweat and my breathing was shallow. Training at Avon Park, I had found every flight to be thrilling. Now, I promised myself that I would never again set foot on a plane. I had been given my warning, and if we landed safely I would ground myself forever.

Camp Lucky Strike was jam-packed with thousands of liberated POWs, but the camp was very well organized and we were issued new uniforms, shoes, and bedding. I had always liked the sturdy look of combat boots, with the buckled top that you could tuck your pants into, but the Air Force was not authorized to wear them. I wore a size 12 shoe, and when the quartermaster said they were out of stock, I asked if they had combat boots in that size. They did indeed, and I chose a pair with a napped finish so I wouldn't have to polish them.

What the camp was not prepared for was the feeding of POWs who had been on starvation diets for months or years. In the cornucopia that is America, not many people had experienced hunger for extended periods, and the officers who ran the mess halls hadn't a clue about how to help us replace the huge amounts of weight we had lost. They decided that milkshakes, loaded with high fat-content ice cream, were just the ticket.

We were delighted with the addition of fondly remembered milkshakes to our diet and chug-a-lugged them with great pleasure, but our shrunken stomachs were not prepared for such a sudden, rich change in our regimen, and we vomited them up as quickly as they went down. Indeed, our digestive systems were ill prepared to deal with most foods, and we had constant bouts with indigestion and diarrhea. We just couldn't seem to win.

Every day at Le Havre was more boring than the next. Time passed even more slowly than it had in POW camp, because we knew that at any moment we might be called to board ships for the U.S. Our major source of entertainment was walking around the area in hope of running into old friends. It was common to hear cries of:

> "Jack, I thought you were dead! I didn't see anybody bail out of your plane."
>
> "Eddie, I lost track of you on the march. Where'd you end up?"
>
> "Lou, I haven't seen you since gunnery. Heard you were in the Pacific."

I was very disappointed that I couldn't find Red or anyone else from my room at Luft IV. Though I often ran into other guys from my old barracks, no one had seen any of my roommates. One day, I was roaming around near a camp gate when I heard a car horn honking wildly as it approached. Guys were running to the gate waving and yelling. The car was a Duesenberg, and in it were my friends who had left me at the airport in Moosburg three weeks earlier.

They regaled us with tales of wild nights in Paris, Brussels, and other stops along the way. I knew that some of the tales were tall, but I didn't doubt that their trip had been a wonderful experience. I mentally kicked myself for days. Just as they had predicted, we would all embark for home at the same time.

Finally, the day came when we were to board ships for New York. It had taken my crew five days to sail from New York to Glasgow on the *Queen Elizabeth*. We were going back on a Liberty ship, and I figured a week at the outside. The problem was that we were in a convoy with many other Liberty ships, and we moved at a snail's pace. It took us eighteen days to reach New York Harbor.

Some of the guys had brought along German rifles they had picked up, and when the ship released its garbage and fish would come up to feed, they would shoot at the sharks.

One foggy afternoon, I went up on deck to stretch my legs and the ship's alarm went off. Out of the mist, a British oil tanker suddenly appeared, headed straight for our port side. I watched as both ships tried to steer away from a direct collision, but the tanker hit us amidships and poked a hole in our side.

Had I survived a year as a POW only to drown in the Atlantic on the way home? Were the guys who had been taking potshots at the sharks now going to be eaten by them? Fortunately, we had been hit well above the waterline and there would be no problems, just a bad blow to my already-rattled nerves.

The ship was small and the water was somewhat rough, so we got tossed around a bit, but I didn't really get seasick. The food was good and the bunks not too bad. It was simply a long, long time to be at sea.

Most of us had very long hair—mine was shoulder-length—and one day the ship's captain announced that several of the crew were excellent barbers and would be glad to cut our hair. Since so many of us wanted to accept the offer, it was decided that we would draw

straws. I drew a high number, so I knew it would be a while before
I was called.

There was an infantry major on board who stopped me on deck
one day to ask, "Sergeant, aren't you going to get your hair cut?"

"Yes, sir, I am, but we drew to see who goes first and I have a
high number."

A few days later, the major stopped me again. "Sergeant, I
thought you were going to get a haircut."

"I am, Major. They haven't called my number yet."

The highest ranking officer on our ship, and therefore in command of all POWs on board, was an Air Force colonel. A fighter
pilot, short in stature but with the particular panache of that daring
breed, he spoke mostly with other Air Force officers.

The next time the major stopped me topside to enquire about
my long hair, the colonel happened to be approaching us, and the
major said, "Sir, can I speak with you a minute? The sergeant here
keeps telling me he's going to get his hair cut, but it's been over a
week and he hasn't done it."

The colonel stared at the major with ill-disguised disdain, then
spoke in a soft drawl: "Major, I'm headed for Atlanta, Georgia to
see a little redhead I've been away from for over two years. That's
all I've got on my mind. I don't give a flying fuck if the sergeant
ever gets his hair cut. Understood?"

The colonel turned and walked away. The major reddened and
took off in the opposite direction. And so I made up my mind that
I wouldn't get a haircut until I reached Memphis.

I had seen the Statue of Liberty for the first time when we left New
York Harbor on the *Queen Liz,* in February 1944, bound for Glasgow.
I had been impressed, of course, but hadn't really felt any great emo-
tional tug. The statue was pictorially as familiar to me as the White
House, but I had never seen either of these national icons.

As we approached the harbor this time, I stood on deck looking at our torch-bearing lady, and tears ran unabashedly down my cheeks. This was my symbol of freedom. This is what I had fought for. Shed blood for. Struggled to survive for a year for. This was my Land of Liberty . . . and I was finally back home.

As I walked down the gangplank shouldering my duffel bag, I saw someone come up from behind and get in step with me. It was the "haircut major."

"Now, Sergeant, don't you think it would have been nicer for your family to see you with your hair neatly trimmed?"

"Oh, I don't know, Major. I think I look right Western with my hair like this."

The major huffed and whirled away, and I never laid eyes on him again.

Chapter Sixteen

HOMECOMING

C amp Kilmer, New Jersey, as a reception center for overseas returnees, had a far different atmosphere than Camp Kilmer, New Jersey, as a port of embarkation for the European Theater of Operations. Nothing about the camp had really changed in appearance. The barracks still appeared austere, even bathed in bright sunlight on a picture-perfect June day in 1945.

The many thousands of troops who had passed through these barracks on their way to combat had left no mark on the camp's character. There was no commemorative plaque to acknowledge that so many of those who had paused here briefly, before heading into the zone of the unknown, would never return. You can't extract emotion, remembrance, grief, or regret from khaki-colored wooden barracks.

But this time I felt very differently about being here. This time I did not face tomorrow with dread, but with hope. I didn't know what the future held for me, but I did know that my life wouldn't be threatened every day and that I would be the one who decided my fate, not cold orders on sheets of paper generated by the millions through inanimate mimeographs.

Part of the processing procedure was a questionnaire asking us to write down the names of all German guards who had committed atrocities against POWs. I had listed several, when a major looked over my shoulder and pointed to the name "Big Stoop."

"You can scratch that one off, Sergeant."

I looked up, puzzled. "He was one of the most vicious guards we had, sir."

"I know, but we've received documented information that he was tracked down by English POWs. His severed head and body were recovered from a roadside ditch."

"Wow! Justice has been served."

"You bet."

My first phone call home was a delirium of disconnected words and phrases, with everyone trying to talk at once through the laughter and the sobbing. I spoke with my mother and father, my twelve-year-old sister, and my four-year-old brother.

"How are you feeling, honey? Are you all right?"

"I'm fine, Mom. Really. I just can't wait to get home."

"When do you think you'll get here?

"In about three days, I guess."

"What can I cook special for you?"

"Whatever you cook will be wonderful."

"We'll close the store and pick you up at the train station, son. Just be sure and let us know exactly when you get in."

"I'll call as soon as I see the schedule, Daddy."

"You won the spelling bee at your school? That's so great, Fay! I'll help you get ready for the city contest."

"Yeah, babe, we'll get a ball and bat and I'll hit you some

grounders when I get home. And I'll take you for a bike ride, too, Alan. Okay?"

I found out that the War Department had had me listed as MIA for nine months before my parents received a German POW letter from me. I also found out that they had sent me numerous boxes of food, wool socks, warm gloves, and a scarf. I'm sure some larcenous Germans enjoyed those packages I never received, just as they did the Red Cross parcels they stole from us.

I didn't expect to see a member of my family until I arrived in Memphis, but on my second day at Camp Kilmer, I was surprised and delighted to be visited by my aunt, Jennye Friedman, and her husband, Milton. The camp was under quarantine, because medical clearance was required before we could go on leave and we had not completed our physicals. Milton was in the Navy, stationed in New York, and he was able to wangle two passes to enter our base.

Jennye was more like a sibling to me than an aunt. Only eight years older than me, and one of my mother's four sisters, she was always my favorite aunt. At twenty-nine, she was very pretty and very pregnant. The following week, she gave birth to Charlie, a future neonatologist.

The Army doctors were not interested in turning debilitated POWs loose in New York City, which was probably a very prudent decision. When I had come through Camp Kilmer on my way to Europe, we were confined to base. Passes were given to no one, and we all resented being so close to New York, yet so far. Now the same restrictions were in effect, and eighteen years would pass before I finally got to visit Gotham.

From Camp Kilmer, I was sent to Fort McPherson in Georgia for more medical tests and placement processing. Because most of my wounds had healed in the fourteen months since I was injured, the doctors decided that it would be detrimental to dig around for shrapnel that was probably not going to cause a problem in the future.

The open sore caused by the piece of shrapnel in my left jaw had never healed, however, and that would require surgery. I was fortunate that an Army hospital was located in Memphis, and I was assigned there so I could be near my family during treatment. The hospital was located at the intersection of Shotwell and Getwell Roads. The names were appropriate, but I found Shotwell a bit too graphic for my liking.

The train ride from Fort McPherson to Memphis seemed to take forever. It was a military train, but not all of us were POWs. Soldiers and sailors were delivered like milk to towns, large and small, all along the way. I couldn't help choking up each time I saw guys step off the train into the arms of loved ones not seen for many months, or even years. As we got closer to Memphis, I began to recognize the names of towns I had once driven through, and I became more and more impatient to get home.

Finally, we pulled into the Memphis station to be greeted by throngs of people, each searching eagerly for that one face they had been waiting to see. There were so many uniforms, disembarking at an agonizingly snaillike pace. There was a shout here. A name called out there. A sweetheart lifted into the air. A mother sobbing into a uniformed shoulder. A father, ill at ease, hugging his son.

Knowing my dad's habit of punctuality, I would have been surprised if he hadn't gotten to the depot at least half an hour before I was scheduled to arrive. But he was nowhere in sight. I waited for fifteen minutes, which seemed more like an hour, then hopped into a taxi and told the driver, "1099 North Parkway." North Parkway was a broad thoroughfare with a twenty-foot-wide section of close-cropped Bermuda grass running down the center, where I used to play touch football.

My mother answered the door and began to cry as she held me tight. Then my grandma, whom I called Mama. Then my sister,

Fay. Then my three aunts, Mollye, Minnie, and Ella, who had taken off from work early to be there.

"You didn't see Daddy?" my mother asked.

"No. I looked all over the place."

"Alan had to go to the bathroom at the last minute. I knew they were going to be late."

My dad finally drove up to the house with my little brother and went through the explanation all over again. Alan was shy at first. I don't think he really remembered me, but when I picked him up, he hugged my neck and fingered my shoulder-length hair.

"My gosh, you really got long hair," said my dad.

"Yeah. I could've gotten it cut on the ship, but I decided not to. It's a long story. I'll tell you about it later."

All of my favorite foods had been prepared, but I could sample only a small portion of each. My mother had baked a loaf of challah, and later that night, after everyone had left, I went into the kitchen to have a slice with a glass of milk. I filled up on the milk so quickly that I could finish only half the bread, and I left the rest on my plate. Fay picked up my glass and was about to throw the piece of bread into the garbage, when I suddenly shouted, "Don't! Don't throw that bread out. I'll eat it later." I was sorry that I had startled her, but better that than to have her see me retrieve the bread from the garbage, which I would surely have done.

I knew that I had upset her, but she didn't tell me until much later that she had gone into the bathroom and cried. She said that she was overwhelmed with sadness that I could become so distressed over throwing away a small piece of bread. Then she realized, for the first time, what it must have been like to be deprived of food for an entire year.

At the Army hospital in Memphis, I was given the most complete physical checkup I had received since my return. My stomach problems had grown worse by the day, but they could not come up with any regimen that helped. Severe cramping and loose stools were an everyday occurrence. My doctor told me that the surgery to remove the shrapnel from my jaw would be delayed for ten days, "in order to build you up."

Since I was only thirty minutes from home by bus, and no testing was done on me in the evening, I had hoped to go home each night and return to the hospital in the morning.

"No dice," said the head nurse. "You're an inpatient. If your doctor wants to turn you loose on weekends, that's up to him. Otherwise, you don't set foot outside this hospital until you're discharged."

When I checked into the hospital, an Army clerk took one sheet of my orders and stapled it to my records. The document stated that I was on thirty-day leave, which included the time required for medical treatment. Usually, there are five or six duplicate pages of these orders, but by some strange quirk in distribution, I had received about thirty copies of the same sheet. Whenever you left the hospital, or returned, it was necessary to show a copy of your orders to an MP.

A little after five P.M. that evening, I left the hospital and went home. The next morning, I arrived back just before eight, changed clothes, and climbed into bed. In a few minutes, the head nurse appeared and proceeded to berate me.

"You left the hospital last night. Don't lie to me about it, I was here a few minutes ago and your bed hadn't been slept in. You must have another copy of your orders, or you couldn't get out and come back in. Hand it over. Now," she demanded, her hand outstretched.

I reached into my canvas bag, pulled out another copy of my orders, and gave it to her. That night, when I went home, I removed the staples from the remaining pages of the orders.

The next morning, she confronted me again. "You have more copies of your orders, don't you? Give them to me. All of them. Give me every last one of them this time."

I pulled three copies out of my bag.

"Now, don't you lie to me. Is this every single copy you've got?"

"Yes, ma'am, it is," I lied.

After that, she ignored my comings and goings—and she ignored me. If I passed her in the hallway, there was not a flicker of recognition.

One day the chief surgeon, Col. Carson, appeared in my room and told me I was scheduled for surgery the next morning. He put me at ease by patiently explaining the procedure and promising that the wound would heal quickly after the offending fragment was removed.

When two attendants came in the next morning with a gurney, I said, "I don't need that thing. I can walk perfectly well."

"We know you can," said one, "but we have orders to wheel everybody into the operating room."

"Okay by me," I said as they lifted me onto the gurney.

Soon after I was transferred to the operating table, a surgeon, an anesthesiologist, and three nurses arrived. They were chatting among themselves, and a mask was placed over my face with the request, "Now, just count backward from ten to one."

I had gotten to seven when I heard the surgeon say something about an appendectomy. I jerked the mask off my face, jumped off the table, and ran toward what I considered my only place of refuge: Col. Carson's office.

Barefoot, wearing a short white nightgown that reached about mid-thigh and was very loosely fastened in the rear, I raced toward the colonel's office with my buttocks flapping in the breeze and three nurses, a surgeon, and an anesthesiologist in hot pursuit.

In a few years, what would Allen Funt have given for this little scenario to appear on *Candid Camera*?

The wooden buildings that housed the hospital were all one story high, so the complex covered a vast area. I ran through corridors for a distance of probably two city blocks, several times passing through outdoor connections, before bursting into Col.

Carson's office. Gasping for breath, I leaned back against a wall, unable to speak.

"What in the world's wrong, Sergeant?"

Seconds later, my five pursuers dashed in, and the surgeon said, "Sorry, Colonel Carson. He was receiving anesthetic, when he suddenly became delirious, jumped off the operating table, and ran to your office before we could stop him."

The colonel looked over at me. "Sergeant?"

Drawing a deep breath, my voice quavering, I said, "They were going to take out . . . my appendix, sir."

The colonel turned back to the five, who were now standing at attention.

"Going to take out his appendix, were you? And how the fuck was that going to get the shrapnel out of his jaw? Huh? Go get his chart. Now!"

One of the nurses flew out of the office and returned in a few minutes with the chart. While she was gone, an oscillating floor fan, which I hadn't even noticed before, suddenly sounded as loud as a B-17 engine.

The colonel stared at the chart. It belonged to the guy in the bed next to mine. "Did you ask the sergeant his name? If you had, you would have found out that he is not Cpl. Walker. And not a goddamned thing is wrong with his appendix!"

I've seen guys get their asses eaten out by some real experts, but none equaled the chewing that Col. Carson delivered that day. As I followed the flagging five back to the OR, nobody spoke. And nobody turned to look back at me, which was just as well, because I was unable to get the grin off my face.

My procedure was rescheduled for the next morning, but a different surgeon performed the operation and no one from the day before was there. It did seem, however, that everybody in the OR was particularly solicitous.

Maybe it's farfetched, but I've often wondered if someone deliberately switched my chart with the guy in the bed next to me. Could the head nurse really have been that pissed off at my shenanigans? I'll never know.

When I was released from the hospital, my stomach problems still hadn't been resolved and no medication was prescribed. I tried to pinpoint the foods that I thought disagreed with me, but quickly realized that *everything* I ate disagreed with me.

About ten days before my furlough was to expire, I received a thirty-day extension. I assumed that the extension had something to do with the newly devised point system, whereby servicemen were being discharged on the basis of their accumulation of eighty-five points. Points were awarded for: each month in service (1), each month overseas (2), each ribbon earned (5), and each additional star (5).

After those with the most active duty records were released, the eighty-five-point requirement would gradually decrease until all eligible personnel had been discharged. Because it would take several months for the records of liberated POWs to catch up with them, furlough extensions were ordered while we marked time. I had more than enough points to be discharged, but the total was a long way from being verified by the Air Force and appearing on my records.

My telephone began to ring often, as more friends got home on leave daily. Milton Brown, my best pal from Humes High School, arrived around the middle of July 1945. He was a bombardier flying B-26's in the Pacific, and he was still suffering from malaria.

My father was good about lending me his car. I had been given a generous number of gasoline stamps for my furlough, so it didn't create a fuel hardship for him.

One July day, I was driving Milton to lunch when he began to shiver until his teeth chattered, and he asked me to close the windows.

July in Memphis is usually about 100 degrees, and the high humidity makes it even more unbearable. I rolled up the windows as sweat poured down my face and waited for Milton to come out of it. Some days later, when his malaria medication began to work, I was pleased for him, as well as for myself.

Milton was going out every night with his high school sweetheart, Frances Willis, and they never failed to ask me to join them. Sometimes I would go swimming with them at Clearpool or to a movie; but unless I had a date of my own, I felt like the fifth wheel to the wagon and usually declined.

It was about this time that I began to have difficulty breathing in close quarters or in a crowd. I felt as if I was smothering, and I could not draw a complete breath. Panic would set in and I believed I might pass out. I would get on a bus to go downtown, and maybe six other passengers would be on board. In a few blocks, the bus would become crowded and panic would set in, and I'd have to get off and walk. At a movie, I would be overcome by the darkness and the feeling that all seats around me were occupied, locking me in, when actually the place was maybe one third full. One day, I left a theater fifteen minutes after I had sat down.

I usually tried to arrive at a restaurant half an hour before the lunch or dinner hour, so I could eat and leave before it became crowded. Often, if the service was slow, other diners were soon seated at tables all around me and I would leave most of my meal unfinished, pay my check, and rush out. It was rare that I would eat at a restaurant close to home; leaving without asking for a doggie bag left me feeling very guilty about the food that I had wasted.

Unexpected noises threw me into a frenzy. I was walking past the Claridge Hotel on Main Street one day just as a taxi driver was unloading luggage. I was only a few feet past the taxi when he slammed the trunk lid with a loud bang. I came completely unglued. My first reaction was to dive for cover. When I realized where the noise had come from, I no longer felt the need to flee, but the psychic damage was done and I stood there trembling.

In those days, Memphis had no bars; so if you wanted a drink, you had to buy a bottle from a liquor store. There was one just down the street, and I picked up a half-pint of whiskey, went into a restaurant and ordered a chaser, then finished the bottle. I understood that this was a crutch and not a cure, but I knew of no other way to treat my problem, and I felt that if I didn't "medicate" quickly, I would go mad.

Toward the end of my furlough extension, I received a letter from the Air Force advising me to take yet another thirty days at home, then to report to Miami for more physical tests and R & R. The additional time at home was appealing, but Milton had already reported back for duty and I was getting a bit antsy to get on with my life.

I went out with friends every night and found that their company distracted me from thinking about my problems, which was a good thing, but I always brought my "medication" along, just in case. On the train to Miami, I sat next to a very chatty lady who had a "beautiful and intelligent" twenty-year-old daughter that "you just have to meet." She showed me a picture of Allison and she was, indeed, pretty. Since I didn't know anyone in Miami, I figured what the heck and promised to call after I got settled.

The armed services had taken over a number of Miami hotels to house combat returnees who were being sent there for R & R. I was quartered at the President Madison, an older but quite comfortable hotel with a large outdoor pool. The food was good and the rooms were more than adequate.

Two people were assigned to a room and, although I met several friends I would have liked to room with, I had to accept the roommate preselected by the "management." When I got to my room, I saw an unopened suitcase on one of the twin beds, so I took the other. As I was hanging my clothes in the closet, my new roomie came in and introduced himself. He was wearing light blue shorts, a lavender T-shirt, and sandals. "Everybody calls me Jinx," he said.

I had never met anyone like Jinx before, in or out of the service. The most striking thing about him was the two-inch streak of platinum blond running through his auburn hair from the center of his head to his forehead. His mannerisms were so decidedly effeminate, I could not believe he had survived the harassment he undoubtedly must have taken from the macho guys who surrounded him. And I was very uneasy about being his roommate.

As it turned out, I didn't need to worry about Jinx hitting on me. He and his "pal" George, whose room was on a different floor, were Chinese interpreters who had just returned from the South Pacific Theater. Neither of them was Chinese, and their linguistic talents were so much in demand that it would have made no difference if they each had two heads. Later, I met George, who was tall, thin, and totally unflamboyant. No one would have questioned his masculinity.

One day, I phoned the "beautiful and intelligent" Allison and made a date for lunch. When I picked her up, her mother was beaming and voluble and I couldn't wait to leave the house. Allison was pleasant to be with and we seemed to hit it off, so I invited her to go swimming at my hotel the next day. When she arrived, she changed in the ladies' room and came out looking tanned and fit.

The pool was surrounded by a sandy area, and Allison had brought a large beach towel, which she spread out while I went to get Cokes. Quite a few guys were lying around sunning themselves, and several had brought dates as well. We had just settled in when I heard someone call, "Norm! Oh, Norm." I looked over at the entrance to the pool and saw Jinx vigorously waving a beach towel.

"Norm, save me a place!"

I waved to him, and he came over and placed his towel next

to ours. I introduced him to Allison, and he was cordial. Then he proceeded to apply suntan lotion to his arms and legs, chattering away.

It was then that Allison's "intelligence" began to surface. Obviously, she had never met anyone like Jinx before, because she asked him, "Do you dye that streak in your hair?" Jinx looked at her as if he had just discovered a worm on the towel and then proceeded to take her apart, word by word.

"As a matter of fact, I do. And where do you send your hair, dearie?" When he had thoroughly eviscerated her, he changed the subject and was very pleasant for the rest of the time he spent with us. After he left, Allison said she was sorry she had upset him and had no idea that he was gay and had put him on the spot. I felt sorry for her, but when she left later, I didn't offer to walk her back home.

Being in Florida stirred thoughts of LaVerne, and in my memory our romance now seemed almost dreamlike. I longed for the return of those idyllic days, but I had no idea where I might find her.

The next day, I was sitting on the edge of the pool talking with a friend, and Jinx and George were lying on a towel behind us on the sand. I couldn't help but overhear their conversation as they described some very extravagant dresses worn at a party they had recently attended. Jinx said, "And did you see the breathtaking outfit that Chris wore? It was mahvelous, with the loooong Bishop sleeves and her hair done up in ever so many fabulous curls."

It took a while for it to penetrate, but I finally realized that they were talking about guys in drag. I wondered what poor naïve Allison would think of that. Sometimes I would have dinner with Jinx and George, and I found their company delightful. They were both very bright guys and, looking back, I regret that I didn't jot down some of their sparkling repartee.

Before I left Miami, I met with an officer who explained my

situation. "Sergeant, your accumulated points still haven't become official, and we're through with you here so we gotta move you somewhere. What I want to do is send you to a base close enough to Memphis that you can go home on weekends. I'm thinking about Blytheville Air Force Base in Blytheville, Arkansas. Do you know Blytheville?"

"Yes, sir. I've been there."

"Well, here's the deal. You'll be about eighty-five miles from Memphis, so it'll be no sweat getting back and forth on weekends. As soon as your points are approved, you'll go home for about a week, then you'll be notified where to report for discharge. How does that suit you?"

"I couldn't ask for a better deal, sir."

"Excellent." He stood up and shook hands. "Good luck, Sergeant."

When I arrived at Blytheville Air Force Base, I reported to a major who was most cordial. "Welcome, Sergeant. Your papers tell me that you were a POW in Germany. That information will stay with me. You're probably not ready to discuss your experience yet, so there's no need to broadcast it. Since you're a radioman and you'll be the highest ranking noncom in the radio section, you'll be in charge of that area. You won't have to do any PT. Your only assignment will be to sit in your office and sign requisitions and other forms as necessary. You can read, listen to the radio, relax. Every Friday, I'll send over a pass for you to go to Memphis for the weekend. If you need anything, just give me a call. Okay?"

It was more than okay. I brought in sodas, books, magazines, wrote letters. I couldn't have asked for a more cushy assignment.

One day, I was sitting at my desk reading, when a lieutenant came into my office. "Hi, Sergeant. Are you real busy right now?"

"Not at all, Sir. What can I do for you?"

"I've got German POWs who're supposed to be moving radio equipment from Building 6 to a truck for transport, and I need to get it done today. At the rate those POWs are moving, we're never going to make it. Do you have time to go over and see if you can speed them up?"

"Absolutely, Lieutenant. I can go right now."

"Great. I've got a jeep out front, and I'll drive you over to check out a .45, then take you to Building 6."

I signed for the .45, buckled the holster belt around my waist, the lieutenant drove me to the site, and I got out.

"Appreciate it, Sergeant."

"Not a problem, Lieutenant."

The guard squad watched as I approached. I saw the POWs, well-fed and wearing clean fatigues, cigarettes dangling from their lips, laughing loudly, each carrying a piece of radio equipment about the size of a can of Spam to the truck, then walking slowly back to the warehouse.

One of the guards came over. "I know the lieutenant is pissed 'cause this is taking so long, Sarge, but these dumb bastards are stubborn as hell."

"Well, we'll see what we can do about it."

As each POW deposited his "load" on the truck, I had him stand aside until I had the whole group assembled. Then I marched them over and indicated that they were to stand at attention with their backs against the building. I spoke to them in German. "Two months ago, I was liberated from a German POW camp. Your fellow Germans treated me like shit. They didn't feed me. They didn't give me clothes to wear. They let me freeze all winter. They didn't treat my wounds. I lost sixty-five pounds, while you were in my country eating good food, drinking beer, wearing warm clothes, sleeping on clean beds, and smoking cigarettes. To me, you are still my enemy. I don't give a goddamn whether you live or die. We need this equipment moved double-time."

I placed my hand on my .45, then walked over to nearest POW

and stuck my index finger in the middle of his forehead. "If you don't load this truck as fast as you can move, double-time, I will put a bullet-hole in your head. Right here. Verstehen Sie dass?"

The POW with my finger in his forehead yelled out, "Jawohl! Jawohl, Herr Feldwebel."

I had no intention of drawing my gun, much less shooting a POW, but I accomplished my purpose. The Germans were racing back and forth with radio parts and the truck was filling up. And I didn't feel at all guilty. Not even one little bit.

The lieutenant came back by in the jeep and waved to me as he passed. Then he slammed on the brakes and the tires screeched as he came to a stop. Putting the jeep in reverse, he backed up until he was in front of me and stared in disbelief at the fast-moving POWs.

"How in hell did you get 'em to do that, Sergeant?"

"I just told them how important it was to get the truck loaded fast."

The lieutenant looked at me dubiously, then got out of the jeep and went over to the corporal in charge of the guards and asked him the same question.

I heard the corporal answer "I don't know, Lieutenant. He spoke to them in German."

Then the lieutenant walked over to a POW who spoke a bit of English. I was out of earshot, so I couldn't hear the conversation, but the lieutenant came back in a couple of minutes and said, "Sergeant, I really appreciate your help. Don't know what I woulda done without you. Come on, let's check your piece back in."

The lieutenant never again needed help with the POWs.

The rest of my time in Blytheville was boring, but I enjoyed being home on weekends. Then I got a call from the major. "Good news, Sergeant. Just got confirmation on your points, and you have more than enough for discharge. You can leave for home tomorrow and wait for orders there. I wish you all the best."

In October 1945, I had been back in Memphis for almost two

weeks when I received orders to report to Lincoln Air Force Base, Lincoln, Nebraska, for discharge. An attached letter informed me that I would be the highest ranking noncom on the trip, therefore I would be in command of the train.

There were over a hundred going to Lincoln, and I was concerned about my duties, but it turned out to be uncomplicated. I was issued meal tickets for the entire group, which meant that wherever we ate, I could pay the tab in U.S. Government scrip. The train was a sleeper and a fairly late model, so we traveled in comfort, but even though I slept with my door open, I still found it difficult to breathe in the tight compartment and would often reach into my luggage for my bottle. There were also more cars than we needed, and the last three were empty. We were a pretty happy bunch, joking, looking forward to becoming veterans.

We stopped in St. Louis for lunch and ate in a large restaurant near the depot. While tables were being cleared for us, I noticed a number of sailors already seated. I had just been served when a sailor came over and said, "Sarge, one of the Air Force guys said you were in charge of this troop train and you'd be going through Kansas City on the way to Lincoln."

"Yeah, we will. Why do you ask?"

"We've got a big problem." He waved toward the other sailors. "They had some mechanical trouble on our train and we got to St. Louis too late to make our connection. If we don't get to Kansas City by tomorrow, we're going to catch hell, even though it wasn't our fault. And we can't get another train for hours. I understand you have some extra space on your train. Do you think it might be possible to give us a ride to K.C.?"

"How many of you are there?"

"Just twenty-five."

"I don't see why not. We've got three empty cars. When we get ready to leave, follow us out."

"Wow, Sarge, that would be tremendous! You're a real lifesaver. I'll go tell the guys."

When he got back to his table, the other sailors all cheered and waved their caps at us.

I had just gotten my guys and the sailors on board when a conductor came up to me and said, "You can't bring those sailors on here. This train is reserved for the Air Force."

"Look, we're pulling three empty cars, the sailors are late because their train broke down and they have to be in Kansas City tomorrow. It's no skin of your nose, so let's take off."

"We're not gonna move till the sailors get off. They're not on our orders."

"How long you been working on the railroad?"

"Eighteen years. What's that got to do with it?"

"Make pretty good money, do you?"

"Yeah, we always make good money."

"Well, these sailors are just back from overseas, and they risked their asses so you could stay home and make a good living. How many times were you shot at lately? Uncle Sam is paying for this train . . . not you. The sailors stay. Now let's get this goddam show on the road."

In a few minutes, the train took off. I didn't know whether I would get flak for my actions later, but I really didn't care. It was the right thing to do.

The discharge procedure in Lincoln was fast. Turn in your GI clothes. Do a quick physical. Sign a raft of papers. In a couple of days I was back home. A veteran. A civilian. A survivor. I felt a little like I had the day after I graduated from high school . . . what now?

Chapter Seventeen

COPING

B etween the back pay I accumulated while a POW, and the money I had saved when working at Fisher Aircraft, I had a tidy sum in the bank. I lived with my parents, and they didn't ask me to contribute anything toward household expenses while I (mistakenly) didn't offer. Financially independent for the moment, I didn't think about getting a job, although many of my friends had gone back to work.

I usually got up around eleven A.M., ate breakfast, and read the newspaper. My stomach problems had grown progressively worse, and the mainstay of my diet had become canned baby food. I existed on Gerber's for almost four months.

I found some pain relief from an old standby called paregoric, a camphorated tincture of opium prescribed by our family doctor for stomach pain. A teaspoonful, mixed with a couple of ounces of water, would turn milky and would deaden your innards almost instantly. Most users became constipated after taking paregoric, but with my intestinal problems I didn't have to worry about that. All it did was make things "normal."

I never spent an evening at home. There was always somewhere to go: a party, a football game, poker at a friend's house, a dance. I continued to treat my psychological problems with alcohol and, of course, the relief was temporary. Sometimes, when I had "medicated" too liberally, I climbed into bed and held on to the sides as the bed wildly spun clockwise for a minute, then stopped abruptly, reversed direction, and wildly spun counterclockwise. At least I didn't feel like the dark was crushing/suffocating me.

At night, I would wake myself up thrashing around on the bed. Nightmares were a constant occurrence, and often they were so vivid that I would spring upright with a scream on my lips and stifle it by shoving my face into a pillow. My startle response to loud noises was instant and devastating, and hours could pass before I began to recover from such an incident. I was depressed because I couldn't make plans to go to school, or to work, and I avoided my parents since they had begun to ask me what I wanted to do.

While in POW camp, I had promised myself that if I was lucky enough to survive, I would personally visit the families of Bill, Sherry, Long John, and Little Joe. I knew now that it would be impossible to fulfill that promise. I could see myself knocking on their doors and collapsing into a convulsive heap of grief at their feet.

When I received an invitation to Daddy's wedding in Atlanta, I knew I would really have to get my act together to be able to attend, but I was determined to be there. I didn't feel it was an obligation, but after all we had been through, I truly wanted to share this happy occasion with him.

Then, less than a week before the wedding, I received a letter from Sherry's sister in Pittsburgh. She said that she didn't understand how six members of our crew could bail out of our plane and leave four others behind. I realized how grief-stricken she was and that Sherry was her only sibling, but I was totally crushed. She was accusing me of fleeing the plane and leaving her brother to die. Did she think I had stepped over his body as I bailed out? Her doubt haunted me.

Survivor guilt was my constant companion. Not a day passed when I didn't think of my four lost crewmates. Why did they die and not me? They were better people. What had I accomplished in life that I deserved to be spared? And now the letter from Sherry's sister sent me into a real frenzy. My breathing was labored and shallow. I thought about driving downtown and jumping off the Harahan Bridge. I drank a water glass full of whiskey before I could stop trembling.

Then I sat down and answered her letter. I explained that my position on the plane was physically far removed from Sherry's station and I never saw him again after we took off from England that day. I told her that our plane was burning, that I was wounded and my clothing was on fire, that I had no oxygen, and that I had jumped through the bomb bay because I knew I'd never make it to the nose of the plane where Sherry was located. I also said that within seven seconds of my bailing out, the plane exploded. I mailed the letter, but I never heard from her again.

I didn't go to Daddy's wedding, and I felt terribly guilty about it. I couldn't go without drinking, and if I went to Atlanta cold sober, I felt that I would embarrass him by hanging around and being spastic. That, coupled with the guilt I was already internalizing, spelled disaster. I drank every day for two weeks. I didn't want my siblings to see me drunk, so after they left for school, I walked to my friend Hugh's house and spent the day there. Hugh, just back from the Pacific Theater, hadn't gone to work either. He and his family were functional alcoholics and drank every night, so I was a welcome guest. In the wee hours of the morning, I would go home and flop into my bed until the next day.

Gradually, I returned to "medicating" only "as needed," and I was able to begin socializing again. The highlight of my week was the Saturday afternoon BYOB tea dances at the Claridge and at the Peabody Hotel, good spots to meet girls. The guys and the girls were both there looking for dates and you had to pretty much be a complete nerd to leave the dance without plans for the evening. After a while, this chase became boring too, and I began dating just one girl. Her name was Ricky. She was fun to be with, a good dancer, and I was comfortable with her.

Of course my parents were concerned with my lack of direction, and when my father found out that I was dating one girl, he quickly opined that marriage would be the solution to all my problems. He knew Ricky's family, and he was convinced that wedlock would "straighten me out." Soon he was constantly urging me to take the step. I told him that I was in no hurry, but he persisted.

In the summer of 1946, most of my friends were getting married. I became an usher in so many weddings that I decided to buy a tux. One afternoon I was donning my tux, and my father came in and started talking about marriage again. "Look, son, why don't you let me buy you an engagement ring."

"If I decide to get married, I can buy my own engagement ring."

"I saw a beauty the other day in my friend Al's jewelry store. I mean a real beauty. It was over a carat! Why don't you come with me next week to look at it?"

"I'm just not ready yet. I'll let you know."

My newly married friends were moving into their first apartments or buying homes with GI loans. When I visited them, it was easy to get caught up in their excitement. I began to wonder if, at the age of twenty-three, I was simply delaying the inevitable. But shouldn't I feel a burning desire to get married, or was this just a romantic, adolescent concept that I ought to have outgrown?

My father phoned one afternoon sounding excited and asked if I had plans for the evening. Puzzled, I answered, "Yeah. Why?"

"Well, don't leave the house. I'll be there in a few minutes."

He arrived beaming, with a small grocery bag in his hand. He shoved it toward me. "Here, open it."

I reached into the bag and took out a small jewel box. "Open it. Open it."

I flipped the top open and saw an engagement ring. It was indeed "a beauty."

"Why did you buy this now? I told you I'd let you know when I was ready."

"I don't know what you want to wait for," he said, spreading his arms with palms up. "You got a nice girl. It's time to settle down. Listen to Daddy one time. Have I ever told you wrong? I gotta go back to the store. Give her the ring tonight. Okay?"

That night, I placed the ring on Ricky's finger and we were officially engaged.

We got married on Thanksgiving weekend in 1946. Her mother gave us a big, formal wedding at the Claridge Hotel, the site of the Saturday afternoon tea dances. I was not prepared to be the cynosure of the event. Surrounded by people, cringing at loud voices bouncing off the music, a frozen smile on my face, I was obliged to stand in one place and respond genially to myriad congratulations. Ricky's family was much larger than mine, and many of the guests were total strangers, requiring an introduction and a painful progression of small talk.

It seemed that Ricky and I were in the middle of a turntable. The center, where we were standing, was motionless, while the perimeter was loaded with grinning guests, all extending their hands as they revolved around us like kids on a carousel, reaching for the ring. Everyone in the room appeared to be enveloped in clear gelatin; swimming around in slow motion; sliding off each other. Their mouths were moving constantly, but their faces were no longer human faces . . . they were the faces of ventriloquists' dummies. Fortunately there was plenty of "medication" around, or I would never have lasted the evening.

At the end of a Jewish wedding ceremony, it is customary for the groom to stamp on and break a glass, which for safety's sake is wrapped in a napkin. This ritual is supposed to identify the couple with the spiritual destiny of the Jewish people. Others say that it signifies the last time the groom gets to put his foot down. I couldn't believe it when my descending size-twelve shoe missed the glass. But it did.

Looking back, I guess that Ricky and I were never on the same intellectual wavelength. She was a bright woman, but her interests were inclined toward clothes and social activities. Things I just wasn't interested in. She adored dancing. She never read a book. She scanned the newspaper for stories about local people she might know, avoiding articles about social issues, the arts, or national politics. She loved reading about celebrities. Her work experience was confined to sales in women's dress shops, and she was good at it because she was very outgoing and loved chatting with customers. Her job also offered discounts on personal purchases, and that appealed to her. Nonetheless, she was a kind-hearted woman and we were getting along well.

My fondest desire was to study journalism, and Ricky agreed it was a career that I would find fulfilling, so I applied to the University of Missouri, whose journalism program was ranked number 1 back then, and also to the University of Oklahoma, number 2. I was accepted at Oklahoma, and Ricky was excited about the idea at first. She planned to get a job in Oklahoma City and, together with the monthly educational subsidy I would receive from the GI Bill, we should have had no financial problem.

We informed family and friends about our plans, said our

good-byes, packed our belongings into the 1936 Buick coupe, and drove to Oklahoma City. We looked up Jimmy Barnes, an old friend of mine from Memphis who managed a theater there, and had dinner with him and his wife. The next day, they showed us around the city and we looked at available housing. Ricky and I drove to the University, and I was impressed with the facilities. The evening before I planned to matriculate, we were lying in bed at our hotel when Ricky said, "Norman, I just don't think I'm going to be able to do this. I can't leave my mother alone for nine months. She's a diabetic. She's overweight. There'll be nobody there to watch out for her. She could go into a diabetic coma at any time. Being an only child, the responsibility is all on me. I know you're really set on going to school here, but . . . couldn't we go back home and you could enroll at Memphis State?"

"How do I answer that, Ricky? I'm not left any choice, am I? You were looking forward to coming here. You seemed to like the place. If I got a degree in journalism from U. of O., I know I could land a good job. I could have the career I always wanted. But, you know damned well I'm not going to stay here alone. So if you just can't be away from your mother, we'll go back to Memphis, tomorrow."

It was embarrassing to go home and let my friends know that we were back. I felt like a failure, even though I'd never had the chance to prove myself, and the circumstances of my return were beyond my control. In my disappointment, I decided to postpone enrolling at Memphis State. With my mind in such turmoil, I didn't feel that I could hack it just then.

Since my work experience was confined to the food-store business, I applied for sales positions with manufacturers who distributed products to supermarkets. My first interview was with a large national company, and I met with their sales manager at a Memphis hotel. First, I filled out application papers, then took an aptitude test. While he and I talked, his assistant graded the test. When she was finished, she laid it on his desk and left the room. He studied the test results for a few minutes without speaking; then he looked up, smiled, and said, "Let's go to lunch."

We went across the street to a coffee shop and after we had ordered, he placed his elbows on the table, clasped his hands, and stared at me intently. "You tested out with one of the highest scores I've seen in a long time. You don't have any sales experience, but you present well, you know the grocery business inside out from the retail level, which is a big plus, and you're articulate. I've been in this field a long time and I've hired a lot of reps. I feel that with some training, and we'll give you that, you can make a helluva salesman. On that basis, I'm going to hire you for this job."

"Well, I really appreciate your confidence, and I assure you that I'll do everything I can to earn it."

We discussed salary, and it was more than adequate. My territory covered the Memphis tri-state area, which meant I would be home almost every night.

When we returned to the room, he picked up my application and began copying information onto a form that I surmised was official notification of my hiring. Then he stopped writing, put down his pen, and looked me in the eye with a strange expression. He said, very slowly, "I wish you hadn't written this down."

"What's that, sir?"

"On the question about your military service, you say that you were a POW. Now, I've been with you for almost three hours, and I'm confident that you're as sound as a dollar, but when this information reaches headquarters and my boss reads that you were a POW, he's going to think I hired a loony. It's not fair, but I know sure as hell what his reaction's gonna be. I can't hire you, son. Just let me give you a piece of advice: *never* put that on any application again."

I was so stunned, I couldn't say a word. I got up, walked out of the hotel, and headed for a liquor store. I sat in a café, sipping whiskey and running his words through my head again and again. "Loony. My boss—he's going to think I hired a loony." I felt like a pariah. Dirty. Branded. Was being a former POW going to tarnish me for the rest of my life?

I didn't apply for another job for a while; then I began answering ads again and going on interviews. I didn't dare have a drink beforehand, and my greatest fear was that my nervousness would be so obvious, I'd be ruled out before I had a chance to pitch myself. My most embarrassing problem at an interview was sweaty hands. Before entering an office, I would dry my palms thoroughly, but they would be moist and clammy again before I shook hands with a prospective employer. Then, when he rubbed his hand against his pants to get rid of my sweat, I wished I could crawl under the carpet and die.

My next best shot was with a company whose brands had been beating all competition on the shelves of America's supermarkets for years. I was interviewed by the national sales manager and by his next in command. I spent about seven hours with them and, at the end of the day . . . I was hired. I was to leave the next week for headquarters in Kansas City, go through three weeks of training, pick up a company car, which I would drive back to Memphis, where my territory was located, and go to work.

"Come in around eleven-thirty tomorrow," the NSM said, "and we'll go over some of the key accounts in your territory. By the way, think you could bring in your wife for lunch tomorrow? We like to talk to our salesmen's wives to be sure they're happy with their husband's job situation."

I floated home on air to tell Ricky about the new job. All evening, we talked about the ways our lives were going to change for the better.

The next day, we went into town together. Passing a department store window, we glanced at our reflection, and Ricky said, "My, what a handsome couple."

The four of us had lunch in the hotel dining room, and the conversation was pleasant. The NSM told Ricky how pleased he was to have me on his "team" and what a good future he thought I had with the company. I declined dessert, but Ricky obliged her sweet tooth with a piece of key lime pie. The NSM said, "Look, I'll stay and keep your wife company with another cup of coffee. Why don't you guys go on up and look at a map of your territory."

We went back to the room and studied the map a bit, and I got a sheet listing the names of the stores I would call on each day, Monday through Friday. The NSM and Ricky showed up about twenty minutes later. We all talked for a while, then the NSM stood up and said he enjoyed meeting my wife and he would see me in Kansas City next Tuesday.

Driving home, I asked Ricky if anything significant was said after I left the dining room. "Not really. Just chit-chat about what a nice city Memphis was and a good place to bring up kids. He did say one thing that struck me as strange. He asked if I was Jewish, and I said that I was. Then he asked, 'Norm's not Jewish, though, is he?' I said, 'Sure, he is,' and he sort of nodded and left it at that."

About seven o'clock that evening, the phone rang and it was the NSM. "After you left today, we interviewed someone else who turned out to be more experienced and we've decided to hire him in place of you." That was it. No apology. No "Sorry." He just hung up.

This time, I was even more disturbed than I was when I got turned down because I'd been a POW. I thought about throwing away my dog tags when I bailed out over Berlin, so I couldn't be identified as Jewish. Was I really back in the USA, or was I still in Nazi Germany? I felt any remnant of self-confidence I had left, burning away like the dripping "skin" of our plane did over "Big B."

I was "flying" a different kind of mission now and getting "shot down" every time.

After that wretched experience, I drove to Memphis State to investigate enrollment and classes. As I was leaving the campus to go home, I began to feel pain in my chest. I figured it was indigestion and kept on driving. After a few blocks, the pain became more intense and I believed I was having a heart attack. I was about four miles from the VA hospital and I decided to go there.

A VA doctor examined me, and I was given an EKG. There was no sign of a heart problem. I was checked in and taken to a large room occupied by three other patients. Over the next five days, I was tested extensively from stem to stern. The doctor finally explained that, other than my ongoing stomach problems, they found no physical cause of my sudden chest pain, which had now disappeared, and that it was probably brought on by an anxiety attack. He prescribed no medication and told me I could go home the next day.

During the night, it became very windy and began to rain. The windows in my room were open, it was quite cool, and I was sleeping soundly. Apparently, the storm intensified and I was awakened by a thunderous crash that sounded like a bomb exploding right on top of me. I sat up in bed, not knowing where I was, and then the lights went on and a nurse came into the room. "What in the hell happened?" I asked.

She pointed to the foot of my bed, where a vase had blown down and shattered all over the floor. It had been sitting on a windowsill and was filled with long-stemmed flowers. The force of the wind blowing on the flowers had toppled the vase.

Frenzied, I began putting on my clothes. "I can't stay here. I'm going home."

"Look, you're being discharged tomorrow. Try to go back to sleep."

"Sleep, hell. I won't be able to sleep for the next week."

"Let me get a doctor. Just sit there till I get back."

I was dressed when she came back with a doctor.

He took my blood pressure and listened to my heart. "I know you're agitated, and with good reason. I would be upset too if that had happened to me. But it was nobody's fault. Your nerves are really shot now, and you don't want to go wandering home by your-self in the middle of the night. Here's what I want you to do. Let me give you a shot, and I assure you that you'll sleep through the night. And I'd like you to stay just one day longer so we can be sure you're over this episode. Will you do that for me?"

He was calm and reassuring. The shot sounded attractive, and I wanted something to knock me out. To help me escape from my disturbed state. I nodded. "Could I come here for treatment as an outpatient? Do you think you could help me if I came in on a reg-ular basis?"

"We can treat you as an outpatient and I'm sure you'd improve, but our regulations require that you come in as an inpatient for three months first."

There was no way I was going to commit to three months of confinement. Suppose, after that time, they decided I needed to stay longer? I would be up shit creek without a paddle. I turned down their generosity.

My nightmares got worse and I never slept through the night. I tried to sleep as close to the edge of my side of the bed as I could, because I would often flail my arms during the night, accidentally hitting Ricky. When I woke up, I'd pour a drink and spend the rest of the night in a living room chair.

Ricky and I never discussed my symptoms. She was concerned about the physical and mental manifestations of my disorder, but she didn't seem interested in knowing the root cause. Sometimes, in conversation, I would pick around the edge of my problems, but what I was saying seemed only to puzzle her and I just gave up.

It was about this time that the *Memphis Belle,* the B-17 flown by the first Eighth Air Force crew to complete their required twenty-five missions and return to the United States, was shipped to Memphis as a permanent home and set up at the fairgrounds. Undecided about the best way to display the plane, the city left it parked in front of the Armory while plans were discussed. The Flying Fortress was not protected by any barrier, and anyone could walk up and climb on board.

About three o'clock one morning, after a particularly disturbing nightmare, I was sitting in my darkened living room when I thought about the *Memphis Belle.* She wasn't *my* B-17, but she was *a* B-17. I got dressed, put a bottle of whiskey into a paper bag, and drove to the fairgrounds. When I turned off the car lights, I was in total darkness.

I walked over to the plane, touched the horizontal stabilizer, then ran my hand along the fuselage until I felt the rear hatch. I heaved myself inside and headed for the nose. Even in the pitch black of the plane's interior, I didn't stumble once walking the familiar path through the waist, the radio room, the narrow catwalk across the bomb bay, past Red's top gun turret and into the cockpit, where I slid into Daddy's seat.

I took a couple of big swigs from my bottle, then leaned back and closed my eyes. I guess I fell asleep, because the next thing I remembered was the four B-17 engines roaring to life . . . and we were flying over Germany. There was the sound of exploding flak and the sporadic ping of shrapnel piercing the plane's "skin." Then the ship reverberated with bursts of machine-gun fire as our gunners opened up on the attacking fighter planes.

I heard Bill's voice on the intercom, yelling excitedly, "I got me a 109! I didn't even have to lead him. He was coming straight in on our tail."

Rum called out, "Bandit, two o'clock high."

"Gotcha," Red responded, as his twin muzzles spat staccato bursts of .50-caliber bullets at the intruder.

When I woke up, I was surprised by my calmness. My hands were steady. My palms were dry. I was able to breathe deeply. And I sensed that I was surrounded by my crew, each one manning his own station. Visiting the *Memphis Belle* became a ritual with me whenever I had a disturbing nightmare.

April 29 has been a downer for me ever since 1944. That's the anniversary of our last mission over Germany. I always try to spend the evening in quiet remembrance of my four buddies who died on that date. My nocturnal visits to the *Memphis Belle* inspired me to do something on the next April 29 to commemorate the fateful day that we bombed "Big B." I decided to have a wreath placed against the *Memphis Belle* in their honor. I ordered a wreath from a florist and told him where I wanted it delivered on April 29. That afternoon, I drove past the Armory and the wreath was propped up against the *Memphis Belle.*

The next morning, *The Commercial Appeal* carried a front-page picture of the wreath and the Memphis Belle, along with my inscription on the card, "For Bill, Little Joe, Sherry and Long John on the anniversary of your death. I still remember."

I was embarrassed by the public disclosure of my sentimentality. My uncle called to ask if I had sent the wreath. I said that I had not. I had thought about making this an annual observance, but I never sent another wreath.

I enrolled at Memphis State to study English and journalism. Contrary to my failed attempt in 1941, when I was seventeen and just out of high school, I loved my courses. The profs were great, and I thoroughly enjoyed the milieu. The GI Bill was a wonderful resource, but the $120 per month subsistence allowance was not going to sustain me financially. I would need a part-time job.

My father asked me to come to work in his food store. I knew that he wasn't just making a place for me. He was not a trustful person and never left the store in the hands of employees unless my mother was there. My presence would free him to have more time off. I hated the six-day-a-week schedule and the long hours, but I had nothing better in the offing, so I accepted his offer. I scheduled all morning classes so I could get to work early in the day. Although the family working environment was by no means perfect, it beat trying to hide my depression and anxiety attacks from an unsympathetic publicly held company.

In July 1948 my first son, David, was born and we needed more living space, so we bought a home in a new subdivision. The house was of brick construction, three bedrooms, one bath, and on a large, level lot. The cost was $10,750, and the low-interest loan was financed by Uncle Sam. Our monthly mortgage payment was $65. My second son, Bob, was born in 1951 and we moved into a larger home.

I had just completed my junior year when my father's back went out. He had serious disc problems and was in great pain. He was hospitalized and, on release, was bedridden for several weeks. After that, he got around with a cane, but was unable to return to work right away. I was distraught at having to drop out of Memphis State, but there was no other choice. It was several months before my father could come back to work. He began by working half days, then started coming in full-time. By then, I had become "indispensable," and I never had the opportunity to return to college.

Chapter Eighteen

A Bite of the Big Apple

For almost twenty years, I was disappointed that I had passed through the Port of New York twice, going overseas and returning, without ever seeing New York City. In the summer of 1964, my now-teenaged sons, David and Bob, were making a strong pitch to go to the New York World's Fair. They didn't know it was going to be such an easy sell. For me, a visit was long overdue, and Ricky had family in New Jersey and Pennsylvania that she often talked about seeing, so in August we piled into our 1956 Buick and headed north.

Other than exchanging Christmas cards every year, I hadn't been in close contact with the guys on my crew. Since Merle Rumbaugh and Waide Fulton both lived in Pennsylvania, I phoned them and made plans to get together. I was very excited at the prospect of seeing them again.

The Rumbaughs lived on a farm near Pittsburgh, and we visited them first. At thirty-nine, I wasn't expecting Rum to be the same twenty-year-old I once knew, but I was looking forward to that big engaging smile and the quick laugh. Unfortunately, I was to see neither. The gravity of his injuries on the Big B raid, plus the long hospitalization after he returned to the United States, had not only taken a great toll on his body, it had also drained his spirit. He greeted me warmly, but the happy-go-lucky demeanor was gone, replaced by a melancholy so heavy it seemed to be a physical presence, as if he were carrying a yoke with the weight of the world across his shoulders. He avoided talking about the past, but he obviously could not avoid the scalding memories that still held his mind hostage. Boy, could I relate, albeit I felt a bit better off than poor Rum.

Rum and his wife had four young children, who seemed somewhat less animated than one might expect of kids their age. From my own experience, I knew that children, even in a loving family, could be affected by a parent's pain and suffering, as Rum's seemed to be. When we said our good-byes and left, I felt a great sadness for my crewmate and his family.

When we reached Philadelphia, we stayed with Ricky's aunt. I invited Waide Fulton over one evening, and he drove out from Oxford, where he was assistant postmaster. His artificial eye was so perfect that most people couldn't even notice. He brought along a scrapbook of his time in the Air Force and even had some letters that my mom had written to his mother while we were POWs. I told him about seeing Rum, and he said he'd visited him before and come away with the same sad feeling. Waide had been married and divorced and had two teenaged daughters.

He looked well, still quite thin and still querulous. He asked, "Do you remember, before we took off for Berlin, you got a .50-caliber bullet stuck in your machine gun chamber and asked me to unjam it? If that wasn't the damndest thing. How the hell did you do that?"

"I was charging my gun and it jammed. You were our crew's armorer. Who else would I ask?"

"If I hadn't straightened that out, you wouldn't'a been able to fire your gun that day."

"You're absolutely right, and I thank you again."

Then he turned to Ricky. "You know him and Red used to go out hell-raisin' every weekend."

"We were kids, Waide. You were already an old man."

The banter went on until he left. We promised to keep in closer touch.

Two days later, we arrived in Passaic, New Jersey at Ricky's cousin's house. As soon as we had unloaded our luggage, the boys started pestering me to drive to Manhattan. Ricky and the boys enjoyed our time in the city. She was thrilled to see several celebrities as we strolled in Manhattan, and the high point of her day arrived in the person of Buddy Ebsen, of the television series *Beverly Hillbillies*, whom she spotted across the street and chased down to get his autograph. The boys were enthralled with just about everything, particularly driving past Yankee Stadium.

I had anticipated the visit to New York for so long, I was surprised that I found actually being there anticlimactic. I had hoped to locate some of my Air Force buddies who once said they lived in the area, but when I thumbed through telephone books I didn't spot a single name, and I was aghast at the sheer size of the directories. Then I decided to check out the myth that if you stood on the corner of Broadway and 42nd Street long enough, you would meet someone you knew. We tarried there for quite a while, watching the throngs of people, everyone in a hurry, but the boys got antsy and we moved on.

Back home again in Memphis, it was business as usual . . . the same long hours, the same boring routine. The kids were usually asleep when I arrived home, and I got into the habit of writing every night. I would eat something light, pour a stiff drink, then write until I fell asleep at my desk. Even though I was exhausted, writing every evening became the one thing I looked forward to, and I was surprised at my productivity. I mostly wrote short stories, but I wasn't confident enough to send them off to any magazines.

Progressive Grocer, a trade magazine for supermarkets, arrived at our store monthly. It was a well-written, slick publication, and I always read it from cover to cover for merchandising ideas. One day, I was leafing through the latest edition when I came across a house ad for an associate editor. Intrigued, I read the ad over and over again, and each time I felt more strongly that it was speaking directly to me. I had all the qualifications requested except for one . . . I had never been published, outside of college periodicals.

I fantasized about the job for hours, and that night I wrote a cover letter, along with my bio, and showed it to Ricky. She said that the letter was good, but was noncommittal about my prospects. I mailed my résumé the next day and never expected a reply.

Three weeks later, I received a letter with the *Progressive Grocer* logo and opened it without enthusiasm, expecting to be informed that they had hired someone with more experience. I was stunned to learn that they were "interested" in me and wanted me to write a sample article. The letter was signed by George Kline, Vice President and Executive Editor. I had seen his byline so many times, I felt as if I knew him.

Writing the article was a real challenge. I finished it in five nights, then edited and rewrote and edited again until I realized that any further attempt to improve it would achieve just the opposite effect. I had done the best I could; I had to let it go.

Weeks went by with no word; then I got a call from George Kline asking if I could come to New York for an interview in a couple of days. I could indeed, and an appointment was set. On such short notice, I knew I'd have to fly, even though I'd sworn twenty years ago that I would never board a plane again and had never been on one since.

At the airport, bags were being loaded onto a huge jet, and my moist hands turned black from the newsprint of the *Memphis Commercial Appeal* I was holding but was unable to read. On the plane, my discomfort must have been obvious, because a stewardess came over and asked, "Is this your first flight, sir?"

I tried to draw in a deep breath, but took in half my lung capacity. "No, I've flown before, but never on a jet."

"Tell you what. I'll come sit with you during takeoff, okay?"

"Thanks. I'd like that."

As we rolled down the runway and lifted into the air, she kept up a steady stream of conversation to distract me, but I still held a stranglehold on the armrests. Ours was a "Champagne Breakfast" flight, and that finally brought some relief as she refilled my glass each time she passed my seat.

At my interview with George Kline the next day, I tried to show a calm I didn't feel, and when he introduced me to the top brass and other editors, I was embarrassed because I wet the palms of everyone I shook hands with. But I must have done something right that day, because after lunch with the publisher and editors, we returned to George's office and he welcomed me to *Progressive Grocer*.

Later, back at my hotel, I called Ricky with the great news. I could sense that she didn't share my elation. "Congratulations, Norman. I know this is what you always wanted, and I'm happy for you. I hope you realize what all this is going to involve. We have to sell the house, move the kids to another part of the country and a strange new school. And David's going to be a senior next year. I don't know how he's going to feel about graduating from a different high school, leaving all his friends behind. There's a lot to think about, Norman."

Since I'd had a big lunch and wasn't really hungry, I went out for just a sandwich. I lay awake for a long time that night pondering what I would do if we all moved up north and then the company decided that my work didn't measure up to their standards.

I didn't know then that George Kline would become one of the most influential people in my life: mentor, confidant, and friend. I also didn't know until some months later that George had been a bombardier on B-24's in the 15th Air Force during World War II, flying out of Italy. In 1944, on a mission to bomb one of the most dangerous targets in Europe, the Ploesti oil fields, his plane was shot down over Bucharest, Romania . . . and he became a POW.

Chapter Nineteen

FROM GENERALIST TO JOURNALIST

T he first week of April 1965, I sat down in my new office at *Progressive Grocer Magazine,* inserted a sheet of paper into a typewriter, and began to earn my living as an editor. The change in occupation was so profound that it challenged my imagination to believe I had actually made this transition. In a couple of weeks, I had gone from a butcher's apron to a business suit; from the hectic atmosphere of a supermarket to the sedate environment of a publishing company. I loved it.

What a joy it was to have dinner with the family every evening, after so many years of getting home at night long after my sons were in bed. On weekends, we could go sightseeing in the city, visit museums, see a baseball game or a Broadway show, or drive to one of the many historic sites in the area.

One difficult adjustment was the downsizing of our living space. We had gone from a three-bedroom home in Memphis to a two-bedroom, two-bath apartment in New Jersey, which would have been totally adequate except that Ricky's mother had moved up with us. Her joining us was not unexpected, since she had become a permanent part of our household four years after our marriage. What created an awkward situation for our entire family was that she was grossly overweight and could not sleep lying down; therefore, a large reclining chair in the living room became her "bedroom." Everyone had to pass through the living room to reach the bedrooms and bathrooms, which was an inconvenience, and we hesitated to watch television after a certain hour in the evening because it might disturb her.

The obvious solution to our problem would be the purchase of a house, but Ricky didn't want to make that investment because David was just months away from finishing high school and she wanted funds available to send him to college.

Whenever I went on a business trip to an interesting city, I would invite Ricky to come along. I thought she would have fun exploring Dallas or Chicago or Miami during the day while I was working, then in the evening we could have dinner at some special restaurant and just enjoy being alone for a change, but she never joined me. Her usual excuse was that she couldn't "leave the children alone," even though David was eighteen and driving; Bob was fifteen; and her mother was there to prepare their meals. We didn't fight about it, but it was an issue of contention. I had hoped that our new lifestyle would draw us closer together. It seemed to be pushing us even farther apart.

It was hard for me to define my dissatisfaction with our marriage. Ricky and I didn't argue. We didn't have any serious, unresolved issues. We cared for each other, but there was no burning fire of desire. There never had been. Ricky was passive, where I was demonstrative, but I had a long hangup about showing affection, while simultaneously feeling that she was patiently waiting to get back to something she was doing. I know that I was supersensitive, but the hurt was deep and I came to resist any impulse, because I sensed it was unreciprocal. I also felt guilty about uprooting her from a city where she'd lived for forty-five years, where she had many friends, and moving her to a new environment.

I know that much of what was wrong with our marriage was rooted in the emotional baggage I carried from my POW past. A past that Ricky was not interested in learning about, nor relating to, therefore she could not understand my mood swings; the dour days when I was uncommunicative; or the times that I would fly into a rage that was far disproportionate to what had disturbed me.

Another factor that impacted our relationship during the first twenty years of our marriage was the sixteen-hour days that I spent working in the store. I was an absentee father. I felt very guilty being away from my family so much, but I had no other choice. I hoped that the "normal" hours I was working now would make up for it a little.

When my sons were younger, I never saw them in the evenings because they were in bed before I got home. Then, when they grew older and stayed up to see me, I was often confronted with a problem as soon as I walked in the door. Ricky had issues with our older son, David, which were not serious, but simply episodes of disobedience, not uncommon in teenagers. These issues were dumped into my hands for resolution at a time when I was exhausted, hungry, disgruntled, and not capable of being a fair disciplinarian. Already angry at my lot, I was often excessive in meting out punishment, which would then send me into a period of guilt, self-hatred, and loathing that would remain with me for days.

I would go without dinner, shower and get into bed, then avoid coming in contact with Ricky . . . whom I blamed for causing me to lose control. It wasn't her fault that I'd lost control. That was my own frailty. But the situation could have been avoided if we had been able to talk honestly and openly about what was really at the root of our problems.

Now, living in New Jersey, doing work that I thoroughly enjoyed, being creative, my emotions were in better balance than at any time since my return from POW camp. It never entered my mind that my marriage was stale. Ricky and I never argued. We were pleasant to each other. I wasn't discontented. I assumed that after twenty years, most marriages sort of settled into a rut, ardor turned into companionship and you accepted the change. Who was I to expect more?

After so many years of dragging myself out of bed at 5 A.M. to go to work at the store, my job at PG seemed like a dream. I was afraid that I would wake up one day and it would be gone. The articles I wrote were drawing good comment, and several of them had gone into reprint, ordered by companies that wanted to distribute them to their personnel. I was invited to address trade associations, as well as the sales staffs of major food manufacturers. I couldn't have been happier. Then, one day, I woke up from my dream.

In 1967, PG acquired an annual publication intended to help manufacturers market their products to the supermarket industry. The previous owner had run out of funds after a couple of editions and was forced to sell. I was surprised when management selected me to redesign the book and launch it as the first product of a new profit center that I would manage. I was also upset, because I truly enjoyed my work as an editor.

My first reaction was to decline the offer, so I met with George to ask his advice. "Norm, you're doing a great job right where you are and it's by no means mandatory that you take this position. On the other hand, I have to point out to you that when someone turns down a promotion, it's rare to be tapped again."

So I became general manager of a profit center and publisher of *Progressive Grocer's Marketing Guidebook.* In need of an assistant, I asked human resources to run an ad, but on the day interviews were scheduled I was called away on business and George offered to fill in for me.

The day I returned to the office, George introduced me to my new assistant, Melanie Buse. Born in Manhattan, just out of Rhode Island University with a degree in English, she was bright, outgoing, and petite. Melanie quickly grasped the fundamentals of our business and was resourceful in developing data-gathering systems that saved time. She also helped train new people as we enlarged our staff.

While new space was being prepared for us, we shared a large office and, during coffee breaks and eat-in lunches, often chatted about subjects other than business. We found that we both had the same political bent, were intense on the same social issues, and also shared an interest in books and in the theater. It was common practice at PG for department heads to take their staff to lunch. Melanie and I ate out together a couple of times a month, and I found it pleasant being with her.

Problems with our first book were far greater than we anticipated, and I spent six weeks at the printing plant in Pennsylvania, proofing and making changes. I was constantly on the phone with Melanie, and her help on that end was priceless. It was almost unheard-of for a publication of this kind to be in the black in its first year, but orders came flooding in and the company was delighted.

Tempted by the vaunted benefits of emerging computer typesetting, management suggested that I try this method for our next book and also that I bring Melanie with me to the plant to help deal with the expected complexities. Meanwhile, I was wrestling with some temptations of my own, because Melanie and I had drawn much closer over the past year. Our conversations were more personal, I complimented her on what she wore, missed her on weekends and looked forward to Monday mornings. Because of my openness with her, she could sense the days when I was down and would deflect office situations she felt might upset me.

I drove to the plant in Ephrata on a Monday morning and picked her up at a small airport in Lancaster just before noon. From the beginning, the sensual tension was electric. I took her bag and put my hand on her shoulder as we walked to the car and she looked up and smiled. The plant president took us to lunch, and the rest of the day was hectic with proofing copy and deciphering typesetting codes embedded in the computer printouts.

After dinner that night, we stopped at a package store and picked up a bottle of Canadian Club. Back at the motel, she went to her room and changed into a short jumpsuit and I into jeans and a T-shirt. Barefoot, we made drinks and played gin rummy on the floor of my room by a balcony overlooking the pool. She asked about my POW experience and sat listening quietly while I spoke more freely on the subject than I had ever been able to before.

It was past midnight when I finally looked at my watch. I said, "It's late and we're gonna need to get some sleep. We've got a lot to do tomorrow." I got up and stretched out on the bed. Though we'd had far too much alcohol to be logical, we each made one futile attempt at logic.

Then Melanie looked at me steadily and asked, "Do you want me to stay?"

The question took a few seconds to sink in. Consequences flashed through my mind and I knew that those I could think of were only the tip of the iceberg. Blithely, like the *Titanic*, I sailed toward: Disaster? Delight?

I sighed deeply and said, "You know, when we get back to New York, we're still going to have to work together. Can you handle it?"

"I can handle it," she said.

As I reached toward the headboard to flick out the lights, I heard the zipper on her jumpsuit. Her body felt tiny against mine. Outside, I could hear the water sloshing against the sides of the pool.

Any psychologist in the country would have given the chances of our relationship surviving a big fat zero. I was married. I was her boss. I was exactly twice her age. My eldest son was only three years her junior. We were from different religious backgrounds. And these were only the beginning of the myriad obstacles confronting us. Bathed in the blinding light of my desire, nothing, least of all common sense, could make me see that by all odds, my intentions were doomed.

I don't know that Melanie was totally sure at this point. She said she was in love with me, yes, but she was more realistic than I in asking, "How in the world do you plan on making this happen?" I had no immediate answer to that question, but I was certain that I wanted to be with her forever and I knew I must find a way.

Back at the office, we tried to break it off. I started to take my coffee breaks with friends on the editorial floor. I stopped going out to pick up lunch and eating at my desk. I ate out every day with one of the editors, or our research director. After six weeks, my theory of separation was working out horribly. Being apart was driving us mad. One evening, I stayed in town and we went out to dinner. The separation had only made our love stronger, and we decided to pursue our impossible dream regardless of the odds.

Melanie thought that we should go away for a week where we could be alone, talk things out, and make some kind of plan. I suggested Atlanta. My brother Alan lived there, and I proposed to pick up his motel bill if he would lend us his apartment for a week.

When I called Alan, he was surprised by the proposal but agreed immediately. "Hey, Big Brother, I don't advise you . . . you advise me. Remember? I'll be delighted to see both of you. And you're more than welcome to my apartment."

A company meeting in Miami was scheduled in two weeks, and I was obligated to attend. I didn't want to wait until after that meeting to go away with Melanie, so I decided that we would go to Atlanta the week before the meeting. I told Ricky that I was going on a business trip to Atlanta, would spend the weekend there with my brother, and then go directly to Miami for the company meeting.

Our week in Atlanta was an epiphany. We went over every aspect of our situation, and it was clear that we couldn't stand being apart. Our six-week separation had been agonizing. We decided to find an apartment in Manhattan that was affordable. Money would definitely be a problem. I was positive that Ricky wouldn't give me a divorce right away, and I was not going to leave her strapped for funds. Also, my younger son was a senior in high school and I was determined that he would go to the college of his choice.

Throughout the week, we talked long into each night and never left Alan's apartment until afternoon. He would call every day to invite us to lunch, but we had just eaten breakfast. He couldn't understand why we were still inside when the weather was so beautiful. All of his classes, as a journalism professor, were early, so he would take off every day to be with us, and he delighted in being our tour guide.

I thought it might be less traumatic to break the news to Ricky away from home, so I decided to ask her to meet me in Miami after my company meeting was over. I knew it was a long shot that she would come, but to my surprise she said she would. Our few days in Miami were shattering. Tears all around. Endless questions that were excruciatingly painful to answer.

"When did all this begin? When you went to the printing plant together?"

"Yes."

"If you had problems with me, why didn't you discuss them?"

"I think our problems were too entrenched to be resolved by discussion."

"You aren't moving out, are you?"

"Eventually, yes."

"What am I going to live on?"

"I'm going to continue to support you, Ricky."

"What about the boys' education?"

"I'm going to see them through any college they want to attend."

"I never thought you'd leave me like this, Norman. I'll never give you a divorce."

She obviously felt that this was a temporary dalliance, a midlife crisis that would pass with time. What an ending to the first time she ever came away with me.

Chapter Twenty

The Ecstasy and the Agony

Melanie found us a fourth-floor walkup apartment on East 66th Street near First Avenue. We sublet it from a friend of a friend, and the rent was $95 a month, stabilized under New York City's arcane rent-control statutes. It was an ancient red brick building that had once consisted of larger apartments, which had been divided into smaller apartments, and the configuration of each unit had suffered from the diminution.

Open the door to our apartment and you faced a hallway, four feet wide by fifteen feet long, leading to a salmon-pink kitchen with a blue lightbulb. Off the kitchen was the bathroom, with a tub that stood on four iron legs and an overhead water tank that was flushed by a pull-chain. The bathroom was too small for a washbasin, so we had to brush our teeth at the kitchen sink. The bedroom was five and a half feet wide. Melanie brought her single bed from her mother's apartment, and in a few days we mastered the art of turning over in it during the night. We became like synchronized swimmers, robotically rolling over in unison to the right or to the left without waking up. The living room was eight by ten feet, with two windows facing the "terrace," an iron-grated platform with an opening at one end for access to the fire escape.

We replaced the blue bulb, repainted the rooms, put up a shelf in the kitchen, and got a couple of bar stools so we could eat off the shelf. It was a little strange eating off a shelf and staring at a wall eighteen inches from your face, but it worked. We bought some cheap floor tiles and stuck them to the kitchen floor with a spread-on, tar-like black paste. We turned off the radiator in the kitchen to keep from broiling. There were risers in the kitchen and in the bedroom carrying heat to the floor above, and they were so hot that Melanie bought foam insulation for the pipe in the bedroom so we could sleep without waking up in a pool of sweat. For the bathroom, we bought a pink satin cord, which we hung from the pull-chain to simulate the elegance of ringing for the butler. During the night, whenever one of us went to the bathroom, we'd call out to the other, "Do you have to pee?" because once you flushed, you couldn't use the john for five minutes unless you didn't mind cold water from the tank dripping on your back. After a few months, when we could finally afford to buy a double bed, we moved the single into the living room, put bolsters against the wall, and used it for a couch. Of course, the double touched the walls on both sides, so we had to climb over the foot of the bed to get in or out.

Since Melanie cooked, I was the dishwasher, and I quickly discovered that I had to wash dishes twice: once after dinner and again before we ate breakfast. Although we sprayed and tried every method we had ever heard of, the cockroaches always came back in full force.

We did have one advantage over the more modern apartment

building facing us across the street: we had a helluva lot better view than they did.

The move to Manhattan was the beginning of the most ecstatic four-year period of my life and, at the same time, the most traumatic. America's involvement in World War II lasted less than four years. Living together was the realization of a dream. Living a clandestine daily existence was a nightmare, the worst, most unrelenting stressor I had ever experienced. We didn't want our relationship known to the company. We could both lose our jobs. But the logistics of keeping it a secret were mind-boggling. Many people who worked at PG lived in Manhattan, so when we walked to work, we would split up about six blocks from the office. Likewise, we never left the office together, but would meet on First Avenue, a few blocks past the United Nations complex.

We never held hands on the street and whenever we saw someone from the office approaching, Melanie fled in one direction and I in another. One Saturday, we walked into Lord & Taylor just as an editor from PG was coming down the escalator. We split up so quickly, he never saw either of us. She was much less fearful of discovery than I, but I had a history of paranoia dating back to two years before she was even born. Our lives were already in enough turmoil without the additional strain of being unemployed.

I began to feel like a true POW escapee again, on the run from the Gestapo, disguised in civilian clothes. The minute we set foot outdoors, anxiety took charge of my mind. I couldn't cower inside our apartment forever, but whenever we went to the supermarket, to a department store, to dinner, or to the theater, I was a basket case until we returned to the safety of our home. I drank every night and needed special fortification if we were going out for the evening. Weekends were especially bad. I found no pleasure in walking through Central Park or around the city. This was Melanie's hometown and she was reasonably comfortable, whereas

I was an over-wound spring, tense and ready to burst at any second if we spied an associate.

And so my private war with post-traumatic stress disorder continued. The only times I felt completely relaxed were when we arrived home in the evening. I'd pour drinks and chat with Melanie in the kitchen while she cooked dinner. We ate on tray tables in the living room, where we could watch television. As long as we were together in our "safe house," my life was sublime. But when Melanie had choir practice in the evening or had to attend some social event, to which I wasn't invited because I was still an unknown entity, I was quickly surrounded by my old demons: claustrophobia, depression, survivor guilt, and the additional guilt of having left my family. That's when I would reach for my bottle, and Melanie was always fearful of the condition she would find me in when she returned.

Every Sunday, while Melanie attended church services, I rode the bus to New Jersey to visit my sons. David, having dropped out of the University of Wisconsin, was still living with his mother, so I saw him every week. Bob was a freshman at Cornell and came home on weekends—when he could get a ride and if he could spare time from his studies. At first there was some awkwardness, but after a few visits we were all more relaxed and able to enjoy each other's company. Ricky was always cordial. Malice was not a part of her makeup, but she wouldn't even discuss the prospect of giving me a divorce and I was afraid to press too hard for fear of pushing her over the edge. She had a history of worrying excessively about the health of our sons and her mother. I remember one day in Memphis, when the kids were in elementary school, I got a call from our pediatrician, Jack, who said that Ricky was bringing the boys in to see him a couple of times a week, and they were normal, healthy kids. Jack and I had been friends since our fraternity days, and he said, "Norman, this isn't good. I really think Ricky needs some help. I'll be glad to refer you to someone if you like."

I took Ricky to see a therapist, and he recommended a local mental health facility. After three weeks and several electric shock treatments, she came home and seemed to return to normality, although her memory was a bit faulty. Over time, there were a couple of other episodes and, although she responded to counseling, I was wary of provoking a relapse, as I still cared for her as a person and did not want to see her break down completely. Melanie was very forbearing, in view of the circumstances, but she wanted to get married and was beginning to despair of my ever getting a divorce.

Flying continued to be a problem for me, and I always fortified myself with a drink or two before boarding a plane. Then, in 1971, my fear of flying disappeared at long last. Melanie and I were living in Manhattan, and I had just arrived home from a business trip when my sister called to say that my mother had taken some medical tests and the results were alarmingly abnormal. She was scheduled to undergo exploratory surgery the next day. I repacked my bags and set out for Kennedy again.

We had been in flight for about forty minutes when I discovered that I was perfectly calm. I wasn't listening to the changes in pitch of the engines. My hands were not perspiring. I tried to figure out the reason for this striking change in my perspective. It suddenly dawned on me that the warning lights in my brain, the ones that told me when to worry about my safety on a plane, were now telling me to worry about the perilous prognosis for my mother. I was thinking about her safety, not my own. My fear of flying never returned, though my claustrophobia still requires that I have an aisle seat.

The exploratory showed colon cancer, too advanced to benefit from surgery. My mother moved in with my sister, whose husband was a doctor and could check on her every day. My brother and I scheduled weekend visits every month. Melanie and I would fly down and he would drive up from Atlanta with Rhoda, his fiancée.

My mother loved the attention. She took to Melanie immediately, taught her to make challah, then thoroughly enjoyed the wonderful French toast the bread provided for breakfast.

Fortunately, she didn't seem to be in great discomfort. She chose to ignore that she had cancer, and none of us ever spoke of it. For her, this seemed to be the better way. She lived each day and refused to spend her precious time worrying about the future. She simply enjoyed the last two years of her life surrounded by my sister's four adoring children, all much younger than mine, who eagerly kept her amused. My boys were old enough to drive down on their own and visited when they could. I'm sorry she didn't live to see Melanie and me get married, but I knew how pleased she was for me on our first visit, when she said, "I don't know when I've seen you so happy."

If my son David was upset by my moving in with Melanie, he never showed it. Within a few weeks, he began to visit us for dinner and never seemed ill at ease. It took about two months before Bob broke the ice, and he usually came over with his brother or with a friend. I knew how tough it was for him, but it was a great source of relief to know that I still had the love of my sons.

Melanie's mother, Renée, didn't know that we were living together. In fact, she didn't even know me. She discovered our relationship by accident. Melanie had given her a key to our apartment, feeling that the gesture would indicate that there was nothing to hide and she wouldn't come snooping. But on Valentine's Day, Renée came by during the day to leave flowers and noticed my clothing hanging in the closet. The cat was out of the bag. Melanie's father had died when she was six and her only relatives, besides her mother, were her brother, Fred, an uncle and aunt, and two female cousins. I can imagine the conversations within the family. They could find no pluses in this liaison, only minuses. Even I would have been hard put to refute their conclusion.

Melanie said, "You know we're going to have to invite Mom over for dinner one night."

Since I went to New Jersey every Sunday to see my sons, I suggested, "Why don't you have her over on Sunday?"

"No. She wants to meet you. You're going to have to meet her sometime, Love." Finally, I couldn't postpone it any longer and we invited her over on a Friday evening. I'd fortified myself with four drinks before she arrived. She was an elegantly dressed, patrician woman wearing a mink coat, and only eleven years older than me. It was one of the most awkward and wretched evenings I ever spent. I made drinks for the three of us and served them in the living room.

One of her first questions was, "I assume there is a Mrs. Bussel?"

"Yes, there is indeed, and we plan to be divorced."

"I see. And when will the decree become final?"

"I don't know that yet."

Having been editor of *True Detective Magazine* for almost ten years, she knew exactly how to question the accused. I had several more drinks while undergoing her third-degree procedure, and although the booze eased the torture to some extent, it didn't add to my coherence and I succeeded in digging myself a very deep hole.

Actually, Renée was a remarkable woman. A French national, born in Italy of an Austrian mother, she had come to the United States at the age of fourteen with her parents and brother, speaking not a word of English. After receiving degrees from Hunter College and a masters in journalism from Columbia University, she became an editor and eventually wrote a book about the Mafia. No one could ever detect from her impeccable English that she was foreign-born.

Although Melanie and I continued to fulfill our obligations at the office (and ours was the most successful profit center in the company), my feelings of guilt grew worse by the day. I was guilty about having left my family; I was guilty about drawing a young woman into the terrible vortex of a POW's nightmare; I was guilty that the divorce was not forthcoming; and, of course, the survivor's guilt that had become embedded in my psyche when our plane blew up over Berlin was just as crippling as it had been more than twenty years ago. Too often, in the throes of a nightmare, I would flail about in my sleep, and sometimes I would strike Melanie. She knew that it was inadvertent, but that didn't lessen the shock of being awakened from a sound sleep by my thrashing arms or legs. Luckily, I never really injured her. Loud noises still destroyed me. The sound of a car's backfire, a neighbor's slamming door, firecrackers, sounds that wouldn't cause most people to even turn their heads, would instantly shatter my nerves and send me running for a drink.

April 29, the date of our last mission, the date that my four crew members were killed, was still a very solemn day for me. I no longer had the *Memphis Belle* to sit in and drink a toast to their memory. On the night of April 29, 1970, Melanie had choir practice and I sat alone in the dark living room drinking from a newly opened quart of Scotch. In the solitude, all my guilt came crashing down on me and I became deeply despondent and self-pitying. I validated thoughts of suicide by the notion that everyone would be much better off without me. Especially Melanie.

By the time Melanie got home, I was pretty well smashed. She didn't ask why I was drinking. I had told her the story of April 29. She took the bottle away, put my feet up on the couch, and covered me with a blanket. I raved about failing to keep my promise to marry her; how worthless I was and how I was dragging her down. "I'm going to leave and let you live a normal life."

"Go to sleep. This is not the time to talk about anything. We'll discuss it in the morning." Then she went to bed.

I couldn't sleep. The more I thought about my situation, the more despairing I became. Through the half-open window, I could hear someone's radio. The Beatles were playing *"When I find myself in times of trouble, Mother Mary comes to me, speaking words of wisdom, let it be-ee."*

I got up, put on a jacket, and went to the door. Melanie heard the click of the lock opening and came running down the hallway. "Where are you going? It's almost eleven-thirty."

"I'm just going for a walk. I'll be back in a few minutes."

"Wait till I get dressed. I'll go with you."

"No, you go back to sleep. I won't be long."

She ran to the bedroom to get her clothes, and I hurried out the door.

There were quite a number of people on First Avenue leaving the restaurants and bars. At first, I just walked aimlessly, looking into the bars as I passed. I wasn't tempted to go in. I had never been a pub crawler. I kept walking slowly, and then I was at the 59th Street Bridge. I didn't like heights, but I walked toward the bridge anyway. I looked at my watch, and it was not yet midnight. I always had a premonition that I would die on April 29. I stood at the railing a long while, staring down at the slowly moving dark water. It looked mysterious, ominous. Frightening. I climbed up and sat on the railing. I thought about jumping through the bomb bay of our B-17 seven seconds before it exploded. Then someone's arms encircled me from behind, dragging me off the railing. I turned my head . . . to see Melanie. Her face was drained of color. She didn't say anything, just took my arm and led me home.

In bed, we held each other tightly and she began to cry. Soon I was weeping as well, deep, racking sobs that convulsed my whole body. She pulled my head to her breast and there I fell asleep.

Days passed before we were able to talk about the incident. I swore that I would never again try to take my life. I asked her how she knew where to find me. She said she didn't know. That it was only a hunch. A wild-assed hunch, and a lucky one.

Melanie thought it would relieve some of the pressure if we could get out of the city on weekends, so we bought a used car. We tried alternate-side-of-the-street parking, which required moving the car every day, a lengthy and frustrating procedure. We finally found space in a nearby parking lot at a monthly fee that was higher than the rent for our apartment.

It seemed that everyone was trying to help me close the generation gap, including my kids. Every Sunday, when I visited in New Jersey, David tried to get me to smoke pot with him. I always said it was a ridiculous pastime and refused. One day, I gave in and said I'd take a few puffs. Ten minutes later, I told him I felt absolutely no different, and he was obviously disappointed. A few weeks later, he induced me to try again, and again I had not the slightest reaction. I said, "This is a stupid waste of time and I can't imagine why you do it."

I thought he had given up, until one Sunday he said, "Daddy, I've got some real good shit this time, and I guarantee you'll get a high out of it."

"Look, when I was a kid, my friends and I used to smoke dried corn silk rolled in newspaper and make believe it was a cigarette. I'd rather smoke a Camel than this junk. At least I get some enjoyment from it."

"Daddy, if you'll just smoke this one joint, just this one, and it doesn't do anything for you, I promise I'll never bother you to try grass again."

"Okay. One last time. And if I don't feel anything, which I won't, don't ever even think of asking me again."

I smoked the joint and . . . nothing. He kept asking me how I felt, and I said, "Not any different than I did a few minutes ago."

Ricky wanted to go to the food store, so David and I drove her there and waited in the car. After a while, we went inside the store. As we stood there watching the shoppers, I began to giggle, and

David asked me what was so funny. "Isn't it hilarious that these people are walking around looking as serious as scientists while they're putting things into their carts? What's so solemn about buying groceries?"

David was delighted. "Daddy, you're stoned."

"Don't be silly. Why do you say that?"

I didn't feel that my thinking was out of the ordinary, but he got a load of satisfaction out of getting me stoned. When I got home, I told Melanie about my experience and she agreed with David. "Were you hungry afterward?"

"Well, yeah, I ate a lot for lunch, but what's that got to do with it?"

"Believe me, Love, he got you stoned."

When I took my jacket off, I felt something in my pocket. I reached in and pulled out two joints. I called David and asked, "Did you put two joints in my pocket?"

He said, "Yes."

"Suppose I had been stopped by a cop? I could be in big trouble now."

"Daddy, you look so damned straight, no cop's ever gonna stop you."

Melanie played the guitar and had a lovely voice, so she was in demand to sing anti-Vietnam War songs. I had never been in favor of the war, but the songs were not familiar to me, so I had to learn the lyrics to ballads like Tom Paxton's:

"Lyndon Johnson told the nation, have no fear of escalation, I am trying everyone to please. Though it isn't really war, we're sending fifty-thousand more to help save Vietnam from the Vietnamese."

Bob would take us over to his friends, Bruce and Sue, for weed and wine parties. Their red house, appropriately called The Red House, was in New Jersey. I remember sitting on the floor at one end of the living room, having a long discussion with Bruce about how the opposite end of the room was at least five feet higher than where we were sitting. The generation gap could never be completely closed, and although I was beginning to have a much better grasp of the boomer philosophy, I found the decibel level of the music shattering. I still didn't dig my sons' concept of "distressed" jeans with bare knees sticking out and hair so long it made the Beatles' tonsorial style look like a crew cut by comparison. But I stopped carping about their appearance and took pride in their desire for peace, equality, and tolerance.

My desperate subterfuge did not improve. It could never improve until I was free to marry Melanie. Even a fugitive from the law could take evasive measures to avoid detection. He could move to a locale where no one knew him. He could affect a disguise. But I could be spotted walking with Melanie anywhere in Manhattan and beyond. I couldn't even be completely relaxed on vacation. We enjoyed going to Caribbean islands but, even though the odds were great that we'd never cross paths with someone from PG, what if we did? And if we didn't travel outside the country, I shied away from large cities. We had sales offices in New York, Chicago, and San Francisco, and our reps covered the U.S. My paranoia was unbounded.

Although my edginess worsened by the day, I was able to remain outwardly calm at the office. People on our staff would comment to Melanie about my aplomb during a publishing crisis. She said she longed to tell them, "Right. You should see him when he gets home."

Ricky called one day to say she was going to Miami to visit relatives. Her cousin Jack, a doctor who had been a friend of mine in high school, lived there, and I knew she would see him. She often asked Jack for advice, and I knew she trusted his judgment. In my desperation, I decided to write to him and ask for his help. I told him how long Melanie and I had been together and that our relationship was permanent. I explained that this charade had been going on for almost four years, that I couldn't handle the pressure any longer, and I wanted Ricky and our children to be able to just move on.

When Ricky returned to New Jersey, I spoke with her again, and this time she agreed to give me a divorce. Whatever Jack told her must have worked. Through the years, I had taken from my income barely enough to subsist on, and Melanie had paid almost all of our expenses. Even though I would now be sending Ricky monthly alimony checks and paying off the large amount of credit-card debt she had accumulated, plus putting Bob through Cornell, I would finally have financial liquidity. And best of all, Melanie and I could be married.

The divorce decree came through on a Monday; we got our marriage license on Wednesday, and on Saturday the ceremony was performed by a justice of the peace in Orangeburg, New York. The service didn't take long because the JP had to take his son to a Yankee game. My son David was my best man. My son Bob didn't attend, I assumed out of what he felt was loyalty to his mother.

Melanie's Uncle Lou lived near Orangeburg, where the wedding ceremony was held, and we went to his house afterward for a reception. Later, we all changed into shorts and played frisbee. It was just a wedding in June, with only eleven guests, but how sweet it was. That evening, we drove back to Manhattan and dropped Melanie's mother off at her apartment on East 77th Street and had our first night together as man and wife.

It was an ending . . . and it was a beginning. It was the end of the most protracted period of mental torture I had ever endured. I'm sure that my POW experience made me much more vulnerable and hypersensitive than I might have been. And it was the beginning of another liberation—freedom from the constant fear of being exposed. In retrospect, I know that my reaction to our situation was grossly exaggerated. What would have been the consequences if we had been found out? We wouldn't have been stoned to death. We wouldn't have faced a firing squad. The worst that could have happened was that we'd lose our jobs. But that's looking at it from a rational point of view, and I was incapable of seeing it from that perspective. Sure, I could have forced the issue. I could have stopped sending Ricky money, and she would have had no alternative except to agree to a divorce, but I couldn't bring myself to impose such an ultimatum and risk the possibility of her having a relapse, or having our children bear the brunt of their parents' dispute.

We spent that Sunday speculating about how management was going to handle our announcement the next day. We both felt that one of us would be asked to leave, but there was a great sense of relief that the pretense was finally over. Melanie said that she would offer to leave because she was making the lesser salary and could find another job more quickly. I said, "I don't think we're going to have the option of making that decision. Let's just wait until tomorrow and see what their reaction is."

On Monday morning, I called our senior vice president and said that I needed to talk with him. He was totally surprised when I told him that Melanie and I had gotten married over the weekend. "Well congratulations, Norm! I didn't even know you two were seeing each other. Wow, talk about coming out of left field. We'll have to figure out how we're going to tell the office. Just hold off on telling anyone until I decide how we're going to announce it."

I went back to my office and told Melanie that we were on hold, while protocol was being examined. As we spoke, my phone rang and it was the senior VP. "Look, I don't see any reason to hold off any longer. You guys are legally married. Hell, tell anybody you want. Okay? And again, let me wish you the very best. I'll have my secretary call headquarters so your records can be changed." His secretary later told Melanie, "When I called to have your records updated, the woman I spoke with said that the company didn't employ married couples, and I told her that my boss said they ran the most successful profit center in the company, so don't rock the boat."

Melanie continued to work with me for the next five years, until she was offered a job with a firm that managed medical-education seminars for doctors. Attracted by the title of vice president, the higher salary, and the perceived glamour of the position, she left PG for what appeared to be greener pastures, only to discover that the minute attention to detail was maddening and the required travel was much more than she had expected. About a year later, she resigned and formed her own company, publishing marketing information for manufacturers who sold products to retail drug store chains. In a role reversal, she became president of her company and I ultimately went to work for her in a business we operated successfully for twenty years until we both retired.

About a year after our wedding, we managed to buy a house in Westchester County, New York, and it was a wonderful change for both of us. After five years in Manhattan, I reveled in the fact that I no longer had to walk to Central Park to see a tree, and Melanie loved the space and being able to have guests over for a weekend.

My brother, Alan, had gotten married and drove up from Atlanta with his wife to spend a week with us. We had a barbecue and invited family and some of Alan's friends from the New York area. He really enjoyed seeing everyone, but he felt a bit tired because of a low-grade fever, which he attributed to recent dental work, and he promised to see a doctor when he returned home.

Alan had been back in Atlanta for ten days when my sister called one afternoon to tell me that he'd been eating lunch in a restaurant near the campus when he collapsed and was taken by ambulance to a hospital. Melanie and I flew down that evening.

When we entered the ICU, he was lying in bed breathing normally, he had good color, his skin was warm to my touch, and the medical apparatus was rhythmically lifting up and down as it pumped oxygen into his lungs. I ran my hand up and down his arm, expecting him to open his eyes and greet me with, "Hey, Big Brother. Fooled you, didn't I?" He was thirty-four years old, just married, already widely known for his journalistic research, only months away from earning his Ph.D. . . . and he was brain-dead. Endomyocarditis, an infection and inflammation of the lining of a heart valve, in his case resulting from a dental infection, had caused him to throw an embolism, which traveled to his brain and quickly snuffed out his young life.

We brought Alan back to Memphis for burial. I knew he had many friends, but I hadn't expected such a large turnout. It seemed that his warmth, his humor, his generosity had touched everyone he ever met, and hundreds came to pay their respects. Shortly, a journalism scholarship program was established in his memory at Memphis State.

Melanie and I went back to New York. Back to work. Back to resume our normal lives. But for me, there was a part of my life that would never be the same again. A little boy who had come into my life when I was seventeen years old was gone. I fed him a bottle; changed his diapers; watched him grow up and become an avid reader; a budding writer; a ham radio operator; an intern reporter; and a college professor. Gone forever. Gone like the four other "brothers" on my crew.

Chapter Twenty-one

POWs Healing POWs

They cannot heal who have not suffered much
For only sorrow, sorrow understands
They will not come for healing at your touch
Who have not seen the scars upon your hands

Anon.

I n 1980, I stopped drinking. There was no plan. No one took me by the hand and led me to an AA meeting. No great epiphany suddenly showed me the light. It came about quite simply. We were invited to Melanie's uncle's house for dinner and arrived in late afternoon. I drank a beer, ate some nibbles, and later had a gin and tonic before dinner. Then I began to feel physically distressed. Nothing gastric . . . more of a wooziness. That seemed too small an amount of alcohol to cause my reaction, and I decided right then and there that my body was trying to tell me something, and I determined that I wouldn't drink again. Now and then, I'll treat myself to a non-alcoholic beer, but I haven't had a drop of the real stuff since. About a year later, I gave up cigarettes. I smoked a pipe for a while; but when my internist asked me if I still smoked, I said, "Only a pipe and I don't inhale that."

"Really. And what happens to all the smoke that floats around your face when you're puffing up a storm? Don't you think you're inhaling that?"

I put my pipes and all the paraphernalia that goes with them into a desk drawer, where they still lie. Which was harder to give up? Well, it wasn't the tobacco. I can mix drinks for guests and I'm not tempted, but when Melanie and I are home alone and she's enjoying a Canadian on the rocks, I sometimes pick up her glass and inhale the full-bodied aroma of the whiskey . . . then hand it back. During the first few years of my abstinence, I often came very close to falling off the wagon during extremely stressful times. Now I know that's no longer an option, and it never crosses my mind to seek out a bottle.

Of course, cutting off my "medication" took away my crutch, and I "limped" through many an evening of emotional turmoil. My mood could change in an instant from mirth to depression. My startle response was so exaggerated that if Melanie dropped a spoon in the kitchen, and I didn't see it falling, I would become so unstrung that I'd leave the room without finishing my meal. I knew that my over-reaction would make Melanie feel guilty; but if I were to continue eating, I would become ill. I explained, "I'm not blaming you. I know that you didn't drop the spoon on purpose. But if I were holding on to a tomato stake while you drove it into the ground in the garden, and you missed and struck my hand, it wouldn't be any less painful because it was accidental."

Without the "medication," my nightmares became more frequent and vivid, as did flashbacks, and I couldn't seem to pull myself out of this mental morass. I talked it over with Melanie, and we agreed I needed help. Our company medical plan covered psychological counseling, but even though this treatment was declared to be "confidential," I didn't dare take the chance. Besides, I didn't believe that private psychologists would be qualified to treat post-traumatic stress disorder. What would they know about combat-related mental problems?

For many years, rumors of veterans receiving inferior care at Veterans Administration hospitals abounded, and not without some basis in fact. But by the time these rumors made the rounds, the accounts had grown into real horror stories and vets stayed away from VA medical centers in droves. Besides, most of them were covered by medical insurance at their places of employment. Since VA hospitals were underutilized, the federal government had a good excuse to decrease funding for expansion or modernization of these facilities. When the Vietnam War ended, the picture suddenly changed as thousands of returning vets sought medical and psychological treatment. VA hospitals were upgraded to accommodate the surge in patients, and all vets benefited from vastly improved treatment.

After reading a newspaper article about a mental health clinic at the Montrose VA Medical Center, about twenty-five minutes from my home, I decided to give it a try. I found the staff there most considerate and sympathetic to my problems, and I was prescribed an anti-anxiety medication. I found that it did help to calm me down, but I used it very sparingly because I feared I would become dependent on it, just as I had been on alcohol.

My claustrophobia, always a problem since my days in solitary at the Frankfurt interrogation center, was becoming worse. I was reacting more to crowded places. I had long ago given up on going to movies, and restaurants were still a problem, as was the hour-long train ride to Manhattan.

I could deal with the commute until all seats were taken and there was standing room only. I always had a seat, because I boarded the train at its origin, but I had to be on the aisle, for quick egress, and if the train became crowded and people were towering over me, I would leave my seat and stand in the open space between cars. The most terrifying situation was going through the underground passage leading into Grand Central terminal during rush hour, when rail traffic was most heavy. At various points in the tunnel, my train would stop to give the right-of-way to another train. Depending on where the pause occurred, the train could disconnect from the electrical power system and lose lights and air conditioning momentarily . . . except for the times when it wasn't only momentary. Those times were not infrequent, and the train might remain immobile for several seconds or several minutes . . . what seemed like an eternity.

I refused to take an anti-anxiety pill every morning in anticipation of a possible crisis on the train, but if I waited until a crisis occurred, the pill wouldn't work fast enough to save me from a desperate incident. Sitting in a pitch-dark, stalled train on a summer day, the passengers seemed to immediately suck all the air out of the car and, with the AC off, the heat became unbearable. At once, it became impossible for me to draw a full breath. It felt as if my clothing had become too tight, squeezing my chest and body, inhibiting my breathing. I would remove my jacket, loosen my tie, unbutton my shirt, unbuckle my belt, and even unlace my shoes. With each labored partial inhalation . . . I believed I was going to lose consciousness.

Around 1984, Melanie saw an ad in a local newspaper inviting former POWs to attend the meeting of a newly installed chapter of American Ex-Prisoners of War. The group was meeting at the United States Military Academy at West Point, New York on a Saturday. I was inherently not a joiner. I didn't belong to any veterans' organizations and was not enthusiastic about going to this meeting. But at Melanie's insistence, I called the number listed and was urged by chapter commander Bob Flood to join them for lunch and to bring my wife.

The meeting was not at all what I expected. Within ten minutes, I was speaking with guys who had been in the same POW camps, on the same marches, on the same train rides as I had. And even though we had never met, we had all suffered the same cruelty and deprivation, and we connected immediately. I had walked into a roomful of buddies, and I felt perfectly comfortable discussing topics that I would never talk about with non-POWs. I was relieved to know that my phobias were not peculiar to me alone. That others suffered the exact same symptoms. It was a great relief to know that I was not unique. That I was not afflicted with some progressive insanity that would one day destroy my mind.

It was also a revelation for Melanie. By talking with wives who had been married to POWs twenty years longer than she had, she discovered that on occasions when I went off the deep end, it was not her fault. She was able to stop beating up on herself for feeling that she had provoked an ongoing syndrome over which, in reality, she had no more control than I.

Soon we began to have lunch with other POWs and their wives in between our monthly meetings. I found out that if I was confronted with a stressful situation, I could call another POW and talk out my problem. There was not always a solution, but it was helpful to have someone you trusted concur with a course of action that may not have been right for the general population, but was appropriate for my POW mentality.

Before long, I was elected adjutant, then chapter commander. I was appointed public relations director for a series of national commanders and finally became president of the American

Ex-Prisoners of War Service Foundation, the charity fund-raising arm of the national organization.

Melanie and I took accreditation courses and were appointed National Service Officers by the Veterans Administration. As volunteers, we help POWs and other veterans file claims for service-connected compensation and other benefits. Many veterans are overwhelmed by the complexities of unraveling the red tape surrounding the claims process and cannot file for their entitlements without assistance. Now, those who are treated at the VA medical center where we work have Melanie and me to help.

Filing claims for former POWs can be particularly difficult, because injuries suffered when they were captured and illnesses occurring during imprisonment cannot be documented. Medical treatment was rare and, of course, there were no records to confirm that a POW had been treated. Eventually, the VA had to address this problem and, prodded by the lobbying of POWs, they decided to approve certain illnesses as "presumptives." No longer did a POW have the difficulty of proving that some infirmities were a result of his imprisonment. Bills were passed that required the VA to presume that they were.

Now, new findings are helping other veterans establish links between combat conditions and illnesses that show up later in life. The Associated Press and the *New York Times* recently reported that a study of 1,946 male vets of World War II and Korea revealed that those with symptoms of post-traumatic stress disorder are at greater risk of heart attacks as they age. This group also has more autoimmune diseases such as arthritis and psoriasis.

A second study of 2,863 soldiers, funded by the Army, found that combat vets from Iraq with PTSD reported worse physical health, more doctors' visits, and more missed work days. The study was published in the January 1, 2007 issue of the *American Journal of Psychiatry*. Laura Kubzansky, of the Harvard School of Public

Health and lead author of the first study, who studies anxiety, depression, and anger as risk factors for heart disease, said, "The burden of war may be even greater than people think."

One of the most frustrating aspects of filing claims for POWs is that most of them are in denial. A good example is a POW who came to our office recently and said with embarrassment, "I don't think I qualify for any compensation. My wife made me come."

"Well, let's go over a few things, and we'll tell you if you qualify. How is your general health? Any heart problems?"

"Oh, no. I recently had a quadruple bypass. My heart is fine."

"Was it very cold in your camp?"

"Aw, man, it was freezing. They didn't give us any coal for our stove. And standing roll calls when the temperature was in the single numbers was brutal."

"Do you suffer in the winter, now, when you are outdoors?"

"No. Well . . . I can't walk in the snow any more. My feet and hands begin to hurt. And even when it's not so cold, my knees kill me."

"Do you ever feel anxious? Are you upset by loud noises? How are you in crowded places?"

"I think I'm okay there. I do worry some about things happening to my family. And firecrackers make me nuts. No, I don't go where it's crowded. If there's a lot of people, I stay away."

Then we asked him to recount his experiences in combat and as a POW for inclusion with his statement of claim.

As he recalled his capture in the Battle of the Bulge and remembered buddies who were killed that day, he began to perspire, wring his hands, and choke up. He had to stop for a minute or two before continuing. It's always difficult to ask combat vets to dredge up those horrible memories, but it is an important part of their record and necessary in evaluating their claims.

A few months later, he was awarded 100% compensation for

several illnesses, not the least of which was PTSD. When he was notified of his award, he called me in disbelief, and I assured him that it was authentic. Now, if he predeceases his wife, his compensation will cease, but she will be eligible for a smaller amount of monthly benefits as his widow.

This is probably the most fulfilling job I've ever had. Helping older veterans and surviving spouses, who are financially strapped, obtain earned benefits is a deeply rewarding experience.

The number of Vietnam War clients we serve is constantly increasing. Most of them are young enough to be my kids. While World War II vets "medicated" themselves with alcohol, our Vietnam counterparts, unfortunately, found other drugs available as well, and some were never able to shake loose from their dependency. Psychological group counseling is offered by the VA, and those who avail themselves of this privilege often show progress; but for some, in the merciless grip of substance abuse . . . it may be too late.

With World War II vets dying at the rate of about 1,500 a day, the era of this military generation is coming to a close. For World War II POWs, the rate of demise is probably a few percentage points higher than for non-POWs. I recently saw an Aussie who had been a POW during World War II, being interviewed on television. He made a trenchant statement about POWs that I totally agree with: "You couldn't make it as a POW without a mate." In Germany, we often had more than one "mate" to look out for us. I've seen POWs nurse buddies back to health. I've seen them watch out for each other's precious food rations. I've seen them bunk together to keep from freezing. And I've seen them help each other walk, as they limped along on marches, when the strength of both combined would not have been enough to lift a bucket of water.

POWs still don't leave other POWs behind. More and more, World War II POWs are becoming unable to drive and they often depend on other POW buddies for transportation to medical appointments or meetings. And they don't feel ill at ease about asking, because they know that, under the same circumstances, if they were the ones still mobile, they wouldn't hesitate one second to offer their assistance. It's interesting that men of so many different backgrounds—educational, religious, social, economic, racial—can come together as brothers, bonded forever by the shared experience of being POWs.

Chapter Twenty-two

My PTSD and My Family:
The Effect in Retrospect

Over the years, I've done enough introspection to know exactly where I screwed up in my life. But my life was not lived in a vacuum, and I also am aware that my decades-long struggle with PTSD profoundly affected my marriage and my children. How and to what extent, I never knew. Frankly, I didn't have the courage to ask. Early on, I honestly didn't want to hear them say that what I had done was unfair, cowardly, or selfish, because that's the way I judged myself. My guilt pail was already full to overflowing; much like the slop bucket on the German boxcar, guilt sloshed over me in an unrelenting torrent. But my memoir would be incomplete if I didn't learn and disclose what impact my years of psychological turmoil had on my sons. I believe that my separate conversations with David and Bob were more painful for me than for them, because I was the one whose actions had caused them distress. They were the innocents. I want to thank them again for their candor, for their sensitivity, and especially for their love and understanding, without which we could never have addressed this subject at all.

No one can live with a PTSD sufferer and come away unaffected. The degree to which a victim of this disorder can control his symptoms is often a fair measurement of the extent to which his family may be affected. Too often, I had difficulty maintaining control. The fact that I worked long hours and was unable to spend much time with my sons when they were small left me with mixed feelings of regret and relief. Regret that those precious years were lost forever, and relief that the boys were less exposed to my dark side. Of course, as soon as the thought of relief because of my absence crosses my mind, I realize that I am indulging in self-pity. Given the chance to relive those years, I know that my sons and I would gladly choose more time together, even at the risk that my often-depressed state might have touched their lives more adversely.

My conversation with each son evoked different memories, except for one mutual recollection: both of them emphasized my hairtrigger temper. David said, "You were very quick to anger, and I was afraid of you because Mom used you as an enforcer. On account of Mom's phobias, Bob and I were much more restricted than other kids. We couldn't go more than a few doors away to play and weren't allowed to cross streets, even though few cars drove through our neighborhood. As we got older, it became embarrassing for Mom to walk us to school every day, especially since there was a crossing guard at the one street with any amount of traffic. Grandma was also a worrier and she reinforced and probably expanded Mom's fears. I remember complaining to you two or three times and you tried to get them to open up our boundaries a bit, but I saw how futile that was and I decided to stop getting you upset by sending you into a battle you couldn't win.

"I guess I was rebelling against what I felt was patently unfair, so I constantly broke the 'rules' in protest, and as soon as you came home at night, Mom would report my misdeeds for the day; you would explode and the household would be in turmoil.

"My years of alcoholism really had nothing to do with you. I don't remember seeing you drunk more than twice. I began to drink because I didn't fit in socially, and then I got hooked. As for my gambling, the thrill didn't come from winning. Even when I won at the track, I would continue to bet on other races because the thrill was in the betting. And no, it wouldn't have made any difference if you'd tried to talk with me. My ears were closed, and nothing would have changed until that period of my life ran its course."

David told me that he wasn't surprised when he learned that I was leaving his mother. He said that he felt our marriage was "contrived" and "lacked substance." I never sensed any resentment on his part, nor felt awkward in his presence. Three and a half years older than Bob, he had lived on his own, taken a few hard knocks, and acquired some worldliness in the process. For Bob, on the other hand, our breakup was a complete surprise, and his heartbreak ripped me apart. When we spoke recently, he said, "I always admired you as such a stand-up guy, and suddenly I felt abandoned and deceived; my world was turned upside down. As a freshman in college away from home for the first time, I was vulnerable and uncertain; so, for me, losing the security of an intact parental unit was enormously unsettling. I don't know why, but David and I never did discuss your moving out. Luckily, I found a group of friends who provided me with a sense of caring and connection that enabled me to weather the shock of your leaving Mom.

"I remember your volatility, your distress when you had to discipline David, your unhappiness working with Grandpa. I didn't know of any way I could chase off the pall of sadness that so often hung over our family, and the only way I could think to help was to be a good kid. Part of that was to do well in school, and that seemed to place me under extra pressure.

"I only recall your drinking a couple of times, when you stayed in the city to have cocktails with some associates, slept on the bus past our stop, and Mom had to drive to the end of the line to pick you up.

"You never spoke with us about the war, or being a POW, so I really knew nothing about your experience. Then, about twenty years ago, you were about to depart for a visit to England and felt that I should know something about your history in World War II. You let me read a statement that you had written for the Veterans Administration, and as I finished it I began to sob. I always thought that you were so strong, but then I realized that the ordeal of your imprisonment had sapped your strength and reduced you to a mere mortal."

David's first marriage could not survive his heavy drinking and compulsive gambling. I guess Ricky and I were both enablers, because whenever his situation became desperate enough, we bailed him out. Therapists told me that he had to hit rock bottom before he could start to recover. I didn't know how much farther he could fall and still be alive.

Then, about ten years ago, he stopped drinking, stayed away from the track, and began going to AA meetings. Today he is happily married to Lydia, works for an office-supply company, and is in his senior year at Rutgers University, where he has exceeded the requirements for the dean's list every semester. I no longer give him a dollar for each good report card, but I'm just as proud of his accomplishments at age sixty as I was at six. I'm glad he's able to forget about yesterday. What's past is past. Happiness is today.

Bob graduated from Cornell in 1973. He finished in just over three years to help me with his tuition costs. When he landed his first job, he called me immediately.

"Hi, Daddy. I got a job!"

"That's great, Babe. Who are you working for?"

"The Farm Worker's Union. You've heard about them."

"I sure have. César Chavez. Pretty good salary?"

"Well, not much to start with. I'll be getting five dollars a week plus room and board."

The puff of cigarette smoke I had just inhaled stuck in my throat, and I couldn't stop coughing. Was this as far as a degree from an Ivy League school could get him?

"Are you okay?"

"Yeah, this cigarette made me cough. Well, that's not a lot to live on. I hope you'll be getting increases right along."

"I'll be able to make it okay. And I'm really interested in what the organization is doing."

"Well, congratulations, good luck, and all that. Let me know if you need anything."

After a while, Bob went to work for the Amalgamated Clothing Workers Union and enrolled in night courses at Rutgers, where he earned a masters degree. He met and married Jewel Nelson and worked to help her through a masters at Alfred University. She, in turn, worked to help him when he returned to Cornell to enter a Ph.D. program in history. Their daughter, Lily, was born in Ithaca, not far from the Cornell campus. Bob was still being a "good kid," and I was making progress in controlling my temper.

Bob continued doing union work, but I had a sense that he missed the halls of academe, so I wasn't surprised when he accepted an offer from Penn State to teach in its labor-education program. While at Penn State, he authored the book *From Harvard to the Ranks of Labor, Powers Hapgood and the American Working Class.* Ten years later, he was recruited to be Director of the University of Oregon's Labor Education and Research Center, in Eugene, and he now resides there with his family, joined by Lily's precocious little sister, Ayla.

Almost every father has the sincere desire to infuse his children with the principles of justice. The accomplishment of this goal is not something parents often speak about. Our pride is evinced by the role our children assume in society, and I am deeply gratified by the fair-minded men my sons have grown to be. But I can think of no greater source of fulfillment than when a child thanks a parent for helping to mold his character. At the end of my discussion with Bob, he said, "Daddy, I also want to say that my sense of right and wrong, and my concerns about injustice, derive in no small part from my appreciation for your heroism in the fight against fascism and your visceral revulsion against all forms of intolerance and bigotry."

I have a jacket full of medals from my service in World War II, and Bob's commendation can't be pinned on my tunic, but it's capable of bursting more buttons as my chest proudly expands than all of the metal ones combined.

And then there's Ricky. Generous, loyal, tireless, with rancor toward none, her life was dedicated to caring for her mother and her sons. We never alluded to the whys and wherefores of my leaving, though we spoke often on the phone. She was always calling to talk about what the kids were doing, or to ask advice about a car problem or an investment. When her uncle died in Philadelphia, I drove her down for the closing on a house he had left her, because she was nervous about handling the details alone.

Ricky and I never stopped being friends, and her inherent kindness even extended to Melanie, with whom she also became friendly. We would go to her place for the Passover seder with the boys and their families, and all of them would join us at our home for Thanksgiving dinner. It was a civilized way for extended families to enjoy holidays, and we spent many happy hours together.

On November 15, 1999, Ricky passed away at her home in New Jersey at the age of seventy-eight. I'm glad that her funeral was a celebration of her life, because that's the way she would have wanted it. Sure there was sadness, but there was also humor as David and Bob spoke about their mother's malapropisms, which were often intentional, her enduring kindness, and her passion in life to feed anything that moved. I shall be forever grateful to Ricky for allowing me to remain her friend . . . and for her assuaging generosity in telling me, so long ago, "Norman, I don't want you feeling guilty about this. I do understand."

Chapter Twenty-three

POW PROFILE

E very liberated POW comes home with emotional baggage. The "weight" of this baggage can't be determined by the severity of his suffering. Most POWs were wounded but received no medical care. Most endured one or more beatings during confinement. All were starved. All were exposed to the elements without adequate clothing or shoes. But the degree of physical injury, or deprivation, can't be used as a measurement of psychological damage. Each individual has his own mental tolerance level, and that is the only deciding factor.

George Hamby, one of my roommates at Stalag Luft IV, is an example of how quickly a POWs mind can be affected by his capture. I didn't know George before we became POWs, but we were both shot down on the same day, April 29, 1944, on a Berlin raid. We were in the first group of sixty-five men to arrive at Stalag Luft IV; we were assigned to the same room and became good friends.

Over the next ten months, George remained tightly wound, manic, always speaking excitedly, always on edge. I last saw him when our camp was evacuated and he was assigned to the group that went on an 800-mile forced march, while I shipped out on a boxcar. We promised to keep in touch, but I wondered if we'd ever see each other again.

I was living in New York, when I read a notice in the ex-POW magazine, the *AXPOW Bulletin*, written by a retired colonel seeking information about a former high school class-mate from North Carolina named Roger Hess. One of my best friends at Stalag Luft IV was my roommate Roger Hess, from North Carolina.

Our standard greeting to each other was always "Ho, Norm!" "Ho, Roge!" I picked up the phone and called the colonel and, indeed, we were looking for the same buddy. He hadn't been able to locate Roger yet, so I gave him my number and said, "If you do reach him, please ask him to give me a call."

A couple of weeks later, we were having dinner and the phone rang. I heard Melanie say, "We're in the middle of dinner right now, could he call you back? And your name is?" After a short pause, she said, "I think he'll want to talk with you now." She came back into the kitchen and said, "It's for you."

When I said, "Hello," I heard a familiar voice respond, "Ho, Norm!" Chills went down my spine as I answered, "Ho, Roge!" We talked for almost an hour. He had stayed in the Air Force and retired after twenty years. Now he lived in Jacksonville and worked in the Navy shipyard. He also had the phone numbers of two other roommates: George Hamby and Nick Vargo. I promised Roge that I would visit him in Florida soon.

I phoned George the next evening and said, "Is this George Hamby?"

"Yes. Who's this?"

"Not so fast, George. Let's go back about thirty years and test your memory. I wanna see if you've forgotten your old friends."

"Who is this!"

"Do you remember the guy you used to come to and say, 'My heart's not beating. I think my heart's stopped beating'?"

There was a dead silence, then a whispered "Is this Norm Bussel? Is this Norm?" Then he was shouting, "Norm, my God. Wow! Oh wow! I've been looking for you for years and years."

In his excitement, his words were stumbling over each other. He couldn't get them out fast enough. He lived in Brookhaven, Pennsylvania, not too far from Philadelphia. He was married to his high school sweetheart, Geri, and had a grown son, George III.

"I'm in New York, George, less than three hours from Philly. Why don't we meet somewhere in between?"

"Well, I don't go that far from home. Maybe you could come to my house."

We set a date, and a month later Melanie and I drove to Brookhaven. George was looking out the window as we pulled up, and he hurried outside to greet us. We both choked up as we shared a bear hug in his yard. He'd gained quite a bit of weight, from the scrawny guy I knew in POW camp, but he was the same old George. Same voice. Same mannerisms. Though he had finally given up on growing a mustache.

As we talked about our POW days, Geri listened intently. She had never heard these stories before. George never spoke about his experiences. Geri said, "I wish George had been able to open up to me years ago. I would have had a much better understanding of his problems."

I found out that George had numerous psychological problems. For the first four years of his marriage, he didn't work. He sat on a chair in their living room, and Geri was the breadwinner. She tried her best to get him to take a job, even a menial job, just to get him out of the house, but without success. For a while George found work as a house painter, but eventually he had to give that up because some days the job might be miles away and he would panic if he had to travel more than a few blocks from his home. George was an agoraphobic, which means that he suffered from a severe anxiety condition that made him fear he might find himself in a situation that would trigger a panic attack. And the variety of phobic situations that might set him off was about as broad as his imagination. As time passed, he consistently decreased his already narrow range of mobility, until the only work he could find was a minimum-wage janitor's job at a grade school three blocks away. He worked there until his retirement, but never did progress to a higher pay standard.

The effects of his illness were broad and constraining. He and Geri could not go out together socially. Geri went on vacations by herself, or sometimes with her brother. She belonged to a bowling league. She walked several miles a day, but could not get George to accompany her, even though he was gaining too much weight from being housebound.

He couldn't go the Veteran's Hospital for treatment, because the closest one was forty-five minutes away. Though Geri's company health insurance was good, it did not cover psychological counseling, and George began seeing a private psychiatrist on his own. The cost was $50.00 per session, a huge sum back in 1950, and it all came out of Geri's salary. The sad part was that the counseling gave George no relief, because the therapist he was seeing knew nothing about treating war-related psychoses.

What is particularly regrettable is that George spent his life under such circumscribed conditions, when he was actually a very intelligent man. He was a talented artist, woodworker, and carpenter. He built a den in his basement, built an enclosed back porch, and completely gutted and remodeled his bathroom. His handiwork is all over my home, from paintings on my walls, to the mother duck and her three ducklings sitting on my lawn, to the wooden fisherman on my porch, sitting on a wharf and dangling his hooked fish over my driveway.

The first time I went to Pennsylvania to see George, he couldn't even go out for lunch in the neighborhood. Around our third visit, I talked him into going to a Chinese buffet restaurant nearby. It was like the first time he had ever eaten out. He marveled at the variety of foods available and appeared to be, if not relaxed, at least not stressed out to the point of not enjoying his meal. He and I sat on the aisle seats of our booth . . . which was good for both of us. When we were finished, I picked up the tab and George asked if he could leave the tip. I said, "Sure," and he took money out of his wallet and laid it on the table. His rustiness at dining out showed again when our waitress passed by and he called her over, pointed to the currency on the table, smiled broadly and said, "This is for you!"

Once, when we came to visit, George wasn't at home and Geri said, "He'll be back in a few minutes. He just went to get his hair cut."

"I didn't know that George drove."

"Oh, yes, he can drive, but the barber lives just around the corner and cuts George's hair in his house. He's not able to drive very far because he won't go through a traffic light."

When I found out that George was getting very little VA disability compensation, I offered to make an appointment for him to take physical and psychological exams at the Philadelphia VA Hospital, then help him file a claim for an increase. "God knows you're entitled to it, George."

"That's almost an hour away, Norm. I can't go there."

"Sure you can, George. Geri will drive you, and I'll schedule your appointment so you'll avoid rush hour."

Even though I was familiar, by now, with George's problems, I didn't anticipate that his resistance to driving to Philly would be so strong. But I kept twisting his arm and finally, reluctantly, he gave in.

When I got back home, I set up George's exam at the VA and called to tell him to mark the date on his calendar. I could hear the anxiety in his voice, but he said he would be there. Two days before the appointment, George called and said, "Norm, I just can't go to Philly. I've been up all night worrying about the drive. I'm vomiting, having diarrhea, I can't breathe. If I won a million dollars in the lottery and had to go to Philly to claim it . . . I couldn't go!"

"Hey, George, it's not worth getting sick over. I'll cancel your exam, and you stop worrying about it. I can't say I'm not disappointed, because I know you could use the money, but let me check around and see if there's anything else I can do."

When I called the VA to cancel, I asked if it were possible for someone to go to George's home and conduct the exam. The person I was speaking with seemed amused by my question and said that wasn't "feasible." In other words, the VA doesn't make house calls.

Then I came across an unusual piece of information. I learned that if a veteran was serving time in a correctional facility and wanted to file a claim with the VA, he was entitled to have someone come to the prison and do the medical exam and the paperwork.

I was acquainted with the Assistant Secretary of the VA, and I wrote him a letter explaining George's situation. I said, "The fact that George is not a felon should not disqualify him from receiving the same courtesy as someone who is incarcerated for commission of a crime."

I didn't receive a reply to my letter, but about a week later, George phoned to say, "Norm, I just got a call from the VA, and they're sending over a social worker to help me file my claim and a doctor to examine me."

I simply said, "That's great, George. Let me know how you make out."

Three months after the medical exam, I got a call from George, and his voice was brimming with excitement. "Norm, I'm sitting here at my kitchen table because I'm afraid that if I stand up I'll keel over. I'm holding a U.S. Government check in my trembling hand for more than $2,000 and it says for the month of May. Does that mean that I'll get a check like this every month?"

"That's wonderful, George! I'm delighted for you. Yes, you'll be getting a check in that amount every month from now on."

"I gotta tell you, Norm, in my entire life, I never made that much money in one month. I don't know how I can thank you."

"You just thanked me by making this phone call, buddy. You don't know how happy I am to have had a part in this, George. Just remember, this is not a gift from your Uncle Sam. This is money you earned by making a great sacrifice for your country. You're entitled to every cent you get, so just enjoy it."

I visited George several times a year and we would talk on the phone frequently. He was invariably cheerful and always interested in hearing about my travels to POW conventions and trips back to my old air base in England. I would send him postcards and pictures from the U.K., and he would hang them on the walls of his den, cherished mementoes. He had every card and letter I ever sent him. I would bring him caps from Stalag Luft IV reunions, each one imprinted with a guard tower. Some of them he wore, but most shared places of honor on his den wall, along with other memorabilia. He even had the greasy flight jacket he was wearing when I first met him, the one with the bloodstained hole in the sleeve where the German fighter pilot's bullet had penetrated his wrist.

George died in a hospital in his hometown of Brookhaven,

Pennsylvania in February 2002. A kind and gentle man who volunteered to fight for his country as an eighteen-year-old kid and paid an enormous price for his heroism. A POW whose body was liberated, but whose mind remained forever chained, captive to the nightmare of his experiences, for almost sixty years. Only his death could set him free.

Chapter Twenty-four

CAPTIVE MIND: FREEDOM ... BUT NOT RELEASE

O f all the combat veterans who serve in the United States military, POWs are likely to be the most silent about our experiences, because those experiences accurately reflect who we are today. And we don't want to share with you who we are today. Who we are today makes us uncomfortable. POWs are different from the rest of society, in ways that are so far removed from the norm that we are embarrassed to talk about them with anyone except other POWs. That's why, in therapy, it's more effective for POWs to meet in group sessions with other POWs, who can relate to their idiosyncrasies.

The phobias that resulted from our confinement are too deeply personal to discuss with friends, family, or, often, even professionals. It could take months for a psychologist, even one specializing in anxiety disorders, to draw out a POW. Some years ago, a psychologist rolled his chair near to mine and raised his voice to drive home a point. I quietly told him, "Back off. You're too close. You make me feel boxed in. And never, ever raise your voice to a POW. If you do, you're looking for trouble." He recently recalled my words of advice and thanked me for "teaching me something important about POWs," which was that POWs lead lives of controlled rage. This is a rage that we have disciplined ourselves to suppress, but smolders still in constant risk of exploding. A rage that began with our capture. We raged at our condition. We raged at our enemy for his inhumanity. We raged that we were so helpless, so hopeless; that we were starving; that we were cold; that our wounds and illnesses went untreated; that we were constantly scratching at sores and lice. And sometimes we even raged at God for allowing us to be captured in the first place.

One of the most unrelenting problems that POWs face is depression. No matter how great a day we're having, this vulture is always waiting in the shadows, ready to pounce at the first sign that our tranquility is beginning to falter.

It is frustrating to become depressed and be unable to pinpoint what triggered your depression. But this kind of despair is often more manageable, because it is general. Because you can't focus on one incident that may have caused your mood swing, you may respond to the question "Why are you so down?" with "I don't really know. I just feel shitty today." You can think of no single source to blame. Since you can't zero in on one culprit, you accept the fact that you "just feel shitty today," and try to pull yourself out of your despond.

But if you believe your mood swing was touched off by an act, or statement, of someone else . . . you may direct all of your resentment toward that person and magnify the smallest blunder into a large and intolerable affront. This is more difficult to shake off, and the resulting gloom can be long-lasting, causing the depressed party to act up unpredictably. Once, when Ricky's aunt and uncle were visiting us, David, then a sassy teenager, mouthed off at her uncle. It wasn't an acceptable act, but it wasn't that reprehensible either. Instead of taking him aside and correcting him, I berated him in front of the family, much more severely than he deserved. I immediately despised myself for my overreaction and fell into a state of depression. After our guests left, I was filled with self-loathing because I couldn't bring myself to apologize to my son.

Today, unexpected noises are as instantly unnerving to me as they were over sixty years ago. Therapists call it "exaggerated startle response." I can go ballistic at exploding firecrackers or automobile backfires, but the world's worst place for an episode of this kind is right in my own kitchen, where the floor is wood and doesn't cushion even a dropped pin. Melanie can put together a gourmet meal faster than anyone I know, but there is a price to be paid for her quickness: she is prone to drop flatware on the floor. Years ago, before I had mastered the art of quickly pulling the drawstrings of my self-control, I would scream "What the hell!" She would be offended, and I would be ashamed by my outburst. Now I simply clench my fists, draw in deep breaths, and wait until I can calm down enough to finish my meal without getting indigestion.

As a POW, the loud voice of a guard might be an order to assemble quickly for a roll call in the rain or snow, or it could be the forerunner of a blow with a fist or rifle butt. The yelling of guards can never mean anything pleasant. So how do you advise a former POW about something, even something mundane, without raising your voice? For example, he forgets to close the refrigerator door. There are many inflections you can give to "Would you please close the fridge," but which are the ones that won't offend him? Is a monotone the best? Should you avoid accenting "please"? Stressing "would" or "close" are certainly not recommended. The above is an extreme example, but it serves to disclose the dilemma.

The possibility of a POW being offended and overreacting to

criticism places an unfair burden on those close to him. POWs don't want those they love to feel that they're walking on eggs whenever they speak. But what a POW may perceive as a reproof appears to be a part of his psyche that even he doesn't understand. For example, if I call upstairs to ask Melanie a question and she happens to be having a dispute with her computer, her responding "Yes!" may come across to me with an inflection that I feel shows annoyance on her part, and I can become withdrawn and go into a funk. As control freaks, it would be a blessing if we could rein in that aspect of our lives and become a bit more thick-skinned. But depression can be a very difficult condition to modify, especially in older people, and that's why it's probably the most prevalent illness for which POWs receive treatment. I'm not a psychologist, but that's my own personal take on POW depression.

Over time, POWs have learned to control the mental powder keg that once was so easily ignited. "Control" is a key word in the POW vocabulary. Most of our phobias stem from loss of control. In earlier years, provocation could quickly explode into rage; now it's more often held in check, but the fuse is still there and, if ignited, can still spark unpredictable reactions. This is yet another trait that POWs conceal. The fact that most POWs are quiet people is not because of an inner calm, but because they have spent many years trying to exercise control over their inner turmoil.

I don't reveal that I will climb many flights of stairs to avoid an elevator. That even in a place of worship, I must sit on the aisle, just as I must on planes, buses, trains, and booths in restaurants. That a very heavy snowfall can make me feel trapped inside my house, inside my skin, unable to draw a full breath, and when I run out into my yard seeking space, the trees extend their bare branches high over my head like elongated fingers reaching out to encircle and crush me, and even the vast expanse of sky is not broad enough to let me believe that I will not suffocate.

Once, sitting in a traffic jam on a torrid day, our motor began to overheat and I was forced to turn off the air conditioner and roll down the windows. I was trapped. I couldn't breathe. On the other side of the road, I saw a café and I thought about how cool it must be inside and how wonderful it would be to sit there and drink iced tea. Then I saw the sign: Closed on Mondays. It was a Monday. Melanie offered to drive, but I refused. As long as I was behind the wheel . . . there was still one thing I controlled.

Hoarding food is characteristic of POWs. I have trouble closing my pantry doors because cans, jars, and boxes extend over the edge of the shelves. I open my freezer door very carefully to avoid frozen chicken breasts falling out and breaking my foot. My basement is stacked high with more rolls of toilet tissue than a convenience store. And bottles of water are everywhere. But I never set aside a dessert that I especially like, to be eaten later. There may not be a "later." The memory of seeing that chocolate D-Bar melting on top of my desk in the radio room, just before I bailed out of my burning plane, left a lasting impression. The same holds true with possessions. If I ever hesitate to wear a new article of clothing because I feel I should save it for a "special occasion," I immediately change my mind and start ripping off the tags. There may not be a special occasion.

To lose a buddy in combat is to be forever aware of the fragility of the human body. To see a buddy ruthlessly killed while a POW is unforgettable. I guess that's why I'm inclined to be overprotective of my family. I try to conceal this anxiety, to keep from inhibiting them, but sometimes I just can't. Melanie is generous in calling me when she arrives at a night meeting or rehearsal, otherwise I wouldn't use the phone until she got back home: I want the line to be open in case she needs me. I didn't let on to my kids that I worried about them when they were out in the evening, but I never fell into a sound sleep until I heard them come in. When my children came home with boxes of candy bars that they were asked to sell in support of school projects, I bought all of the candy myself because I didn't want them knocking on the doors of strangers who might berate them for the interruption. Despite their protests of "But this isn't the way we're supposed to raise the money!" I wouldn't relent.

Travel can be challenging for a claustrophobic. I try to keep my limitations to a minimum by researching the area I plan to visit. On a trip to San Francisco, we ate lunch at a lovely restaurant overlooking the bay, with a great view of Alcatraz. Melanie mentioned that there were conducted tours of the infamous old prison. "I don't think I'm interested in seeing the inside of a jail," I said. "Been there. Done that."

Sightseeing in Jerusalem, we went to the Church of the Holy Sepulcher, and Melanie, along with other tourists, crawled under the small opening at the foot of the sepulcher to see the inside. I was content to wait for her in front of the church. No tight places for me.

The "Chunnel" was in operation the last time we traveled from England to France, and people were rhapsodizing about how quickly the train moved beneath the English Channel to Paris. The ferry ride across took about five hours, but I was perfectly happy sitting in one of its several restaurants drinking coffee and eating chocolate croissants.

You would think that survivor guilt would ameliorate in some measure over the years, in my case . . . more than sixty years. But that's not true. I will always ponder why my buddies died and I was spared. They were better people than me. I'm sure Sherry's sister felt that way, too, and I will forever be haunted by her letter. This question of who should have survived is never far from my mind. I know it's illogical to look for reason in the event, but my perception has nothing to do with reason. I'm incapable of reason on this subject. In my guilt, I believe that the wrong person was spared. I'll always believe that.

At the New York State Ex-POW annual convention, there is a solemn ritual that is performed every year. A container of sand is placed on a table, and every POW is invited to come forward and place a small American flag in memory of deceased comrades. As we call out the names of those we wish to commemorate, we choke up and our eyes well with tears. We're probably more emotional then than we are when we visit the graves of family members. It's not that we care any less about departed family or friends. The difference is that most of our loved ones died in bed after enjoying normal life expectancies. Our buddies were killed by our enemies, lives cut short at a tender age when they had seen very little of life at all.

In this twilight period of their lives, what do World War II POWs wish for? It is paradoxical that, despite their continuing reluctance to talk about their past, what I get most from my fellow POWs is the concern that the history of the hardships they endured will die with them. Because POWs are not hesitant to talk with other POWs, the late Col. Bob Bieber, a POW in Germany, arranged to hold interviews at national POW conventions and videotaped the experiences of numerous attendees. Some of the videos are available for viewing at the National POW Museum at Andersonville, Georgia, as well as at the Veterans History Project of the Library of Congress in Washington, D.C. Hopefully, future generations will avail themselves of these accounts of a generation who served their country, first in combat, then as POWs. Some POWs say they fought in two wars. In the first, they battled the enemy with weapons; and in the second, they struggled to survive incarceration by using their wits.

Most of our physical wounds have healed with time, but the wounds that will never heal are the psychological wounds. The wounds caused by starvation. The wounds caused by brutality.

The wounds caused by inhumanity. These are the searing, raw, yet invisible wounds. The wounds that plague our days. The wounds that haunt our nights. The wounds that torment our dreams. The traumatic, incurable, emotional wounds that POWs live with every day of their lives. These are the wounds that will never cease to give pain . . . until we go to our graves.

I still have some mixed feelings about things Germanic, though Melanie and I often converse in German. Having spent half of her senior year of high school in Vienna, Austria, where her family lived, she speaks Hoch Deutsch and is more fluent than I, who picked up my vocabulary from German guards. But I think my Southern accent softens my German a bit, just as hers is mellowed by her sweet soprano voice. On the other hand, if we're in Manhattan and I hear others speaking the language, usually German tourists, my immediate reaction is still fight-or-flight. Afterward, I'm merely annoyed by the guttural rasp of their voices. To my ears, it sounds like they're talking around a mouthful of hot potato.

In 1960, I arrived home from work one evening and discovered that Ricky had bought our son, David, a bicycle made in Germany. I immediately exchanged it for one made in the United States and, even today, I avoid buying products made in Germany. After World War II when Volkswagen advertised *Everybody's getting the Bug,* I was tempted to write on billboards: "Maybe someone will develop a repellent."

I will never again set foot on German soil. Ich bin *nicht* ein Berliner. To me, the earth that Nazis trod is forever toxic. I've gone out of my way to avoid flights that stop, however briefly, in that country. I was enraged when President Reagan visited a German cemetery in Bitburg, where SS troops were buried, and I wrote letters to newspapers in protest.

When I came home in 1945, I was surprised to learn that German POWs in the United States lived as well as our own military.

They enjoyed good meals, clean beds and clothing, excellent medical care, library privileges, and movies, and they even bought cigarettes and beer from the PX. I could deal with that, but what *really* pissed me off was the Saturday parties where POWs danced with American girls.

This "Kraut coddling" in the American camps was enormously in excess of the Geneva Conventions mandates for the treatment of POWs; but, upon reflection, I would rather have seen the Germans overindulged, than have them suffer the same deprivations that we did at the hands of our captors. It was self-satisfying to feel that my country was too civilized, too honorable to brutalize POWs. Boy, was I knocked off my smug pedestal when the atrocities against Iraqi detainees by our troops at Abu Ghraib were discovered and the interrogation methods at Guantanamo exposed. Every POW friend I spoke with about this felt as indignant and as ashamed as I did. What a shock to find out that we are no better than our enemies.

I'm very glad that I don't hate all German people. It makes no sense to harbor an animus for generations; to visit the sins of the fathers upon the children. When I saw throngs of German tourists in Israel, I was surprised to learn that they comprise a large percentage of that country's visitors. I have worked productively with Germans who came to America after World War II. Some of them were veterans of that conflict, yet we were able to discuss aspects of the war without awkwardness. Melanie and I have a number of German friends with whom I'm very gemütlich.

I shall forever be indebted to the German guard, Old Joe, who befriended me at Stalag Luft IV and made me realize that all Germans were not bad people. He was almost shot by a superior officer while trying to release me from a boxcar just before our train was bombed by Allied planes. He risked his life one night by surreptitiously raising loaves of bread, speared on the end of his bayonet, to a window in my boxcar after we had not eaten for three days. I remember when I first met him at Stalag Luft IV and was puzzled because he wanted to help me. When I asked him why, he said, "You look very much like my son who is a POW in the United States." If we resembled each other physically, and if Young Joe had genetically inherited his father's deep compassion, was there that much difference between us?

I truly regret that I never tried to get in touch with Old Joe, but my demons wouldn't have permitted me the research. How wonderful it would have been to meet with him in, say, Paris. We'd have had a lot to say to each other, and I don't think he would have been fazed to learn that I was Jewish. Maybe his son could have joined us. I'm sure he got back to Germany all right, because we treated the German POWs in our country very well. I hope Old Joe's life was all good thereafter. He made some everlasting changes in the way I look at the world. I've never been embarrassed by the tears I shed the day we parted in that railroad yard in Nuremberg; the day he waved his red bandanna in final farewell. Yes, I loved that German guard like a father.

Chapter Twenty-five

RATTLESDEN REVISITED

In the early nineteen-eighties, some guys from my old Eighth Air Force Bombardment Group, the 447th, got together and decided to hold biennial reunions back at Rattlesden, England, the village where our air base had been located. A gunner from our group, Eddie Leighty, a Pennsylvania native, had fallen in love with a Rattlesden girl while he was stationed there, came back to England to marry her in 1945, and had lived there ever since. This was fortunate for the reunion planners, because it gave them a buddy on the scene to help with the logistics.

Then they learned, to their delight, that our old air base still existed as a flying field. This was most unusual, because almost every former U.S. air base in England had been plowed under after the war and returned to crops.

The site where our base was located was owned by the Lee family and leased to the United States government for the duration of the war. Afterward, the Lees gave some acreage to a local glider club, and the club maintained one runway for gliders and other small aircraft. The real icing on the cake was that the original control tower was still in use and kept in excellent condition. There had been one change made to the tower, which the U.S. Air Force would certainly have frowned on . . . the glider club had installed a pub on the second story for use by its members.

After I began attending the reunions, I was talking with Fred Lee, one of the sons, at the air base one day and he said, "You know, Norm, on the day the last B-17 took off from this field on its way back to America, I was standing on this very spot with my father, and he said, 'Fred, there goes the last of the Yanks, but I assure you they'll be back. These boys will go home, get married, and then they'll be coming over with their children to show them where they were during the war. Just remember, when they come back, you be nice to them. They're the ones that saved our England.'" Well, the Lees took their father's words to heart. We couldn't have been treated nicer if we'd been royalty.

When I first heard that the 447th had begun holding reunions in England, I wasn't even slightly tempted to make the trip. I had been there less than a month before I was shot down. Red and I had gone into Rattlesden several evenings to drink at the pub, and we had once visited Ipswich to see a movie, but, other than that, I felt no deep connection to the area. And I was shot down with my first pass to London in my pocket, so I never even came close to that historical city.

Waide Fulton, waist gunner on my crew, had gone to a couple of the reunions and kept telling me about what a great time I was missing. Finally, I agreed that we would go to the next one, never dreaming that I was opening a door to new and old friends, with memories enough to last a lifetime.

On my first trip back, as our group assembled at Heathrow

Airport, I met a few old friends and a few former POWs, but most of the returnees were guys who had arrived in England as replacements long after I was shot down, when fighter escort was vastly improved, and they had completed their missions.

We boarded buses for the two-hour drive to Ipswich, where we were staying. Rattlesden was too small and remote to support a hotel, so we had to seek out larger towns for adequate accommodations. Ipswich is about fifteen miles from Rattlesden, as the crow flies.

As we left the airport at Heathrow and drove through the countryside, it looked like "ancient history" to us, because America is so comparatively young. Driving through small towns, we saw architecture that hasn't changed in hundreds of years. Some two-story wooden buildings leaned precariously after many years of settling, defying gravity for ages. Homes with thatched roofs are still enchanting, no matter how many times you see them.

Then there were the "plague churches," standing starkly alone in the distance and seeming to stare reproachfully at the cars and lorries as they sped down the highway. The plague churches are forsaken reminders of the plague in the Middle Ages, when many towns were torched to prevent the spread of the disease. The churches, built of stone, resisted the inferno and still rise sternly against the horizon as a grave reminder of man's mortality.

The next morning, we climbed back on the "coaches" to go to Rattlesden. A few miles from the village, at the Woolpit exit, we pulled over onto the shoulder and rolled up behind a convoy of military vehicles, U.S. Army troop and weapons carriers and jeeps, proudly flying American and British flags from staffs bolted to their fenders, waiting to escort us to the air base. Driven by local residents, members of 447th/England, a group formed by the Lee family to plan our reunions, the trucks had been bought from U.S. Army Surplus and maintained beautifully, belying their forty-plus years of service. Later, we were given rides around the base in these vintage conveyances and found that they still had the same unforgiving springs that our butts tenderly remembered from World War II.

Returning to England for the first time, I had no great expectations. In fact, I really didn't know what to expect. Certainly, I wasn't looking for the warmth and the enduring gratefulness the Brits expressed to us for our coming to their aid during WWII. How paradoxical to come to England and receive the acclaim we never got at home. It all began when we were going through customs. The agent who checked us through was probably in his late twenties. He looked at my blue cap with the picture of a B-17 in flight and "447th Bomb Group" imprinted below it and asked, "The 447th, that was near Ipswich, wasn't it?"

"That's right," I said. "You're awfully young to know that."

"Oh, I'm a World War II buff. I know where most of the B-17 bases were located. Welcome back and have a very good stay, sir."

That was just the beginning. When our coaches entered the grounds of the airfield, there were rows of cars parked in front of the control tower. The same control tower that had seemed to show such an air of grimness when we were taking off on missions, now appeared to be just another friendly site, welcoming us home as returning warriors.

People were standing beside the cars, and each of them was holding one or more large books. As we left the coaches, they came forward to greet us, introducing themselves and extending their books for our signatures. They wanted our names, our ranks, and the squadrons we were in. They were eagerly seeking our autographs. Each book contained pictures, some clipped from forties newspapers, some actual photos, of B-17's taking off and landing, many returning to Rattlesden severely damaged. Many of these Brits were not old enough to have been alive during the war, yet their knowledge of the history of the 447th and its missions was astounding. One 447th fan, in his twenties, had traveled all the way from Denmark to be with us.

In nearby Bury Saint Edmunds, I was browsing in a Marks and Spenser department store, and a saleswoman saw my 447th hat and came over and asked, "Sir, were you here during the War?"

When I answered "Yes, I was," she said, "May I shake your hand and thank you so much for all you've done."

The same scene was repeated while we were sightseeing in Ipswich and Cambridge and in towns all over England, even in London. People who think that the British are so reserved don't really know them.

To the citizens of Rattlesden, we were their "boys," and they made sure that our social calendar and our stomachs were full. In the afternoon, inside a Nissen hut at the airfield, a band played songs popular during World War II and the local ladies prepared barbecued chicken, burgers, and bangers, and served fresh vegetables from the surrounding farms. Wonderful strawberries were in season, and they were coated with clotted cream; and all the desserts were homemade.

After our meal, the sound of the band in the Nissen hut reached a decibel level that was too painful for my ears to tolerate any longer. I wandered outside and was greeted by a truly spectacular sunset.

The sun was slowly sinking beyond a stand of trees, and I walked down to the runway where I could view it more quietly. As I stood there alone watching, I almost expected the treetops to burst into a ball of flame. It was that intense. There was something almost spiritual about this vivid sunset, but then I have always had a mystical feeling when I'm in Rattlesden.

What is so special to us about this old airfield? Why do we keep coming back? After all, our actual combat experience was many miles away. My plane blew up over Big B on April 29, 1944, but I have no desire to visit Berlin.

Perhaps it's because Rattlesden was the site of our coming of age. Perhaps it was where we first faced the moment of truth, acknowledged the harsh reality that our youthful fantasies of immortality were just that—fantasies. It took no more than one mission to for us to realize that we were extremely vulnerable, that this game was for keeps and our odds for survival were very slim.

On one of our trips to England, we went to the RAF Molesworth airfield where we were greeted by Col. Zimmerman, who commanded the USAAF troops at the base. We were treated to the most impressive flag ceremony I have ever witnessed, in honor of those who lost their lives during WWII. There was a 21-gun salute, then a squad in full dress uniform performed a moving, slow-motion folding and presentation of the flag.

Afterward, Col. Zimmerman informed us that he had a "special treat" in store for us that evening, at a hangar dance on the base. We arrived back at Molesworth about eight P.M., and our coaches pulled up before an immense hangar whose doors were closed so we couldn't see inside. We were told to form a column of fours, and then a Scottish bagpiper suddenly appeared before us in full regalia. The wide hangar doors swung open, and he tootled us inside.

As we marched through the doors, we were stunned to be greeted by twelve hundred wildly cheering, whistling, applauding people. Most of them were Brits, and some were American soldiers stationed at the base. But, even more astonishing, it was like a gigantic military masquerade ball, because almost everyone was wearing a WWII uniform. Some wore American uniforms, some English. There were officers, enlisted men and women, soldiers, sailors, Air Force, and Marines. The women and men who were not in uniform were dressed to the nines in forties finery. A sixteen-piece Tommy Dorsey-type orchestra began playing hit songs of the era, and the huge dance floor was soon filled with guests dancing to the strains of *"There'll be blue birds over the White Cliffs of Dover, tomorrow just you wait and see."* It was an emotional and breathtaking scene.

We were quickly surrounded by the British, many of whom wanted us to sign their autograph books and others who simply wanted to talk with us about our experiences. There was food and drink, and the convivial atmosphere had a dreamlike quality to it because it was so improbable. Maybe this is the way the Beatles felt when they first appeared on the *Ed Sullivan Show*, then toured the United States to bask in the unrestrained acclaim of adoring Americans wherever they went.

Our coaches were scheduled to leave at 10:30 P.M., and the time passed too quickly. We formed a column again, and the bagpiper played as we marched out between throngs of guests lined up on both sides of the aisle. People were rushing forward to shake our hands and wish us well. A man a few years younger than I took my hand in both of his and said, "Thank you! Thank you!" Then he burst into tears. I had a hard time trying to keep from becoming teary myself.

It was indeed a stirring and emotional evening. The Brits are not only gracious and hospitable, but they have never forgotten our partnership in defeating the Axis. And what is even more gratifying is the fact that most of the attendees at the hangar dance were born long after WWII. That's why we keep returning to Rattlesden. That's why many of us bring our children and grandchildren. We're nurturing a friendship that will extend to future generations.

The powerful magnet that draws the men of the 447th back to Rattlesden is our urge to reaffirm the fact that we survived this most challenging episode of our lives. And we can only relive this unique experience by reminiscing with others in our Bomb Group—friends old and new—because they are the only ones who remember.

One would think that our reunions at Rattlesden might become repetitious, but nothing could be farther from the truth. Each reunion is delightfully unique. Each has something different to offer. Something nostalgic. Something poignant.

For example, on our second reunion, we were invited to visit the elementary school in Rattlesden and be entertained by the children in a program they had been rehearsing for us. Students were assigned to show us around the school, and we drew Penny Moore, an eight-year-old whose brother Peter was six. She took her guide job very seriously as she conducted us on a tour of the school. Later we met her parents, Geoffrey and Jean, and our families have remained close over the years, visiting each other's homes, keeping in touch by E-mail.

A couple of years ago, Penny graduated from Cambridge just before our reunion, and when we arrived in England, she invited Melanie and me to go punting on the Cam River. "The Cam" is a narrow, slow-moving stream, and the lovely old university, steeped in tradition, is situated on its banks. A punt is a long, flat-bottomed boat with square ends, accommodating about eight to ten people, and it's propelled like a gondola, by someone standing aft and pushing backward with a long pole. Penny said that her balance might be a bit more reliable than mine, a premise that I couldn't argue with, so she provided the womanpower and I sat in the prow guiding our craft with an oar. It was an utterly delightful afternoon. The river was chockablock with punts, many filled with young tourists from Japan, Italy, and Germany, all screaming with mock alarm as their boats bumped into other boats, each navigated by equally inept punters. We splashed each other with water and worked together to separate our boats when three of four of them ran together, clogging the river and creating a traffic jam.

During the punt ride, I recalled the first time we had met Penny, a third-grader conducting us on a tour of her school. How lucky I was to see her through the years as she grew into this bright and vivacious young woman. Our closeness to the Moore family was yet another ingredient that cemented our bond with England.

One of the most moving ceremonies at every reunion is the 447th memorial service on the High Town Green, where the people of Rattlesden have erected a memorial to our Bomb Group. The street is closed off to vehicular traffic and filled with people as the whole village turns out for this event. There is a military band that plays as we all join in singing the American and English national anthems, and flag-bearers display the colors of both countries. Perhaps the most emotional moment is when we sing the enduring hymn *O Valiant Hearts*. The words are so appropriate to the ceremony:

> *O valiant hearts, who to your glory came*
> *Through dust of conflict and through battle flame,*
> *Tranquil you lie, your knightly virtue proved,*
> *Your memory hallowed in the land you loved.*
>
> *Proudly you gathered rank on rank, to war,*
> *As who had heard God's message from afar;*
> *All you had hoped for, all you had, you gave*
> *To save mankind—yourselves you scorned to save.*
>
> *Splendid you passed, the great surrender made,*
> *Into the light that never more shall fade;*
> *Deep your contentment in that blest abode*
> *Who wait the last clear trumpet call of God.*

Sunday service at St. Nicholas, a charming old Anglican Church in Rattlesden, is another high point of every visit. Built in the thirteenth century and renovated in 1546, it is the only church I've ever known to display a plaque honoring a United States Air Force Bomb Group and to have constructed a chapel as a memorial. The Lees are members here, and we've come to know many of the parishioners.

On each visit, a choir robe is produced and Melanie is co-opted to sing in the choir. With her love of choral music, it's not necessary to twist her arm. The sermon is in recognition of the 447th, and members of our group are called to the lectern. At the 2005 reunion, a handcrafted bench was set up in the churchyard in memory of a popular 447th president, who was also a POW, Byron Schlagg.

After church services, the parishioners of St. Nicholas invited 447ers, in groups of three or four Yanks per household, to lunch. Melanie and I were privileged to join choir director Geoffrey Moore and his family at their home, along with the vicar, Rev. Robin Excell, and Lord and Lady Morris, who prefer to be called Michael and Nicola.

Lunching with the British is very special. It is one thing to walk through English villages and view dwellings from the street, but you can't really relate to how people live until you're invited into their homes. We all came away with a much better picture of our friends in Rattlesden and of their lifestyles.

Our final stop before departing for London is always the Imperial Air Museum in Duxford. There you can find WWII planes of almost any nation that was involved in that war, on display. Of course, we always head straight for the B-17. On my first trip back, I recall my surprise to find Brits from teens to middle age, clustered around the American planes, waiting with their autograph books for Yanks to arrive. They wanted to know what position we flew, the name of our plane, and if we'd ever had to ditch, crash-land, or bail out. They knew that England was covered with United States Air Force bases during World War II and that it was rare for a day to pass without groups of former American airmen showing up at the museum. But we don't hang around the museum very long, because we know where another B-17 is resting on its hardstand nearby, and this is one we can board and clamber around on.

This plane is named the *Sally B,* and she is the only flying B-17 in England. She's famous for her performance as a stand-in in the movie *Memphis Belle*. The *Sally B* is maintained entirely by donations, and the cost of keeping her in airworthy condition is considerable. We are greeted warmly by our good friend Derek Smith, who works for the B-17 Charitable Trust and always invites us aboard the venerable old bomber, where we regale each other with stories of missions remembered. One by one we struggle through the rear hatch, not as nimble as we once were, nor nearly as lithe. There aren't many ball-turret gunners around who can still fold themselves into their old position.

The year that I brought my son Bob along, I proceeded right to the radio room with him. He had never been aboard a B-17 before and was fascinated by the old girl. I took the opportunity to explain the circumstances of my last mission, April 29, 1944, when my plane, *Mississippi Lady,* was shot down over Berlin. I can never describe that mission as graphically as when I'm aboard a B-17. Finally, Bob understood exactly what had happened to us on that fateful day, and how we lost four of our crew when our plane burned and exploded.

We lost our dear friend Eddie Leighty a couple of years ago. The last time I saw him was in 2003. He was having cardiac problems, and a young man pushed Eddie in a wheelchair to the 447th memorial ceremony on the High Town Green. At the end of the program, we always set up a photo-op in front of the monument so that members of each of the four squadrons may have their pictures taken by family and friends. The young man stopped the wheelchair on the street and, when Eddie stood up with his cane, took his arm to help him walk to the monument. Eddie jerked his arm away defiantly, determined to walk to the monument alone. As he struggled to move forward, tottering on his cane, I knew he'd never make it and a fall could prove disastrous. I ran up and took his arm and said, "Eddie, may I walk with you?"

He turned his head toward me with a glare, then relaxed into a smile. "Sure, Norm. Sure. Let's walk together." So we made our way to the monument and Eddie kept his pride.

Eddie died before the 2005 reunion, and services were held at St. Nicholas. Friends from Rattlesden told us that as the funeral cortege moved from the church to the waiting hearse, the *Sally B* did a flyover, bomb-bay doors open, engines purring, wings waggling gently in a final salute. Wow, Eddie! What a way to complete your last mission.

At our 2001 reunion, we affixed a bronze plaque to the control tower at a ceremony in honor of 2nd Lt. Robert E. Femoyer, a 447th navigator who was posthumously awarded our nation's highest military decoration: the United States Congressional Medal of Honor. His citation reads: "For conspicuous gallantry and intrepidity, at the risk of his life, above and beyond the call of duty near Merseburg, Germany, on 2 November 1944. While on a mission, the bomber, of which 2nd Lt. Femoyer was the navigator, was struck by three enemy antiaircraft shells. The plane suffered serious damage and 2nd Lt. Femoyer was severely wounded in the side and back by shell fragments, which penetrated his body. In spite of extreme pain and great loss of blood, he refused an offered injection of morphine. He was determined to keep his mental faculties clear in order that he might direct his plane out of danger and so save his comrades. Not being able to arise from the floor, he asked to be propped up in order to enable him to see his charts and instruments. He successfully directed the navigation of his lone bomber for two and a half hours, so well it avoided enemy flak and returned to the field without further damage. Only when the plane had arrived in the safe area over the English Channel did he feel that he had accomplished his objective; then, and only then, he permitted an injection of a sedative. He died shortly after being removed from the plane. The heroism and self-sacrifice of 2nd Lt. Femoyer are in keeping with the highest traditions of the U.S. Army."

At every reunion, we schedule a stop at the American Cemetery at Madingley. Our wreath-laying ceremony is always a sobering experience, but in 2005 it was particularly solemn because, only a few days before our arrival, many innocent people were killed or grievously wounded in a London subway bombing carried out by Muslim terrorists. As fate would have it, this attack came on the 60th anniversary of the end of WWII. The best way we could show our solidarity with our English friends was to proceed with our reunion . . . and not one reservation was cancelled.

The mere sight of thousands of white markers, row on row, makes us remember that these Americans, whose lives ended so abruptly, made their great sacrifice, not by chance—but by choice. They chose to place themselves in harm's way because our freedoms were threatened. And they left us with a legacy of patriotism and heroism that will never fade from our memory.

For years, I had been trying to find out where my four crew-mates who died on our last mission were buried. On one of our early trips to Madingley, I was introduced to the cemetery super-intendent, and I asked him how I would go about locating my bud-dies. "Very simple," he said. "Just follow me into my office."

He went into his computer, and in five minutes he handed me a printout of the information I wanted. Sherry's body had been returned to the United States and he was buried in Pittsburgh. Bill, Little Joe, and Long John were interred in France, in the American Cemetery at St. Avold. We had been to France before, as a side trip after our reunion. I told Melanie that the next time we came over, I wanted to go there again and see those gravesites.

Two years later, we went back to France. While we were in Eng-land, our luggage was loaded onto our coaches and unloaded by bellhops, whenever we changed hotels. Now we were traveling by train in France and had to haul our own bags on and off at every transfer point. When we arrived at St. Avold, we found that we were still several kilometers from the cemetery. We had reserved a room at a motel next to the cemetery, actually just three hundred yards away. Fortunately, Melanie is fluent in French, so we had no trouble ordering a taxi and getting to the motel, a totally unpretentious little inn of about twenty rooms.

After breakfast the next morning, we walked over to the cemetery and, just as in Madingley, the grounds there were superbly maintained. We went to the superintendent's office, and he was most helpful in directing us to the gravesites. Is there anyone who walks through a cemetery without stopping to read the inscriptions on the grave markers? I think not. We paused to note those who had still been in their teens; those who died within days of the end of the war; and those who died after the war was over from combat wounds so severe that they were unable to survive them.

When we located my guys, Melanie took pictures of me at each grave, standing with my hand on the cross. Until I visited Sherry's grave in Pittsburgh, I had never taken a picture in a cemetery. I had always felt uneasy about it. I guess I still do. It seems to me in some way intrusive on the serenity of the reverential site. But then, aren't gasoline lawnmowers an even greater invasion of the tranquility? Now I am glad I have those pictures, so that I can relive my visit whenever I hold these images in my hand.

At each grave, I pictured a buddy who lived in my mind's eye just as he had more than half a century before. A young kid. Forever young. Never to raise a family. Never to enjoy the fulfillment of a career he had planned. Never to know the unmeasurable pleasure of playing with grandchildren. Theirs not to reason why.

I touched each smooth stone cross, cool to my hand, unyielding, yet I had the feeling that I was in some way communicating with the deceased. I spoke to Long John and to Bill, offering my regrets.

I gave my belated thanks to Little Joe for saving my life when he tossed my parachute across the radio room, keeping it from burning. I will never get over my grief at their loss, but it was a kind of catharsis to make this trip and communicate with them spiritually. I hope that I was able to convey the sentiment that I still remembered and would always remember. And with regard to my survivor guilt, the visit to St. Avold did provide a modicum of release to my still-captive mind.

I wish every American military cemetery, both at home and abroad, would have the following inscribed over its gates:

> *Rest here in eternal peace and tranquility, and know that whenever the word COURAGE is heard on these hallowed grounds . . . it will be uttered in your honor.*

Sgts. on crew of *Mississippi Lady* (left to right, from bottom): Vasilios Mpourles, William Peters, Norman Bussel, Merle Rumbaugh, Waide Fulton, Joseph Guida.

EPILOGUE

After that fatal mission from Rattlesden, England to Berlin, while I was a POW in Germany, I promised myself that if I was lucky enough to return home, I would write a detailed account of this calamitous event so that the families of those who were killed, as well as those whose loved ones died in the camps, would know exactly what happened on that fateful day and beyond.

More than sixty years passed before I was able to set forth a single word about that mission, although the minutiae were still as vivid in my mind as ever. I guess I wanted my account of this tragedy to be perfect; but, as an editor, I knew that writers must trade off the idea of "perfect prose" in exchange for meeting deadlines.

I also knew that my "writer's block," or whatever excuse I might come up with for my failure to record the most traumatic day of my life, was simply that . . . an excuse. I hadn't written about it because I was afraid of the subject. I was petrified that I might not be able to describe these events exactly. That my reprise would not be "perfect."

Well, my own mortality finally became a factor, and I knew that this story would never be told if I didn't soon overcome my fear of reliving those terrible times, my fear of dredging up painful memories I had fought for decades to suppress. So I wrote several chapters, but then I was elected President of the American Ex-Prisoners of War Service Foundation. My new duties gave me another excuse for procrastination, so the manuscript curled up comfortably in my computer, to sleep undisturbed for four years.

One day my granddaughter, Rachel K. Bussel, also a writer whose father is my son David, came to visit and asked to see this work not in progress. After reading what I had written, she said, "Grandpa, this is very good. I never knew about this part of your life; you didn't speak about your experiences before and I was always reluctant to ask. You've got a book here; you just need to finish it."

With her encouragement, I got back to work, and about nine months later *My Private War: Liberated Body, Captive Mind* was done. As anticipated, it brought back memories I had long sought to avoid, depressing memories that disturbed my sleep. But in honesty, it became a sort of catharsis as well, and now I am able to look at the past and see glimmers of light rather than total darkness.

To the best of my ability, I have recorded the history of unforgettable events that took many lives and reshaped many more in a war that prevented the enslavement of the free world. I have written in sincerity, in candor, and in awesome remembrance. To those who died, and to those who suffered mental anguish and physical deprivation as POWs, I apologize for any imperfection in this work, because nothing is perfect.

ACKNOWLEDGMENTS

F irst I want to cite my granddaughter, the writer Rachel Kramer Bussel, without whom this book would still be languishing in my computer. After reading my half-done work she said, "This is a part of your life I know nothing about. Won't you please finish it. For me?" What grandfather could refuse such a compelling request. Then she connected me with an agent and became my preeminent publicist. I am indebted to Dr. Kenneth E. Reinhard for his professional advice on the subject of anxiety disorders. To my agent, Helen Zimmermann, who strongly believed that my story needed to be told, for her peerless guidance in helping me improve my original manuscript and her notes of encouragement in the margin, which so often drove away doubts that plagued my progress. My perceptive editor at Pegasus Books, Jessica Case, quickly spotted omissions in my story, issues that I had deliberately avoided because they were too painful to remember, then gently convinced me to write about them. It was worth the anguish of recalling these events; otherwise my memoir would have been incomplete.

Special thanks to my sons, Bob and David, for sharing their memories of growing up with a former POW father; my niece Cynthia Marker and my sister Fay Marker for their enthusiastic support and historical recall. My kid brother, Alan, whose tragic death at age 34 ended a promising career as a professor of journalism, would have been so proud that I finally was able to complete my story of World War II, as would my mother, Rose, who began taking me to the library more than eighty years ago and instilled in me her love for books.

To George Hamby, my POW roommate, who did not live to see the publication of this book, I owe much for his help in recalling events which affected our lives forever. For 93 year-old Waide G. Fulton, my only surviving crewmate, who lost an eye on our fateful mission to Berlin, but never lost sight of the patriotism which carried him through his ordeal, my thanks for pictures which are included in this book.

And for my wife, Melanie, who for months put up with my mood swings as I relived parts of my life that I preferred to forget, helped immensely with research and editing but, most forbearing of all, kept inserting floppy discs into my data processor to transfer what I had written to her late model computer, then to a CD, because I was too stubborn to stop using my comfortable clunker, so ancient that its dictionary does not recognize the word: e-mail. I can't come up with anything more expressive than, "Thanks," at the moment my love, so I will forever seek new ways to show my gratitude.